Lady (Howard) Vincent

From China to Peru over the Andes

A Journey through South America

Lady (Howard) Vincent

From China to Peru over the Andes
A Journey through South America

ISBN/EAN: 9783743318830

Manufactured in Europe, USA, Canada, Australia, Japa

Cover: Foto ©Andreas Hilbeck / pixelio.de

Manufactured and distributed by brebook publishing software (www.brebook.com)

Lady (Howard) Vincent

From China to Peru over the Andes

OVER THE ANDES

A JOURNEY THROUGH SOUTH AMERICA

BY

LADY (HOWARD) VINCENT

AUTHORESS OF "40,000 MILES OVER LAND AND WATER,"
"NEWFOUNDLAND TO COCHIN CHINA," ETC.

WITH REPORTS AND LETTERS ON BRITISH INTERESTS
IN BRAZIL, ARGENTINA, CHILI, PERU, PANAMA
AND VENEZUELA

BY SIR HOWARD VINCENT, M.P.

WITH NUMEROUS ILLUSTRATIONS

LONDON
SAMPSON LOW, MARSTON & COMPANY
Limited
17a, PATERNOSTER Row, E.C.

TO

THE PEOPLE OF CENTRAL SHEFFIELD

THIS ACCOUNT OF

OUR THIRD WORLD JOURNEY

IS

AFFECTIONATELY INSCRIBED

PREFACE.

> "Let observation with extensive view,
> Survey Mankind from China to Peru."

So wrote Samuel Johnson, and it has been my keenest desire and my good fortune to act upon the injunction.

"Forty Thousand Miles over Land and Water" told of the impressions made upon me in the United States of America, Australasia, and the vast Empire of India.

"Newfoundland to Cochin China" detailed my experiences in the Dominion of Canada, amid the fascinating Japanese, and around the Walls of the Forbidden City at Peking.

This volume speaks of a third journey, whereof the furthermost point completed our "survey of mankind from China to Peru." At the request of many friends and for our warm-hearted constituents, the people of Central Sheffield, these records are printed and published.

ETHEL GWENDOLINE VINCENT.

1, Grosvenor Square.

CONTENTS.

CHAPTER I.
OVER THE SOUTH ATLANTIC 1

CHAPTER II.
THE HAVEN OF BRAZIL IN REVOLUTION . . . 12

CHAPTER III.
UP THE PLATE TO BUENOS AYRES . 28

CHAPTER IV.
THE CAMP OF ARGENTINA 55

CHAPTER V.
ACROSS THE ANDES 87

CHAPTER VI.
CHILI AND THE CHILIANS 122

CHAPTER VII.
THE NITRATE-FIELDS AND THE DESERT SHORE 145

CHAPTER VIII.
PERU, AND FIVE MILES TOWARDS HEAVEN . . 167

CHAPTER IX.
TO THE ARCHIPELAGO OF OCCIDENT . . . 198

APPENDIX.

	PAGE
I.—To the Land of Revolutions	219
II.—British South America Won and Lost	233
III.—The Paris of the West	240
IV.—Argentine Politics	244
V.—Argentine Travelling in 1827	250
VI.—Over the Cordillera	252
VII.—The English of the Pacific	256
VIII.—The Nitrate Fields of Chili	261
IX.—Peru and the Peruvians	267
X.—Venezuela and England	272
XI.—The West Indies	277
XII.—British Interests in Brazil	283
XIII.—British Commercial Interests in Argentina	291
XIV.—British Trade in Chili	302
XV.—British Interests in Peru	309
XVI.—The Panama Canal	318
Index	327

LIST OF ILLUSTRATIONS.

	PAGE
St. Vincent, Cape de Verd Islands	2
Pernambuco	6
Corcorado and the Sugar Loaf	22
Plaza Libertad—Buenos Ayres	40
Rosario de Santa Fé	68
Posada on the Andes	102
Road over the Andes between the Argentine Republic and Chili	110
Santiago de Chili	124
Bridge on the Valparaiso and Santiago Railway	134
The Esplanade, Valparaiso	136
Nitrate Works	156
Scene on the Oroya Railroad	178
Monte Meiggs, Summit of Oroya Railway	184
Panama Canal Company's Hospital	200
Panama Canal Works	318
View of the Panama Canal	322

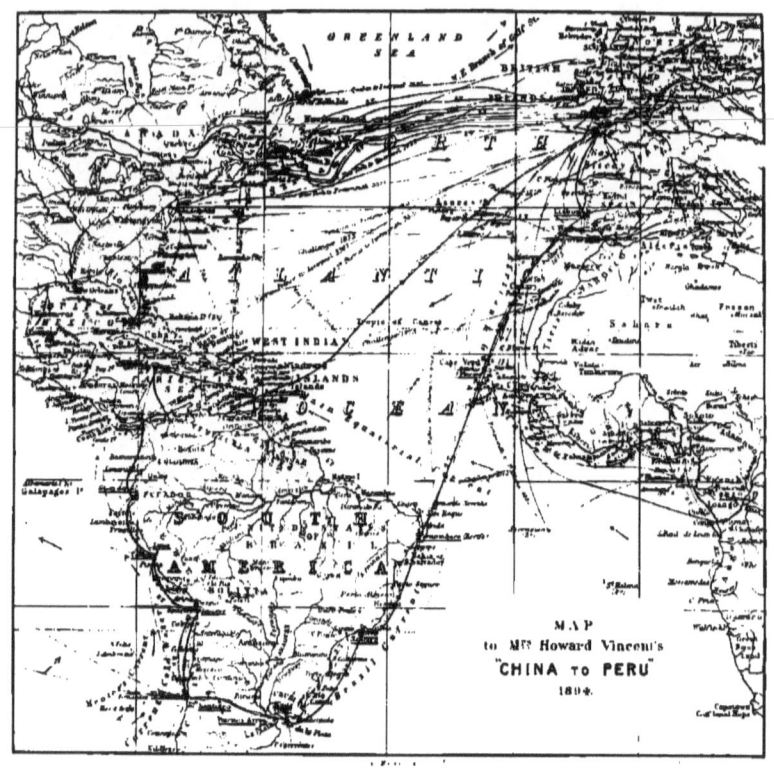

CHINA TO PERU.

CHAPTER I.

OVER THE SOUTH ATLANTIC.

A LITTLE green bay surrounded by olive-covered slopes, with the white and buff town of Vigo lying above it, gives the comfort of shelter, after a dreary day of tossing in the Bay of Biscay, for all on board the Royal Mail Steamer *Thames*.

We embark a goodly number of emigrants, who come out in flat-bottomed lighters, sitting enthroned amongst their household gods, and getting wet through, ere a lucky jump lands them on the gangway.

The next morning we are steaming merrily up the Tagus, past the bar and lighthouse and the Tower of Belem, and Lisbon lies white and smiling in the sunshine, its white and pink houses terraced one above each other, high up on the hill.

We take a run up to Cintra ; beautiful Cintra, with its green valley, amid the barren mountains, filled with splendid Spanish oak and chestnut trees, its overhanging gardens gay with every tropical creeper ; where the fuchsias grow in bushes and the magnolias flower on full-sized trees. Such a view too over many bare brown ranges, out to the ocean, whilst always immediately above us is the grey parapet of the ancient Moorish fortress, running up and down, to right and left, on the high-most peak.

On the evening of the second day after leaving Lisbon, we could just distinguish, on a cloudy moonlight night, the pale shadowy outline of the great rock peak of Teneriffe, rising out of a translucent grey range of mountains on the Island of Grand Canary. To port, Las Palmas, another island of the Canary group, is marked by a single lighthouse.

Four days afterwards we are up at six o'clock to see the morning mists roll away from St. Antonio and St. Vincent, two of the islands of the Cape de Verd group. Weird and fantastic are the volcanic peaked rocks of the mountain ranges—now rising in conical needle peaks, now massed like craggy castles or opening out into deep craters. Abundant rain must have fallen lately, for St. Vincent is not the bare and barren island so oft depicted, but shows a pale green vegetation, very fresh and sparse, but which, mixed with the bright chrome and madder tints of the volcanic strata, gives to it a curious and not unattractive character. It reminds us much of Aden, possessing, like that place, a varied grandeur of its own, produced by Nature trying to make a play of colour with the sparsest materials.

Lying in the absolute centre of the Bay of Porto Grande is the most curious freak of creation: a little pinnacled rock island, tapering to a natural peak, which in its turn is crowned by a white lighthouse. The base is completely hollowed out by the action of the continuous swell of the South Atlantic breakers,

ST. VINCENT, CAPE DE VERD ISLANDS.

forming a black cavernous circle around, which is broken into perpetually by clouds of foam and spray.

This bears the commonplace name of Bird Island, and looks as if it had just been placed there on purpose to carry the dazzling white lighthouse, with its steep zigzag path and final approach by a balustrade and stone steps, whose faithful light guides the ships to a safe anchorage.

There are the red-roofed cluster of houses, with the large white building of the Brazilian Submarine Telegraph Station, which makes up the whole of the town. We land to find a few clean paved streets, peopled chiefly by negroes and negresses, and proceed to the telegraph station. About forty clerks, under the care of Mr. Lloyd, live here, and transact the business of the electric current, joining South America with Europe. Cable messages pass through the operating room we visit in every language, but as codes are chiefly used it must be dull work, hour after hour, writing off meaningless words from the ceaseless click, click of the instrument. The only amusement of these exiled clerks is cricket, and their chief excitement as to whether incoming vessels will stay long enough to enable them to get up an opposition team for a match. St. Vincent belongs to the Portuguese, and one cannot help regretting that it is not one of England's possessions, as forming an invaluable coaling station. We may, however, take comfort in the fact that all the ships in harbour this morning, with the exception of a Portuguese gunboat, carry the Union Jack, showing, as always, the complete supremacy of England on the seas in all parts of the globe.

Sunday in the Doldrums! with the most awful heat. Some little amusement may be extracted from the manner in which passengers, at the extremity of endurance, lie panting on the deck, and for once our unpleasant Portuguese and Brazilian passengers are somewhat subdued. Everything but most absolutely necessary clothing is discarded, and everybody gasps and perspires during this loss of our hitherto pleasant companion, the north-east trade wind. This true experience of the tropics is succeeded by the day of tropical downpour, which is generally found just north or south of the equator, where the different wind-currents meet.

The following day we crossed the line about midday; but with a cool breeze on the port side it is difficult to believe we are on the equator. With the picking up of the south-east trade wind in another day, the extremes of temperature are over.

A word about the Royal Mail steamer *Thames*. She is a splendid vessel of 6000 tons, and commanded by Captain Hicks, the best captain that in our many sea voyages we have sailed under. She is very comfortable in all respects but one. The largest part of the passengers are Portuguese and Brazilians, indeed they appear always to support the line, and to use it more than the English. Suffice it to say that their manners, habits and customs do not harmonize with ours, and indeed appear to us repellent. The contents of the cruet are poured over the food, or you may see several raw eggs broken into a tumbler, with wine and Worcester sauce added impartially thereto. Add this drawback to an unfair proportion of children and a greatly overcrowded ship, and our month's sojourn on the *Thames* is otherwise like any other long sea voyage.

A scudding white-crested breeze, with a bright sun chasing shadows across the green island of Fernando Noronha, the Convict Settlement of the Brazils, is the next point of interest. The island has a most curious natural phenomenon. From the green hills that slope gently upwards from the centre of the island springs an horizontal basaltic pyramid, 1000 feet high. In the far distance it resembles a steeple, but as you come nearer it appears to be a great mass of rock, balanced on, and shelving outwards, so as to overhang, the mountain on to which it is accidentally thrown. We clearly distinguish the pink and red houses of the penal settlement, with their broad thatched roofs, the red prison where they are confined at night, the road running through the centre of the town, and the white stone house, probably the Governor's, about half-way up on an open space. The further end of the island is covered with forest, and at its extremity is an archway, cleanly cut through the rock, called the "Hole in the Wall," and through which we get a glimpse far out to sea. On the beautiful yellow beach the sapphire waves, crested with foam, roll continuously in.

Fernando Noronha is four and a half miles long, with a population of 2000, out of which 200 are women convicts. It is garrisoned by a company of Brazilian soldiers, commanded by a major, who acts as governor. The island seems too pretty and attractive a spot for a penal population, and efforts are being made to persuade the Brazilian Government to form a quarantine station here for the northern ports.

"Land on the starboard bow!" calls out the look-out, in the customary monotonous yet melodious pitch, in place of the usual "All's well," that echoes through every hour of the night, as the bells strike, and here is our first view of the green-blue line of the great continent of South America, our first view of the coast of Brazil, which forms one-fifth part of this same continent, and again one-fifteenth part of the whole world.

Pernambuco, the Recife of the natives, and the second largest city in Brazil, is coming into view, and soon we are opposite the bold green-clad height of Olinda, with its verandahed houses scattered amongst palm-groves. Well may its appearance have caused Decarte Coelleo, as he explored the coast to exclaim in Portuguese: "O linda stuaceo para se funda una villia." "Oh! beautiful site for a town." Exclamation immortalized as being used in part, to furnish the name of this pretty suburb.

Pernambuco, with its houses all white and red-roofed, lying among groves of tufted palms, seems to rise out of the ocean. Brilliantly shines the sun in tropical clearness. The sea is the usual perfect ultra-marine of this South Atlantic, with never a trace of the green of the North Atlantic in its unfathomable depths.

Creamy-white is the foam that girdles the reef, thrown high in mid-air from off that wonderful natural breakwater. Truly may Pernambuco be called the Brazilian Venice, with its many intersecting streams, and its quiet lagoon lying inside the bar.

This Recife (the native name for reef) is a mighty coral reef which extends along nearly the

PERNAMBUCO.

Page 6.

whole extent of the northern coast of Brazil. For five miles from Pernambuco, it continues without a break, and is laid so exactly straight and even that it resembles a breakwater of concrete. There is one opening opposite the town, and vessels of no great draught can pass the bar, and anchor alongside the wharf. From our deck it appears as if the spray dashed on to the wharf itself, but in reality there is a green lagoon, between the reef and the dock. At low water the reef is exposed and seems formed of a hard, dark brown rock which, when broken up, resembles yellow sandstone containing imbedded bivalves. A coralline reef it must have been, constructed laboriously during perhaps, hundreds of years, by the patient, industrious hives of submarine life, and when deserted by them, has become filled up with sand and shells.

Our yellow quarantine flag flies mast high. Some forty passengers, all packed and ready to land, await with feverish eagerness the result of much signalling from the shore, whilst the remainder discuss the prospects of landing ; for Pernambuco is exposed to the fury of the great Atlantic rollers, and a jump into a boat as it is carried swiftly by the gangway on the crest of the wave, or even being lowered in a basket, is as nothing compared to the soaking with spray as you cross the bar. Therefore is opinion divided as to the prudence of landing.

A boat is sent off from shore. All watch it dashing on the heights of the rollers, and then ploughing into their troughs. The doctor stands, papers in hand, on the gangway ; but when the green flag comes within speaking distance, a polite little official stands up and delivers himself of a fiat of quarantine. No mails are to be received or delivered, no cargo disembarked, no passengers landed, our clean bill of health not even inspected, but an unreasoning arbitrary order for the ship to proceed to Isla Grande, 1200 miles down the coast, and the nearest and only quarantine station for this vast seaboard of Brazil.

Blank disappointment, utter dismay, is depicted upon the countenances of all, as we turn away from the bulwarks, but we feel the greatest commiseration for those who have nearly, so very nearly reached home, and to whom it means a journey at their own expense of 1200 miles, quarantine and fumigation at a lazaretto, and a tedious return by a coasting steamer. Worse even is the case of the second-class passengers and steerage. Many will have paid away their bottom dollar in passage-money, and here they will be landed in a strange country, far from their destination, without means for return. Quarantine is the curse of the European inhabitants of South America, and the Government with its arbitrary orders delays the development of trade and progress in the country.

With sad little groups scattered about the decks, discussing the situation and picturing worse future evils, the anchor is quickly weighed and once more we are ploughing our way through the brilliant blue waves.

The "might have been's" of life! Yesterday we should have touched at Maceio, the capital of the Province of Alagoas, a thriving town with a large trade in sugar and cotton. To-day we should have cast anchor in the Bay of All Saints' before Bahia "a gulf formed by nature for the emporium of the Universe."

Out here in South America we are constantly on the track of the ancient Spanish mariners, the discoverers of the New World. It was from Bahia that Americus Vespucius, in 1503, carried home from the newly discovered country a cargo of the dye wood, which when cut in pieces resembled "brazas" or "coals of fire," from which circumstance it was called Brazil wood, indirectly giving the name of Brazil to the country.

We should like to have landed at Bahia, on the four mile long Praya, or beach, of the old town and business quarter. Thence ascended to the newer and more habitable quarter of the town on the hill by a steam lift. We should like to have seen the negresses, the finest in South America, and the fattest, who are thus described by an American author: "The women who hawk fish or pine-apples in the streets, are marvels of physical development and grace. They are as straight as palms, and as lithe as willows, and they walk like Greek goddesses. With purple, pink, or blue waists cut low in the neck, they display arms of the finest modelling, and a development of muscle and sinew and an erect and queenly carriage, which must be the envy and despair of the Brazilian ladies of the highest rank." We missed, too, taking on board the luscious pineapples, and pipless oranges for which Bahia is celebrated.

But, alas! we are steaming on past all these Brazilian ports, until on a cloudy Sunday morning, slowly Cape Frio loomed up before our eyes, a stately mountain of rock, the beginning of a range of sixty miles, which ends abruptly at the entrance of Rio Harbour. Here we are, sailing straight past the haven where we would be. The mountains open out. The entrance guarded by the twin islands of Pai and Mai is seen, the Sugar-loaf, Corcovado, Tijuca, recede before us. Another sixty miles and we are anchored at our quarantine retreat, at Ilha Grande.

Painfully intense is the long wait before the launch sets off from the pier, appallingly long seem the lengthy and deliberate turnings over of the ship's papers, and the parleyings between the doctor and health officer. Experience has made us nervous. We crane over the ship's side to catch the first intimation of our fate. It comes. Glad news. A day's fumigation on the morrow, and we may return to Rio on the day after.

Early next morning we are turned out of our berths, and the health officers come off and order all the mattresses and bedding to be thrown into a barge and borne off to the fumigating buildings we see lying low in a sandy cove. Soon comes an all-pervading smell of carbolic, from a watering-can which sprinkles disinfecting fluid freely, leaving a little puddle of the same in each cabin, whilst fore and aft from the steerage rise columns of sulphurous fumes.

We escape ashore in the afternoon. Now Ilha Grande is very far from being the desolate quarantine station you might suppose. It is a very pretty peaked island, tropically covered and fringed with palms, with the pink lazaretto nestling by the water's edge. A ramble round the white sands of the beach, where the waves lazily wash ashore shells and seaweed, up and down the hillside, entrances us with visions of

Tropical America. There are the sword-like leaves of the banyans clustering under the cocoa palms, tall clusters of white belled datura growing beside the glossy leaved bushes of the coffee plant, all covered with its exquisite white starred blossom, giant cacti, clinging and growing upon the rocks of the sea-shore, orchids nestling on the branches of trees, and every specie of tropical fern and creeper grow in this luxuriant isle.

The lazaretto and adjoining buildings form quite an imposing square on the landing-stage. The former is very large and really well-furnished, and they show the apartments where the late Emperor and Empress performed their quarantine in common with their humbler subjects. The expense of building was over 60,000$l.$, and the maintenance of such a large establishment must be costly in proportion. Yet when we remember the deathly scourge of yellow fever, which yearly claims its hundreds of victims, we can scarcely wonder at their precautions to refuse admittance to an equally deadly enemy, cholera. But a very few weeks ago an Italian steamer came into port with 120 cases on board and sixty deaths to report.

At 11 p.m. we are still waiting for our bedding to return, and it is a ludicrous sight soon afterwards to see all the passengers turning over piles of mattresses and pillows in search of their own. When secured we find them emitting a strong perfume of sanitas and wet through, for it is raining diligently.

CHAPTER II.

THE HAVEN OF BRAZIL IN REVOLUTION.

TORRENTS of rain usher in the morning of our return to Rio de Janeiro, and continue whilst we retrace our course. Soon we see the sleeping outline of the "Gavia" or "Look Out," which forms the extremity of the Tijuca range of mountains. Now we are under the towering summit of the Corcovado, such a perpendicular peak of rock, but the umbrella on its summit tells us that; from the other side, facing the harbour, a railway renders it accessible. Lastly, from amid the mist and spray, slowly emerges the great Sugar Loaf.

The similitude from the entrance is absolute. The Sugar Cone is rounded and graduated to perfection. With the waves sullenly booming round the base, this unscalable mass of rock, without chink, jut, or cavity on its entire surface rising up immediately at the point of entrance, forms a fitting introduction to the most beautiful harbour of the world. It inclines slightly over, leaning towards the sea and from inside, a green shoulder projecting from halfway up joins it to the peninsula.

Two flat little islands, called Pai and Mai (father

and mother in Portuguese) guard the entrance, and threading our way between them we are passing within a stone's throw of the battlemented Fort of Santa Cruz, mounting a triple row of a hundred guns. The tiny islet of Lage, with another fortress, lies as nearly as possible midway between Santa Cruz and the Sugar Loaf, completing a perfect defence to the entry of the harbour. Villegaignon another island fortress and naval depôt, is a little further to the left, and, see, it flies the white or rebel flag, having gone over to the enemy but yesterday. Little did we imagine that two hours later, all these same forts would be booming forth smoke and fire, and that the whole sea would be surging with a hail of shot.

How describe the harbour now we are well inside it? We seem to see an intricate panoramic succession of wooded mountain peaks, many of them terraced with brightly coloured houses undulating round the curves of the bay, and a little condensed as they touch the water's edge. Sydney Harbour is perhaps more beautiful and is certainly larger, but Rio is the grandest. The town proper of Rio is difficult to distinguish, so numerous and far extending are its suburbs. Numberless green islands stud the deep blue of the harbour, whilst the fluted tops of the Organ Mountains form a completing circle to the further edge of the bay. Now the sun gleams forth lighting up the spires and towers of Rio, and bringing out the brilliant green of the tropical vegetation.

The political situation, however, detracts from the interest of the harbour, for now we see that all the shipping is collected at the head of the bay opposite to Nichteroy, the capital of the province, possessing the arsenal, and that the men-of-war of all the European powers are anchored near. There is the British cruiser *Sirius*, and two gunboats, the *Beagle* and *Racer*. The first is commanded by Captain Lang, who performed for the Chinese navy what Gordon did for their army. One French man-of-war, two Italian, two German, and two United States, are all near together. The rebel fleet with top-masts lowered, and decks cleared for action, lies in different parts of the bay. Over there is the *Aquidaban*, the flagship of Admiral Custodio de Mello, the leader of the Naval Rebellion. Its deck is crowded with people.

On anchoring confusion reigned supreme on board, but we were extricated by courteous letters from Mr. (now Sir Hugh) Wyndham, the British minister, and Captain Lang, who had sent a steam launch from the *Sirius* to convey us ashore, and in a few minutes we were on our way thither in his genial company.

There to the left is the Ilha das Cobras with the red cross flag hoisted on the Marine Hospital. It is also the site of the Naval Cadet College, commanded by that admirable man, Saldanha da Gama, and it is mainly owing to his good influence that up to now the cadets have maintained an attitude of neutrality. Thus Ilha das Cobras and another adjoining island, also remain neutral, and their partisanship is eagerly desired and sought by both parties.

We land at the Naval Arsenal, near the Custom House, remembering that it was from here that the late and last Emperor, Pedro II., was taken on board the gunboat, at dead of night, and last set foot in Brazil.

A few days ago the Government attempted to seize Ilha das Cobras, so the *Aquidaban* anchored at the buoy we see about 200 yards away, and commenced to bombard the lower part of the town which contains the business quarter. The steeple of the Church of the Pescadores was knocked down, and the shell exploded in the room of a house below, which we afterwards saw with the wall blown out.

We land and take a "bond" (or tramcar) through the Rua Primo de Marco, past the Hospital of the Misericordia lying by the harbour shore, until we reach a steep street where we get out. A climb up some winding steps brings us to the house and garden of Mr. Mendes, the well-known purveyor to the British Navy, under the familiar name of "Portuguese Joe." Mr. Wyndham, unable to get a room in any hotel, is lodged for the present here. All the Legations are situated at Petropolis, Rio being too unhealthy as a place of residence. We are assured that the hotels in the lower part of the town are unsafe, and whilst they telephone for rooms at the Hotel International at St. Thereza, we are put in possession of the political situation.

On the morning of September 6th, Rio awoke to find that the navy under Admiral Custodio de Mello had rebelled against the military dictatorship of General Floriano Peixoto. All the officers happened by a curious coincidence to be ashore that night, and by morning Mello was in possession of twelve vessels of war, five torpedo boats, five coasting steamers, and two steam launches, twenty-four vessels in all. The arsenal at Nichteroy was bombarded, and Mello issued a manifesto. Being in possession of the harbour, he was able to cut off supplies and all communication by water. On Wednesday there were signs that the city was to be bombarded by the rebels. Suddenly at ten o'clock, firing commenced. It was the signal for a stampede of women and children, and a general exodus to the mountains. It is estimated that one-third of the population left the town. The banks and places of business were closed. Few casualties were reported, but the press censorship is so rigorous, that the newspapers are a perfect blank as to current events.

Once or twice the bombardment was renewed, and some shots and shells fell in the lower town, one unfortunately killing a young English clerk standing on the balcony of a restaurant. Gossip says that he was one of four clerks who came out together from England last October. Three died of yellow fever within three months of landing, and now the fourth has met with a violent death.

On September 25th the fleet notified their intention of bombarding the city. Mr. Wyndham issued a manifesto to the English to leave Rio as quickly as possible. The same notice was issued by the other ministers to warn their countrymen, and it was arranged that in case of necessity, the Europeans were to assemble on the Palace Square to be taken off to the various men-of-war. Two rockets from the town, answered by one from the cruiser, were to be the signal for landing some 700 bluejackets from the united fleet. All the European powers are working harmoniously together, with the strange exception of Germany, who holds completely aloof, perhaps because the French Admiral happens to be the "doyen" of the fleet on this occasion, and they do not choose to work under him.

The intervention of the foreign Powers, headed by Mr. Wyndham, served to avert the destruction of the city. The Government consented to dismount the guns on the heights just above the lower town, on condition that Admiral Mello undertook not to bombard the city. The desertion of Villegaignon, one of the three forts in the harbour, on the previous day, has been one of the severest blows yet received by the Government.

Such is the position of affairs. We find Rio in a state of siege, and yet the apathy of the people is astounding. They assemble on a good vantage-point to watch the firing, as if it had been a sham battle. Partisanship does not run high, but as many arrests have been made, men fear for their opinions. We gather that the rebels are gaining ground. The National Guard has been called out, but comprising as they do the worst elements of the town, more is to be feared from their excesses perhaps than from the landing of the rebels. A strange incident happened the other day. A boat flying the British flag was seen at the customary anchorage of the *Aquidaban* (foreign launches and boats have been allowed to land when bearing the flags of their nationalities). On investigation by the British flagship, it turned out that an American named Boynton and an Englishman were preparing with a torpedo to blow up the Brazilian ironclad; the former averring that he had been offered a large sum of money, 10,000 dollars of which had already been advanced, if he succeeded in blowing up the centre vessel of the mutineers. They were taken prisoners to their respective cruisers.

Rumours being current of a bombardment between the forts this afternoon—indeed they appear only to be waiting for two sailing vessels to clear out of the way—we hasten to take the "bond" to the funicular railway. In a few minutes this lifts us far on our way up the mountain. Another bond, drawn by four mules, drags us up the steep, winding mountain road. The views over the harbour are superb; the vegetation, with its glowing, tropical colouring, enchanting; but—boom! boom! we hear the thunder of the cannon, and we can think of nothing else until, with a final tumble and scramble, the mules land us under the walls of the hotel, on the heights of Santa Thereza.

What a sight meets us as we reach the terrace! Great columns of smoke puff out from Santa Cruz, as one after another her guns open fire on the now rebel fortress of Villegaignon. A flash of fire, a volume of smoke, and then a reverberating boom that shakes the ground, even at this height and distance, under our feet. Now the fort of Lage, appearing only a tiny speck on the blue waters of the harbour, joins in and contributes the thunder of its guns to the bombardment; and a masked battery on the peninsula of San Juan occasionally sounds forth, as shown by the column of smoke that rises from this green spot. But the rebels answer gamely. Villegaignon pours a storm of shot around Santa Cruz and Lage, and the *Aquidaban* with the other war vessels open fire.

Rumble, rumble, as of distant thunder! flash, flash! boom, boom! as the artillery thunders forth murderously on all sides. All the intermediate sea around Santa Cruz and Lage is agitated by a hailstorm of shot. Frequently a shell falls, sending up a column of spray into mid-air.

What was that? A great flash of fire, succeeded by a cloud of smoke, rises out of Villegaignon. We imagine a shell has burst inside the fort. But we heard afterwards that a Whitworth gun had exploded, killing one man by cutting his body into three pieces, and wounding seven others. Then a shell burst just short of Santa Cruz, with a great flash of flame and smoke, succeeded by a fountain of water over the place where it fell into the sea. We see a ship sailing gaily in under full canvas, past Pai and Mai, towards the entrance of the harbour. They must be astonished at the boom of cannon, but as they may have been sailing for thirty days out from England, and know nothing of the revolution, probably they imagine it is some national festival of rejoicing. Whiz!—a shell went very near their mast and fell a few yards off. They begin to think something is wrong, and soon come to anchor.

For two hours does this vigorous bombarding proceed, and then clouds descend in heavy rains, and early darkness sets in. The firing dwindles and dies away. What has been the result? Nothing gained on either side. They say a few shots landed in Santa Cruz, one in Lage, and some bullets hit the heavily armoured side of the *Aquidaban*. We had seen with astonishment that the shot and shell fell promiscuously short—in fact so bad was the aim that we almost concluded that it was done on purpose. Thus ended without damage another of the series of pantomimic conflicts.

We find a very damp room and beds in a *dépendance* of the hotel, which is crowded with refugees; but we think ourselves fortunate to be safely encamped on the heights of Santa Thereza, beyond the range of the stray bullets of these incompetent gunners.

From our beautiful mountain we take a bond the next morning, winding down the hillside. The white stone aqueduct made by the Jesuits, who were some of the first settlers in Brazil, and whose good work for the country is constantly present, bears us company for some way. Around us is a jungle of dense tropical growth of gigantic palms, bright-green banyan trees, eucalyptus, flowering bushes with bright, waxy leaves, wreathed with ropes of creepers, all mingling together in dusky confusion. Maidenhair fern grows freely in the crevices of the walls of the overhanging gardens, with their gaudy hedges of crotons, whilst the views over the harbour, lying serene and bright in the clear morning air, are simply indescribable. For between fifty and sixty miles its beautiful contour indents the coast, with numberless islands of vivid green jewelling its placid surface, whilst the Sugarloaf stands ever in sentinel watch at the harbour entrance, and the Tijuca range forms a magnificent background of brightest emerald-green.

Our enthusiastic delight over this panorama of beauty ends with the funicular railway, which brings us quickly down to the lower town, past the roofs of many houses. One minute we are on the mountainside, looking down far below; the next we are landed in the street. A "bond" takes us to the centre of the town. The term "bond" applied to the tramways comes from the English company who started them, giving bonds or coupons. There is little choice of locomotion in Rio, for carriages are scarce and the only alternative is the regular old-fashioned French tilbury, lined with crimson plush, and holding but one person besides the driver. The streets are so badly paved, and formidable holes and pools of water so frequent, that a bond is the preferable mode of travelling, and patronized by all classes. They are all drawn by mules, who, with bullocks of far-branching horns, are the only draught animals. These mules are fine animals; sleek, strong, and wiry, looking ridiculously small to draw the large open tramcar, but they go a great pace, and keep on their legs in a wonderful manner, picking their way on the uneven cobble-stones. The whip used is a flat leather thong, which comes down with a resounding thwack on the mule's back. The bond is stopped by a "tschut," a noise peculiar to Brazilian lips.

There is nothing to see in the town. All the beauty of Rio lies in the wondrous setting of the harbour, and the pretty surrounding suburbs. The streets are very narrow, winding, and overhung with the broad eaves of the roofs and tiers of balconies, rendering them sunless and cheerless. Yet many of the houses have a good appearance, from the marble-veined stone, sparkling with mica and quartz, of which they are built, and which bears a resemblance to alabaster. The fretwork of the iron railings and gateways is attractive, and they have imported from

Portugal the pretty custom of tiling with blue and yellow porcelain the lower storey of the dwellings. Squalid as are the houses of the smaller streets, they are redeemed by a certain picturesqueness of oriental colouring. These are some of the tints we see: grass-green, sky-blue, heliotrope, pale pink, chocolate, dark brown, yellow, and carmine.

Rua Primo de Marco seems to be the busiest commercial street, which we reach by the Ministry of Foreign Affairs. Opposite is the palace of the late Emperor, looking on to Palace Square, with the allegorical fountain representing the four principal rivers of Brazil—the Amazon, the Parana, the Madeira, and the San Francisco. To this palace Dom Pedro hurried from Petropolis, where he permanently resided, on the news of the first breaking out of the revolution on November 14th, 1889. It was here that, after a sleepless night, surrounded by the Empress, the Crown Princess Isabel, and the Conde d'Eu, he resigned the throne, to be hurried from the palace the same night and placed on board a gunboat. So ended the revolution of the "Three Glorious Days." We are beholding the sequence to the Emperor's abdication in the civil war in progress.

Numberless kiosks, hung with painted poles, facilitate the sale of lottery tickets, which are used for all purposes, including that of collecting money for charitable objects. A mixture of races is seen in the Brazilians with their small persons, sallow faces, and brown eyes; Portuguese, who are of finer and stronger build; and the emancipated negro slaves, and the negresses, with their turbaned heads and flat-footed, swinging gait.

CORCOVADO AND THE SUGARLOAF.

The Haven of Brazil in Revolution. 23

We turn into the Rua Ouvidor, the principal street of Rio. It is a narrow alley, dark from the meeting balconies overhead, where no traffic is permitted. This is perhaps as well, for in other similar streets the bonds come so close to the pavement that it is as well to step into a doorway as they pass. The *coup d'œil* of the Ouvidor, with the narrow vista obscured by the overlapping flags, is original. Chief among the flags is the Brazilian ensign, green with a white centre, whereon is depicted a blue globe with celestial stars. Each constellation represents a province of Brazil, whilst across all is inscribed the motto, " Ordem e Progresso," " Order and Progress." It is a satirical comment on the present condition of the country. The Ouvidor is the Bond Street of Rio. The shops are full of Parisian goods, and hundreds use it in the evening as a favourite lounge. Times are unsettled now, and we see the Ouvidor somewhat deserted.

The afternoon finds us on our way out to Botofogo, a rich suburb extending for five miles to the Botanical Gardens. We see some of the palaces of the merchant princes, for Botofogo shares with Gloria, Larangeiras, and Thereza, the popularity of these breezy suburbs, with their pretty views over the harbour. It is a lovely drive, for to the left we draw near to the leaning Sugarloaf, whilst Corcovado is hanging immediately over our heads, on the right. We pass gardens full of flaming blossoms, orange, red, and purple. The alamanders grow on bushes, the poinsettias spread their scarlet petals along the dead branches of their trees, flaming salvias and spreading oleanders grow to the dimensions of huge shrubs.

while the hibiscus, single and double, is in full bloom. Trails of purple bougainvillia cover the moss-grown walls, and the orange-trees are weighed down with their golden fruit. Yet the Brazilians seem to prize our simple English flowers the most, for in those gardens that are most carefully tended we see our own familiar roses, carnations, asters, pansies, and even a few small autumn dahlias. They look so tender and delicate, beside the large and flaming blossoms of a tropical country.

The Botanical Gardens lie at the foot of the Tijuca Mountains. That magnificent avenue of palms, the finest in the world, grows here. Fifty palms form a lateral avenue; they are intersected in the centre by a double avenue, running longitudinally, of fifty more palms on either side. Each rises from a neat glass plot, throwing a perfectly straight, unnotched grey stem high in the sky, ending in a fringed cluster of palm-leaves. The perspective of these avenues is perfect, their fringed tops, in ever-diminishing height, seeming to meet together and descend in a vanishing line together. Since the deposition of the Emperor the gardens have fallen into bad order, and are now dismal and uncared for.

Rain has recently fallen, and we find Rio pleasantly cool and damp; but Nature has been too lavish, and these mountains that encircle the town shut out the breezes, and in the hot weather leave it a prey to stifling heat, which brings disease in its train. Yearly the population of 400,000 is ravaged by fever, and it is truly said, "Yellow Jack is the Emperor of Death, for whose downfall and permanent exile Rio de Janeiro despairingly hopes."

A disturbed night. At midnight we are awakened by the booming of cannon. The search-light, which sweeps the harbour incessantly at dark, has discovered that the *Marilio Dias* is cruising outside and attempting an entrance. Notwithstanding the firing, she manages to slip by the forts without injury, and gain entrance into the harbour.

At 6 a.m., having first assured ourselves that the Peak was clear, we prepared to ascend the Corcovado. But ere we had finishing dressing, down came the clouds, the mist even covering the harbour. Still we persevered, and joined the mountain railway at a midway station. This train shirks nothing. Up the steepest grades we go, the engine pushing from behind. The line is cut through the tangle of tropical growth, and as we rise quickly upwards, we are constantly looking down into the prettiest valleys and getting lovely peeps over the harbour. The sun gives forth a pale gleam, and we are hopeful, for this ascent gives quite the finest view of the whole of Rio ; indeed it is difficult to understand its topography without seeing the panorama of Corcovado.

The railway can go no further than Paneiras and the hotel platform, for the rebels have seized so much of the coal supplies that fuel is running short. Nothing daunted, we commenced to walk, and after getting very hot and tired, the clouds came down and damped our clothes and our ardour, and we descended, sadly and dispirited, to the town.

To-day is a national holiday. They are celebrating the discovery of America by Christopher Columbus, and all the offices are closed and the streets hung with flags. We had luncheon with Mr. Wyndham at the fashionable restaurant in the Ouvidor, the "Londres," where the *cuisine* is French. On the table are alabaster vases filled with flowers made of feathers, a fashionable industry in Brazil. They are clever imitations, but too gaudy to be pretty. More worth buying are the green beetles and dragon-flies that make up into pretty pins and brooches. We usually connect Brazil with the nuts bearing that name. Strange that all through the country you never see a Brazilian nut on the table. They are used only for export, and the rectangular shape arises from the way several nuts are packed together inside a pod.

On going down to the Arsenal wharf to embark for the *Thames*, we find the landing-stage has been fortified with iron plates, trusses of hay, and sand-bags, whilst a Maxim gun is being wheeled into position by some soldiers. Steaming safely under the protection of the British flag of the *Sirius's* launch, we reach the *Thames*.

There is great excitement on board. The rebel launches guard the ship, whilst some officers parley with Captain Hicks. It appears that we have as passengers some sixty deserters from the rebels, who are being sent by the Government to man one of the war vessels at Rio Grande do Sul. Admiral Mello demands their surrender with their firearms, refusing the *Thames* a passage outwards. Their luggage is being searched, but after some delay and consultation Captain Lang orders the *Thames* to proceed, and signals to the men-of-war, "Stand by; English mail going out." We get up steam and proceed forth, passing right under the stern of the *Aquidaban*.

Slowly we steam past, but not a shot is fired. On past Villegaignon and Lage we go, where we can see no damage from the bombardment. Opposite Santa Cruz we hang out a board inscribed with the password of the day, " Dino," but the look-out is so bad that we have passed ere they discover us, and give a tardy salute. With the Sugarloaf and Corcovado wreathed in mist, we sail past twin Pai and Mai, out into the open ocean.

CHAPTER III.

UP THE PLATE TO BUENOS AYRES.

It is the weary story oft repeated of quarantine all down the coast. We feel sadly impatient with this fresh disappointment and delay.

The colour of the ocean has undergone a change. It is muddy and torpid from the volume of water pouring down from the River Plate at the rate of fifty-two million cubic feet per minute. We halt at Flores, a little rock-bound island, the quarantine station. Here we learn our fate, and that there is no landing at Monte Video. We put ashore several boatloads of passengers, to join 270 others who are performing their penance. Then they have the impudence to send off and say that it is raining too heavily for them to disembark any more, and we are kept anchored for the night. Thus it is ever, one more wearisome delay upon another.

We proceed to Monte Video, the capital of Uruguay, the Oriental State as it is always named, being to the eastward of Argentina. The people delight in being called "Orientals," and some of the oldest Spanish blood is in their veins. They are chiefly an agricultural and pastoral people, so the name seems misapplied.

Up the Plate to Buenos Ayres.

Monte Video has no port. Intended by nature to become one of the most considerable commercial capitals of South America, for lack of safe anchorage it languishes. The current is extremely dangerous. We lie out in the open roadstead, which is exposed to the full fury of the "pampero" as it blows off the mouth of the Plate. In ancient time there were so many sandbanks that the sailors named it Boca de Infernus; and so it seemed to us this morning, for with a fresh breeze, the yellow, muddy waters of the Plate foamed into billows, and the lighters that came alongside rolled and pitched desperately, leaning to every angle of the compass. Even safely anchored as we are, the ship rolls and lurches, shuddering from stem to stern as we occasionally bump on a sandbank. The horrors of landing in the launch alongside, reconcile us somewhat to our missing a visit to Monte Video.

Across this troubled expanse of water lay the long-drawn line of the town, with the turret of the cathedral a dominating point. But the most prominent object to the left is the green Cerro or Mount, which gives its name to Monte Video. Rising to 500 feet, it bears on its summit an old Spanish fort, from the centre of which springs a lighthouse, with a revolving light, visible twelve miles out to sea.

The afternoon wears on. The wind blows, the waves rage around, and everything that comes out to us is under water the whole time. The lighters rocking wildly alongside receive our cargo of sacks of coffee. Then a sad accident happens. A little girl of six, looking out of a port-hole in the steerage, is caught in the rigging of a lighter and falls into it.

The latter has sprung a leak and threatens to sink; they hasten to shore, and only some hours afterwards we learn that the child's neck was broken by the fall, and that she was killed on the spot.

If the Republic of Uruguay is not very familiar to us at home, at least it produces two well-known household commodities. Paysandu ox-tongues are exported from Paysandu, one of the principal ports on the River Plate; and at Fray Bentos, many miles further up, is the Saladero, or beef saltery, which manufactures Liebig's essence of beef.

A little voyage of only 120 miles across the estuary of the River Plate brings us opposite to La Plata. It is hard to believe that this wide sea is only the mouth of a river. But so it is.

For four weary days are we kept stationary at this anchorage opposite La Plata, surrounded by a large number of other vessels, our companions in misfortune. Daily does the health officer call in on us, on his round of inspection. We watch the launch visiting first one vessel and then the other. Our turn comes. It is always the heart-sickening answer, "To-morrow, perhaps." The weather is cold and cheerless; a great process of cleaning up the ship commences, and day after day of blankness rolls by until, on the morning of a certain Friday, we feel sure that our release is at hand, and that the eight days' quarantine from Rio de Janeiro have elapsed. We are all packed and waiting. The launch and health officer begin the usual visitation. But hour succeeds hour. "He cometh not," is the despairing cry of all on board, and we sit down in spiritless despair for yet another dull day of inaction on board.

We are just commencing dinner that evening, when a gentleman comes up the saloon and speaks to the captain. The good news spreads like wildfire. It is the doctor, and we know that we have pratique.

The Argentine Government are doubtless right to impose a strict quarantine against arrivals from Brazil. Yellow fever is an epidemic that would spread quickly in their insanitary towns, but a ship's clean bill of health might avail something in shortening the period of detention, and a sailing-ship sixty or eighty days out from England, and that has not touched at any intermediate ports, might be given free pratique at once. Reason and judgment should prevail against red-tapeism. At least we have been saved the horrors of Martin Garcia, the quarantine island; the French mail is just landing her passengers there.

Very early the next morning we are inside the long breakwater with its fringe of rustling willows and reeds, whispering in the still morning air, and passing the docks of Ensenada. The low, swampy ground is covered with great clumps of pampas grass. Soon the *Thames* is turning, with the help of two valiant little steam-tugs, in a narrow basin, and safely docked at La Plata. These docks are a great engineering work, and were built by a Dutchman, Mr. Wardrop, costing 3,000,000*l*.

Whilst the confusion of passing the luggage through the Custom House progressed, we had time to take the train to La Plata, about three miles distant. The country was intensely flat, and intersected by dykes and swamps covered with coarse grass. The train, after passing through the street in the centre of the city, landed us at a magnificent terminus, a typical introduction to this deserted town. La Plata is a city of paper. Founded in 1882, during the years of the boom, when the docks then being constructed would connect it with Ensenada, La Plata was designed by its founders to be a great commercial port, the capital of the province, and the rival of Buenos Ayres, the national metropolis. Magnificent public buildings rose quickly to order, boulevards were laid out in wide blocks, and sites set apart for the Provincial Assembly, the City Hall, Museum, etc. It was designed to be like Washington, a city of "magnificent distances." Land speculators operated largely and found a fertile field for their nefarious dealings. In a year or two the census numbered 30,000 inhabitants. But they soon tired of the quiet life, and longed for the pleasures of the capital. The exodus began. Now La Plata is a city of the departed. The streets we see are grass-grown and deserted. Rows of carriages stand awaiting a fare, but none ply in the streets. The trams even are empty, and were it not for the law obliging provincial employees to reside here, it would be a city of the dead.

We see the wide Plaza, with the scrubby palm avenue that connects the local Parliament Buildings on the one side, with the Government House on the other. This latter with its magnificent Corinthian columns is half finished, one wing being minus windows and its outer veneer of stucco. A tramway takes us past the police barracks, and towards a great triumphal arch which leads nowhere. Then among the groves of eucalyptus-trees we pass the museum, the only thing worth seeing, and so forth again on to the dreary plain and back to the docks. La Plata, placed down on a swamp, vast and treeless, sheltered only by the eucalyptus which have grown up quickly since the foundation of the city, was without a *raison-d'être*, and doomed to a speedy death. We see it senile and decaying. Yet is it interesting. The abstract was so grandiloquent, the concrete is so infinitely dismal.

We return to Ensenada at the same time as the special train, which brings glad hosts of friends to greet our passengers. This is a great Argentine custom, the greeting and bidding farewell to travellers, and the railway-stations are always crowded with groups of these affectionate friends. Very amusing and "sentimental," as an American lady said to me, were some of these welcomings; for the Argentines are a very affectionate race, and if their women are not remarkable for their intellectual qualities, at least they are very fond and devoted mothers. You also see here, what you never would in England, married sons and daughters living under the parental roof, and not seeking a house of their own on marriage.

Our Custom House inspection, thanks to the courtesy of the officials, was purely nominal, and we were soon in the train going up to Buenos Ayres.

South America looks very untidy. That is our first impression of the country as we pass through a large, flat expanse of land, almost bare save for a luxuriant crop of large-leaved, rank thistles, on which many cattle preparing for export are feeding. Now we run through a large estançia, with the pretty house hidden among some woods of eucalyptus.

D

These trees make such a curiously even wood or forest, planted in regular lines, and with nothing but grey stems visible below, with no undergrowth or bramble to break their even ranks. We become at once acquainted with a leading feature of life on an estancia. I refer to the bleaching and rotten carcases that lay strewn in all directions. Where they fall, there they lie, the skin only being thought worth preserving, and all the pampa of South America is strewn with these ghastly objects. We are delighted to see another distinctive feature of this southern hemisphere in a flock of ostriches, flapping their wings and striding away from the train

This little journey of two hours, intensely ugly as it is, is characteristic of the Argentine Republic. The deadly level monotony of the country, the utter flatness, is typical of the whole. The untidy fences, the shanties roofed with corrugated zinc, the parched earth, the rank growth of thistles, the large herds of cattle, are metaphorical of the whole of Argentina.

We approach Buenos Ayres through the most unsavoury portion of the city, the Boca, where, in the most wretched " conventillos," or wooden houses raised on posts, gather together the lowest of the Italian immigrants. The streets are full of holes, covered with green slime, squalid and festering with disease, a very hotbed of crime. The tower of the church of San Domingo is passed, where hang the flags of the English regiments, dark memory of a great national reverse. Then the docks of Buenos Ayres, with its sea of rigging crowded together in the narrow channel of the little stream of Richuelo, come in sight. There are sailing vessels from every port of the world, busy lading barrels of sugar, or dried hides, which lie stacked high on the docks; and some day when the Government have finished the great excavation works of the new docks, from this little stream the largest vessels will be able to come up and anchor before the wharves of the city.

We arrive at the Central Station, and, thanks to the kindly help of Mr. Green, the courteous agent for the Royal Mail Company, we find ourselves in a few minutes at the Royal Hotel. This hotel marks a new departure in the social status of the city; for hitherto, as we had been warned, the indifferent comforts of the Grand and the Provençe were all that the traveller could expect. Henceforth Buenos Ayres has a first-rate hotel, newly furnished from Paris, and well equipped in every way. The American system of an inclusive charge, generally varying from six to ten dollars a day, is general.

Buenos Ayres is the most important town in the southern hemisphere. It surpasses Rio de Janeiro, Melbourne, and Sydney in population. It is the Paris of South America—the first thing that strikes you, however, are the tramways—the number of trams, and their noise. The pavements are very narrow, barely room for two abreast; and the tramcars usurp some of this space, the horses touching the curb as they stumble along in the gutter. A horn dangles from a string in front of the driver, and at every cross street the sound of this penny trumpet re-echoes, or even the more ambitious notes of the bugle recall a hunting morning at home. Again, you may liken it to the cat-calls of a Punch and Judy show, or the braying of an ass. Night is made hideous by it, and, awake or asleep, this noise in the streets below is perpetual and harassing. The second thing that calls for notice is the paving of the streets with large, uneven cobble-stones, full of holes, and seamed with tram-lines. On all sides you have the most painful spectacle of horses falling, slipping, and recovering themselves on the greasy stones. Driving is a penance, with the carriage-wheels being constantly wrenched against the tram-lines, and the relentless jolting over ill-laid blocks. The horses are small and mean-looking. Excellent as they are for hard work, the drooping head and flopping ears of the native horse make him a peculiarly ugly-looking animal. It is a sign of the cheapness of horseflesh that all hired carriages have a pair; in fact, a vehicle drawn by a single horse is almost unknown.

A policeman is posted at every transverse crossing. His neat uniform of blue cloth, with cape and white spats, is very smart; whilst standing near him, hobbled, is his horse, ready for him to mount, in pursuit of justice. He is provided with a whistle, and every quarter of an hour all through the night it sounds, and is answered by the man at the next point, and so on all through the city. If he receives no answer from his comrade, he mounts his horse and gallops to the next point to see if anything is wrong. Thus all through the night, the citizens who lie awake, are constantly reassured of the presence of these watching guardians.

Buenos Ayres is a typical American city, laid out in the wearisome regularity of the chess-board. Each block—called a manzana—is 140 yards by 140, on each of its four sides, and contains about 100 houses. These blocks are intersected with another street about every 150 yards. Thus the geography of the city is simple, though occasionally you forget the inordinate length of a street, and find you have further to go than you like, for many of the streets contain 1300 or 1400 numbers. Rivadavia, the central artery, is several miles in length, and has over 7000 numbers. We find many national events commemorated in the names of the streets, such as Calle 25 Mayo, the day of independence from the Spanish yoke. Every South American city thus honours the 25th of May. Or again, great generals, such as Belgrano, General Lavalle, and Rivadavia, give their names to a Calle.

Were the streets wider and the houses higher, Buenos Ayres would be a handsome city. As it is, even the best quarters of the town have a mean and cramped appearance. The houses are only one story high, with a flat roof called the "azotea." The windows are on a level with the pavement, and guarded by iron railings, and shuttered, which gives rather a grim, dull appearance to the dwellings. Many of the houses and public buildings have a handsome exterior, as they appear to be built of massive blocks of stone and granite. Pleasing delusion! for here is a half-finished building of rough brick and mortar, and it awaits the veneer of stucco that completes the illusion. The old Spanish custom is universal of the houses being built round a "patio." Very pleasant and cool look these pretty patios, of which we catch passing glimpses through the light filagree grille that guards them from the street, with their tesselated marble pavements in blue and black, their palms and flowering shrubs clustered round a splashing fountain.

We were amused to see that the Buenos Ayreans ensure a fresh supply of milk, by having the cow, with its calf, brought to the door. Thus you constantly saw a cow being milked under the householder's supervision. Another feature in the dairy supply are the gauchos, with long, flowing ponchos, riding in from camp on the roughest horses. Attached to the saddle are leathern receptacles, covered with cow-hide, some small, others large, arranged in tiers. The smaller tins contain the cream and the larger the milk, and the former is made into butter and churned as the animal jogs along. A sheep's skin covers the saddle and cans to prevent the sun from turning the cream, and the gaucho rides atop, with his legs dangling forward over the horse's neck.

We attended church on Sunday morning. There was a poor congregation; but the English, from the absence of the usual Saturday half-holiday, adopt the custom of the Catholic country, and spend Sunday in amusement. Mrs. Pakenham, the wife of our Minister, took us out to the Polo Club at Belgrano. Buenos Ayres has many suburbs, the chief of which are Flores, Belgrano, and Quilmes, and here most of the foreigners reside in pretty quintas, or villas.

It was a long drive of six or seven miles through the Avenida General Alvear, and beginning with some of the palatial residences of the *élite* of Spanish society. These splendid houses, with their *porte-cochères* and recessed balconies, their pretty gardens full of palms and banksia roses, command a view over the River Plate. Formerly they were the scene of many magnificent entertainments, but since the boom and subsequent crash they are given over to a quiet solitude. There is scarcely any entertaining done now, and retrenchment and economy are the order of to-day. Buenos Ayres has awakened from its mad revel of profligacy, when foreign money poured in plentifully, and great public works gave opportunity for jobbery. It is wiser and sadder, and healthier times are coming, when public confidence will be restored. In every city we came upon the remnants of this great boom, in the shape of magnificent public buildings, half finished, and falling into decay. On all sides we heard of the semi-ruin of the great Spanish and Argentine families. We had left England with the same tale of ruin and disaster to all interested in South American stocks ringing in our ears, only to find a repetition of it in another hemisphere.

The pretty gardens of the Recoleta lead us into the broad, dusty avenue, lined with casuerina-trees, which extends for a dreary length past the Penitentiary, the Waterworks, and the park of Palermo, towards Belgrano. There are the two racecourses, and the "barranca," or high cliff, where several pretty houses are in possession of one of the few elevations around Buenos Ayres. It is a dusty, untidy-looking bit of country, and Belgrano, when we reach it, looks somewhat dull, with its rows of barred and shuttered windows, ill-paved streets, and clouds of dust, enlivened only by a few pretty quintas and their rose-laden gardens.

The polo-ground and its pavilion, are situated amid most dreary surroundings of half-finished houses and broken-down palings. The native horses seem to make most excellent polo ponies, and we witnessed a very fast game. Hurlingham is another polo and cricket ground, an hour away from the city. Altogether Buenos Ayres, with 4000 English residents, seems to show decidedly sporting tendencies with its twenty-four athletic clubs, which include eight cricket, five football, two polo, six rowing, one tennis, and a hunt and a kennel club.

The most enthusiastic traveller would find it difficult to discover much to see in the city. Plaza Victoria, with its single circular row of palms around the square, is the civic centre, and contains all the characteristic extravagant work of Juarez Celman. Here is the Government Palace, the Capitol, the Law Courts, the Cabildo, the Bolsa, where, amid scenes as feverish as those in Wall Street, fortunes were made and lost in the palmy years of 1888 to 1890. The Cathedral and Bishop's Palace occupy the best part of one side. The imposing façade of the cathedral was given by General Rosas, " a tyrant who needed to do something for religion to atone for his crimes against liberty." The portico is upheld by twelve Corinthian columns, and represents Joseph embracing his brothers, in commemoration of the reunion of Buenos Ayres with the other Argentine provinces. But the *coup-d'œil* of even all these fine colonnaded buildings, with their Grecian capitals and recessed balconies, is quite spoilt by the intervals of unfinished houses, or flat-roofed, dingy shops, whilst the centre of the square is bare and unattractive, notwithstanding its two patriotic monuments.

PLAZA LIBERTAD, BUENOS AYRES.

Up the Plate to Buenos Ayres.

Every Englishman must soon turn his steps towards the church of San Domingo, rising from a marble platform, with its right-hand tower thickly embedded with cannon-balls. It contains a sad sight for us. On each of the six pillars of the nave is a handsomely carved gold frame. Within it, protected by glass, an ancient flag, not an emblem of the Church, not a record of the march of Christianity; but a monument of the defeat of the English in 1807.

In the year preceding, General Beresford, with the 71st Highlanders, a battalion of Marines and a few gunners, had taken possession of Buenos Ayres. The expedition was planned by Captain Sir Home Popham upon his own responsibility. The Spanish Viceroy fled at the approach of the English, and 40,000 people surrendered on June 27th, 1806, to 1000 British infantry, with 16 horsemen, 2 howitzers, and 6 field-guns. A million sterling of treasure was despatched to London, and received with popular rejoicing.

The idea of Pitt was to repair the loss of the United States of America, by the acquisition of the far richer Southern Continent. Had it been realized how different would have been the lot of these politically distracted Republics! Strong reinforcements were prepared. Merchant fleets set sail for the new El Dorado. They left England triumphant. They returned despondent.

Beresford the Brave had done all that was humanly possible to maintain his position. He had conciliated the inhabitants, paid for all his supplies, guaranteed the freedom of religion. Had he declared his mission to be the expulsion of the Spaniards, and the establishment of South American independence, he might have won the people over completely. But he had no instructions. By degrees the weakness of his position became apparent. By the help of a French soldier of fortune—Captain Liniers, afterwards styled the Reconqueror—Spaniard combined with Argentine, and surrounded him on all sides. Beresford was compelled to surrender.

The relieving force was under the ill-fated command of General Whitelocke, of reputed bar-sinister royal. He was either knave or fool—perhaps both. He had an army of 12,000 men and the support of a large naval force; but after criminal delay he marched on Buenos Ayres on July 5th, 1807. Only raw levies were opposed to him, but his defeat was signal; he surrendered at discretion. These flags in San Domingo are the trophies of the reconquest.

They consist of the King's and the regimental colours of the 71st Highlanders; a red ensign of the Royal Marines, the "R.M.B." conspicuous in the centre, and the legend, "Ubique per mare, per terram"; a Union Jack and a plain red ensign, said to have belonged to H.M.S. *Diadem;* a red flag with a Death's head and crossbones thereon.

One of the prisoners of the 71st, whose brave deeds in America and Hindostan, in Africa and the Peninsula, at Waterloo and Sevastopol, are not diminished by their action at Buenos Ayres, wrote with charcoal on the wall of his cell the following doggerel Spanish epitaph :—

Up the Plate to Buenos Ayres. 43

"Aqui yace el fomoso Regimento nombrado del Ingles 71.
Jamais vencido de enemigo alguno,
Que en lides nil. Salio lucimento.
Aqui yace postrado su ardmento
A la fuerza y valor de unos soldados,
Que sin brillo, sin lustre y desertrados,
Abaturon su orgullo en un momento
Llora la Inglaterra esta disgracia,
Serviendo de escarimento à su osadia
Al saher sucumbieron por and acea
Cerca de dos nil bomberes que mania
Intentar dominar su ineficacia
Del Argentino el brio y valentia."

Which may be paraphrased :—

"Here lies the famous Regiment numbered 71st by the English—the hero of a thousand fights, never vanquished by a foe—its ardour laid low by the valour of a few soldiers, without tradition or experience. In a moment they lowered its pride. But let this misfortune be to England a warning that Argentine, the brilliant, is not to be overcome by some 2000 men."

It is said that once since that sad day, the Argentine Government was disposed to restore the colours to her present Majesty in proof of amity and good will, but that the British Minister replied, "that when we wanted them, we would come and take them." There is probably no truth in this, for although our diplomatic representation in South America may not be brilliant, it is not discourteous. The rumour probably arose from a Chilian gentleman having written in 1882 to H.R.H. the Duke of Cambridge offering to restore a standard of the 71st, taken by his grandfather at

Buenos Ayres in 1806. The letter being referred to the Argentine capital, gave rise to a municipal commission, which, after full investigation into all the facts, declared that no other flags were taken save those in San Domingo, and a banner in the Cathedral, and that no Chilian troops came to the succour of the Argentines.

On the other hand it was probable that in the popular enthusiasm over the Reconquest, which is still celebrated on many a street, flags were made, as souvenirs, in imitation of the captured ensigns.

The Recoleta, the great cemetery of Buenos Ayres, lies on a bluff, surrounded by a pretty garden. It presents a strange spectacle. The coffins are not buried, but each is placed in a separate temple of its own. Thus you walk through broad, palm-bordered avenues, where a strange medley of marble memorials are thickly crowded together. Some have a canopy supported on columns, with a life-sized statue of the deceased seated beneath. In others you descend into a cool marble grotto inside the vault, where a bust of the departed crowns the altar. There are obelisks, pyramids, and rock-hewn caves without number. But the most favourite way is to enshrine the coffin in the marble altar-piece, leaving a space where it is visible among the candles, crucifixes, and tawdry decorations of artificial flowers and bead wreaths. The doors are often left open, and it is customary for relations to come and tend the decorations. Some again have vaults, seventy feet deep, with sliding doors, and you can look down and see the compartments, some quite full and others awaiting their occupants.

Many of the chapels contain a family, and it is touching to see the babies' coffins and those of children of all ages, buried with their parents. A placard announces that this sepulchre is to let. Possibly the relations have omitted to pay the rent, in which case the occupant is unceremoniously turned out and sent to the common cemetery; for only the rich can afford to be buried here, the price of a vault in perpetuity being about 2000*l.* Those who cannot afford the luxury of a chapel must be placed in the thick wall divided into niches, where the door is sealed with a marble tablet with the name of the deceased. The big bell of the neighbouring church of the Recoleta tolls ceaselessly, and the barbaric pomp of the funerals is very impressive, with their enormous retinue of mourning friends. But the near contact with death around and above ground is oppressive, and with a shudder we emerge through the gloomy portals, where the sable bier in the adjoining sala awaits the next comer, to mingle with the gay throng of carriages wending their way towards the park of Palermo.

The Mendicants' Asylum occupies the old convent of the Bethlemite friars, on this same bluff. Forty years ago the few poor persons there were in Buenos Ayres made their rounds every Saturday on horseback, wearing a police medal, and soliciting alms, being sent away sometimes with the formula, "Pardon me, brother, for giving you nothing." Now they are gathered into this poor-asylum under the care of the Sisters of Charity.

We drove one afternoon to see "Celman's Folly," and arrived at a building rich in Rococo encaustic tiling, resplendent in blue and brown and yellow Doulton ware, wrought into pilasters, rising tier above tier into a magnificent pile. We thought at least that it was the city hall or some great public building. What was our surprise to learn that all this splendour contains only a vast series of water-tanks, raised in separate stories, each huge tank occupying one side of the building !

As we ascended, the sound of many waters reached our ears, tons of water pouring from the topmost cistern and filtering down to the lowest. These waterworks cost the shareholders 6,000,000*l.*, over 100,000*l.* of which was squandered in this ridiculous palace of pipes. The water supply is obtained from La Plata. The drainage also flows into the river some way distant. There is some idea that in certain tides and winds they get intermixed.

At the "Frontone" or ball-court in the Calle Cordova, we witnessed the national game of "Pelota." It is a most graceful pastime, the "cesta" or long basket scoop receiving the ball with a skilful swoop, and then shooting it out again to a great height. It requires much dexterous skill to play well. The "frontone" resembles our racket or fives court, and the four players are called a quinetta, and play up to forty points. The excitement and shouting is intense in the betting-ring below, bets being offered on each volley and frequently on each stroke, if the volley is long sustained. A Spanish team receives an enormous sum to come out here, and a professional player will make perhaps 2000*l.* for the season, whilst it is no uncommon thing for the stakes to amount to 3,000,000*l.* in one year. It seemed to us that the strain on the wrist, where the cesta is attached by the winding round and round of a leather strap, must be trying. It would be a charming novelty to introduce into England, now that the day of lawn-tennis is waning. The size and space occupied by the frontone, however, is a difficulty, though small courts are constantly found in the grounds of Spanish houses.

A lovely afternoon found us on our way out to Flores, where are the prettiest quintas (or villas) of the Spanish and English merchants. We left the town at the commencement of Calle Rivadavia, and after going out into the country some six miles, still found ourselves in the same street and at No. 7000 odd! Very pretty are these villas, built in bungalow style, everybody choosing what appears best to his taste, be it Gothic, Corinthian, or Moorish, castellated or crenellated, arched or square, with balconies, terraces, and marble steps; each surrounded by a garden full of palms, and with such voluptuous hedges of roses, whilst pale-yellow tea roses form creepers of tropical growth on the walls and balustrades, and fountains play into a basin of gold-fish. The variety is infinite and pleasing. For several miles this suburb of Flores extends into the country, with its double row of quintas.

Returning we visited the post-office, which, though the only one for the whole city, is in a curious dirty, rambling building, situated quite out of the centre of the town, and surrounded by a fretwork of poor streets. Next we came upon " Tattersall's," which, borrowing its name from the great Knightsbridge emporium, fulfils much the same functions out here, only the sale of stock is included in its programme. All the great sales of thoroughbreds and stock from the well-known estancias are held here, and only last week the great yearly "ramate" of Captain Kemmis' yearlings took place, though the prices realized were rather disappointing compared to better times.

We ended up the afternoon with our usual stroll in the Calle Florida, that fashionable Regent Street of Buenos Ayres, with its Parisian shops and large crowd of *flâneurs*, whilst smart carriages with their gaily clad occupants gallop past on their way to Palermo.

One evening we paid a visit to General Bartolomé Mitré, an old and revered servant of the Republic, who has taken part in many campaigns, and filled the office of President. Full of years and honours, he passes his declining days in the seclusion of his library, translating Dante's "Inferno" into Spanish. With pardonable pride he took us up to his wonderful library, and showed us the 15,000 volumes, catalogued and classified, of every work and book published on the American continents, North and South. Adjoining and opening into his house are the offices and printing-press of the *Nação*, of which General Mitre is the able and fair-minded proprietor and editor.

Our social functions included a ball at Comte and Comtesse de Sena, in their palatial residence, when we were introduced to the *élite* of Argentine society and *porteñas*, as the ladies born in Buenos Ayres are called. The señoras, with their clear complexion and lustrous black eyes, their Parisian toilettes and gleaming diamonds, seemed to us beautiful and brilliant. Many of them had had English governesses and spoke English well, the others French.

We regretted to see that the English and Spanish society are quite apart. There is no social intercourse between the two nationalities, no interchange of courtesy. The English residents lose much that is pleasant thereby, though it is possible that the older families of the Republic may not care to be associated with our representatives, who are all intimately engaged with commerce. One must, however, allow that this is generally the case with the English colony abroad; we are too narrow-minded and prejudiced to associate cordially with other nationalities.

Another night we visited the Opera in Calle St. Martin, and heard a good performance of Donizetti's "Favorita." The opera season is over, and the ladies attend in morning dress, but earlier in the year full dress is compulsory. The house presents a much more brilliant spectacle than our Covent Garden, from the division between the boxes being merely a low balustrade; thus the *coup-d'œil* of the house is greatly enhanced. They have excellent opera companies, French, Italian, and Spanish performing during the season.

A luncheon given us by Mr. Welby, the delightful and popular First Secretary to the British Legation, at the Café Paris, made us acquainted with that fashionable restaurant, the rendezvous of the principal men of business for the mid-day *déjeuner*.

The darkness of the Café is redeemed by the excellence of its juicy beefsteaks, its delicious asparagus, strawberries, and fresh cream from the quinta.

Buenos Ayres supports two racecourses, one at Palermo, the other at Belgrano, called the Hippodrome. It was to this latter course that, on a lovely Sunday morning, we were driving in Señor Manuel Quintana's (son of the Minister of the Interior) smart victoria. The Derby of the year, the great international race with Monte Video and the Oriental Republic, was about to be run. The stand was gay with fluttering flags, and a vast crowd of some 8000 persons were present. We were conducted to a box above the space reserved for the Jockey Club, with a view over the pretty course, bordered with weeping willows, and with the carriages grouped on the ground on the other side of the railings. The paddock and weighing-rooms were excellent. We only missed the lawn in front of the stand, in place of the dusty space that took its place, to make it like Ascot. The colours were as varied and prettily combined as in England. The jockeys are all Argentine; English ones are never successful. It is whispered that jealousy is the reason, and not want of skill, and that an English jockey is always hustled in the race. There are no bookmakers. The betting is all through the Pari Mutuel, and in the large circular pavilion, with its separate guichet for each horse. One hundred and ninety-six thousand tickets were taken at this one meeting. The State charges a percentage on the winnings, and the Jockey Club or owners of the racecourse do the same; thus the two clubs are always well in funds. The horses parade round, and up and down a long time before each race. This enables people to judge the favourites, and a last rush to the Pari Mutuel then takes place. The boxes, with their low divisions, were full of smart ladies dressed in lightest summer attire forming a mass of brilliant colour. In this clear atmosphere pale vivid colours seem appropriate, and I often wondered at the daring shades of magnolia, orange, and pink that were worn with great effect by their fair owners.

Two former Presidents, General Roca and Dr. Pellegrini, were conversing in a box below us, and we saw and were introduced to many well-known people. Then the Jockey Club served a magnificent luncheon in a private room in the stand. The interest was gathering up, and excitement became intense as the hour for the big race drew near. Some 300 Montevideans had come over expressly to witness the race, and how they shouted for their favourite as slowly but surely it was beaten, and Buenos Ayres, the Argentine champion, won easily. The enthusiasm was enormous, and an ovation was accorded to horse and jockey as he was led through the crowd.

Of all the things that surprise you as you land in this South American capital, perhaps the park at Palermo is the most startling. Here, between the hours of five and seven each evening, but more particularly on Thursdays and Sundays, you will find hundreds of smart equipages, in a quadruple rank, going at foot's pace round and round the oval enclosure of the park precincts. Prettily laid out, it has an historical interest, having belonged to the great tyrant Rosas. The carriages are mostly closed or have the hood up. Ideas of propriety and the duenna hover over society, and the belles are hidden behind glass panels. Moreover, these Hispano-Argentine ladies never walk in the streets. Their lives are very dull, as they scarcely read or work, and their greatest pleasure is the daily airing in the Park, where they can display the lavish extravagance of their costumes and the cosmetics of their faces. It is no exaggeration to say that all are alike painted and powdered freely, from the highest ladies to the grisette. This procession of smart broughams, landaus, victorias, phaetons, and buggies, with liveried servants and splendid horses with cruel bearing-reins, does not betoken hard times. But here all is on the surface. They may not be paid for. What matter? The Argentine would rather live meanly at home than not make his outward parade.

A few horsemen mingle in the throng returning from the Rotten Row, where it is curious to see the riders ambling or "pacing" along in place of a trot or gallop. It looks a somewhat effeminate motion to us, but this is the natural gait of the horse, and he must be trained to other paces.

Now the gay throng turns homeward through the Boulevard Santa Fé, and you would think life depended upon getting home first, for the coachmen race with each other at full speed—indeed, they refuse a place where it is forbidden.

Paris has two great imitations, the one in the East, the other in the West—Bucharest and Buenos Ayres. It is rare to find two cities so far distant, yet so resembling one another. Both are largely given up to pleasure. In both every available cent is spent on outward show. In both French shops and restaurants fill the streets. In both French habits and customs are imitated in exaggeration. The resemblance is complete.

Buenos Ayres is a most pleasure-loving city. The Opera is always crowded, and the attendance at twenty-six theatres averages 3000 per evening, or one in every 180 of the population. The restaurants remain open all night, and tram-cars scarcely cease running. It is also a very cosmopolitan city, with its mixed nationalities of Brazilians, Spanish, Italians, Argentines, Germans, French, and Basques. The latter perform the domestic duties for the residents, whilst the Italians, whose immigration is enormous and successful, are the masons, the bricklayers, the gardeners, and day-labourers of the Republic. There are 700,000 Italians in the country, a good seventh of whom remain in the capital. Their children will become Argentines. Spain will give place to Italy. The Germans, hard-working and industrious, number some 5000; the Frenchmen have 9000, employed chiefly in shops and restaurants; England is represented by some 5000 residents, but the working men who have come out have done badly. On every hand we hear this fact confirmed.

The *haute commerce* of the country, the banking business, the great import and export houses, the large financial firms, the landed interest, is mainly in English hands, but they make no permanent home in the River Plate. Their eyes are ever cast towards their native shore, and their fixed idea is to return home so soon as their fortune is assured. The Germans are more prominent in *le petit commerce*. If a profit, however small, is to be made in a transaction, they will work hard to earn it. The French settle in the country. They are sympathetic to the foibles of the Argentines.

Hospitality and kindness had been showered upon us during our stay, and we left Buenos Ayres full of regrets, and full of gratitude to our kind hosts and hostesses.

CHAPTER IV.

THE CAMP OF ARGENTINA.

It was one of those perfect spring days, when we feel it a pleasure to exist, for our excursion to the Estançia San Martin, belonging to an Argentine gentleman, Señor Vincente de Casares. An hour in the train on the Sud Ferril Carril, passing through an absolutely flat country, occupied by many quintas and estançias, gave us our first impression of the "Camp." It is a curious expression this, signifying the country, and it takes a little time to habituate oneself to "living or going into camp" simply meaning to live or go into the country.

On arrival at the Station Vincente Casares we found a break and a magnificent four-in-hand team of blacks awaiting us, but our first view of the latter was somewhat untoward, for the leaders were standing on their hind-legs and fighting vigorously with their feet. After some trouble they and their harness were disentangled, and we proceeded along the road, a typical camp one. Space is not valuable, so the track is enormously wide, and barely indicated by some crooked railings. Road it cannot be called, for it is composed of the virgin soil of loose earth, now in dry weather a cloud of dust, rising in a monsoon behind us. In wet weather it becomes a morass, with lakes and ruts. The horses are never shod, nor do they have their hoofs pared. It is unnecessary, for the road is only their native earth.

Magnificent iron gates, lead us through a rich crop of alfalfa or lucerne to the pretty house, with a deeply recessed piazza leading into the surrounding rooms. Radiating from all sides of the house are grand avenues of eucalyptus, with far-reaching vistas. They flourish and grow rapidly, and are thus valuable in this treeless country. Just behind the piazza is an archway of willows, in the purest, freshest green. These weeping willows are found all over South America; they form a pretty and uncommon vegetation. Just now in the spring of the year they are rejuvenated and clothed in tender virgin green of brightest tint. The garden, with its fountains playing, its fawns and lions of bronze, was full of palms, gueldre roses, great red-headed poppies, and borders of cloves and pink. We thought San Martin a charming place, and would willingly have passed a month there.

The San Martin Estançia comprises something over thirty leagues, a league being three square miles in extent, or equal to about 6000 English acres. Over 6000 head of cattle are reared on this vast estate. But you soon grow accustomed to large figures in camp life, and deal in thousands where in England we should speak of fifties. The mayor domo, as the agent or estate manager of an estançia is designated, did the honours for M. Casares, who sent us a telegram of regret that he was accidentally prevented from coming himself.

The brilliant sunshine and pleasant breeze, the glories of a spring day, are enhanced by the exhilaration of this delicious climate. Overhead is a deep-blue sky, paling to a translucent grey tinge on the sweeping line of the horizon, always a noticeable feature in this flat pampa country. Birds are building their long, conical nests, amongst the budding branches of the trees, and on every gate and post are plastered their mud hives. The ptero, resembling our plover, wheels circling round, uttering its wild, piercing cry. Owls sit and blink in the sun, beside the earth holes of the bizacha or prairie dog. The short grass is just putting forth a new growth. We drive over the breezy uplands to inspect the herds of cattle. There are magnificent Durhams, Herefords, and black and white Dutch cows grazing with their calves. Their enormous size, broad backs, and weight of flesh would delight the judges of fat cattle at the Islington Agricultural Show, and I doubt finer animals being there exhibited than we were now seeing.

All the paddocks were covered with great clumps of thistles; but they are not like our ugly wayside weed, the favourite food of the donkey, but have beautiful silver leaves, long and drooping and gracefully scolloped. Their fertile growth is an indication of good land. During seasons of drought the cattle feed on them, as they retain the moisture, and even during the driest periods a little green grass is generally found under their spreading leaves. During the months of January and February the thistles attain to a height of six or seven feet, and present a very handsome appearance with their glow of purple blossom.

Then we drive across to the Central Dairy. We have noticed the various little buildings, scattered at far distances on the horizon. They are the milking-sheds, which collect and forward the milk to their great receiving centre, and we see the rough country carts, drawn by a troika of shaggy horses, containing the milk-cans, continually driving up before the platform. Here their contents are emptied into a great tank. I don't think that on any English dairy farm we should see a veritable corrugated zinc tank full of milk, the contents being passed through a pipe to the bell-shaped separator in the centre of the building. Here it was wonderful to see the milk pouring out of one tap and the cream from the other. The churn, the butter squeezer, and the separator are all worked by machinery; the churn-handle pumped vigorously up and down, and the wooden roller revolved round the circular board, pressing and squeezing out the butter-milk from great yellow-coloured masses of butter, by invisible means. The inside of this dairy was somewhat sloppy and untidy, and I must say that in this wholesale process one missed the clean tiles, the well-scoured milk-pans, and the irreproachable cleanliness of an English or Danish dairy. Sufficient butter and milk are sent away from St. Martin to supply a shop in the Calle Florida.

A drive a little further on brought us to a collection of ranchos and the sheep-pens; the shearing for the year is, however, finished. These ranchos are very rough huts built of mud bricks, with earth floors. Sometimes, indeed, they are made of wattles, plastered over with earth, and form but a frail protection on these exposed plains. Another paddock contained some of the valuable blood-mares and their foals. A single guanaco was feeding amongst them. We returned to wander round the farm buildings. One was surprised to see how rough was the stabling, with mud floors and matchboard partitions, where some exceedingly valuable mares and stallions were lodged.

It was pleasant to rest awhile amid the groves of eucalyptus, with the drowsy humming of insects, the singing of birds, and splashing of the fountain mingling together in the noonday heat, whilst luncheon was preparing. This turned out to be a native feast, beginning with "Tuchero," a favourite Spanish dish, and a staple dish in the domestic economy of South America. It consists of slices of mutton boiled until dry and stringy, and served up with salad cabbage and turnips. The *pièce de résistance* lay in the sheep, which we had watched, under the charge of a peon, being roasted whole in an adjoining grove. Cut open and extended across a spit, the carcase slowly revolved over a small fire of sticks. It was now produced, hacked up into unknowable portions. Pale-green strawberries, quite ripe but of this unusual colour, cream thick and rich from the dairy, with asparagus large, succulent, and jucy, and such as we in England never see or taste, completed this rural repast.

A last treat was reserved for us. Don Vincente Casares is celebrated for his stud, and no estançia in the Argentine boasts finer horses than were now produced. Gaily caparisoned with white and scarlet pad-cloths, decked with prize rosettes, led each by his particular stable peon, they pirouetted and pranced round and round the gravel drive. There was the bright chestnut thoroughbred, winner of a flat race a week ago; there were Clydesdales, and roadsters, and thoroughbred hacks and racers, as fine as any stud in England could produce, and we never tired of watching these magnificent animals trotting and capering round, now pawing the air with their fore-feet, now showing a clean pair of heels. A great deal of trouble has lately been taken by leading estançieros to improve the blood stock, and large sums have been expended in bringing over valuable sires from England. Ormonde, who was bought for 15,000*l.*, is only an instance of this determination. South America is already beginning to show the results of this improvement in breeding, and where horses can be reared so cheaply, the time will come when they will be largely exported to England. Already we were told, that a horse which will fetch 20*l.* in England, pays his expenses and leaves a margin of profit for the owner. An ordinary criollo horse can be bought for a sum varying from 1*l.* to 3*l.* Hence it is that even the poorest colonist or settler, the shepherd, the farm labourer, the wandering gaucho, all possess a horse. All ride in this country, and no man thinks of walking. The saddle is his home, and the horse his faithful companion.

We returned to Buenos Ayres to make our final departure west on the following day.

A last rattle over the holes and ruts of the capital brought us to the Once de Setiembre Station at

The Camp of Argentina. 61

6.30 a.m. The two trains per day on all the lines, leave, the one very early in the morning, the other late at night.

We are to travel in regal luxury, for Mr. Bouwer, the Metropolitan agent, and Mr. Craik, the manager of the Central Argentine Railway, have combined to do all in their power for our comfort, and have given us the use of a private car. We find ourselves in a long telescope coach, consisting of a sitting-room furnished with sofas, armchairs, writing-table, and looking-glasses, whilst the passage leads to two bedrooms, with hanging cupboards and every luxury, including a bath-room. The kitchen is at the further end. Domingo, the car attendant, is quite a character. He is an excellent cook, and overwhelms us with the number of meals and courses that he is only too anxious to serve, and insisting, contrives to get his own way. Attached to the end of the train we can enjoy our platform, with its uninterrupted vista of the twin rails, unwinding themselves in parallel and diminishing lines, across the great waste.

This is the pampa of South America.

Imagine a great barren plain of burnt, brown pasture, monotonous as the ocean, without a ridge or hillock or rise, reaching to the horizon ; a plain thus extending, without break or change, right from the Atlantic seaboard of Argentina to the foothills of the Andes. More cultivated and populated with men and cattle, it resembles closely the prairie of America. It has its counterpart also in the prairie of Canada. Like those great lone lands it has a peculiar fascination of its own, acquired from the extreme even monotony of the stretch, ending in a yellow circular line sweeping around the horizon and joining on to the pale, transparent sky-line, fading gradually together into space. It is a fascination, appreciated in some measure perhaps by those dwelling near the Downs at home.

Yes, the pampa exercises a great enchantment. During the four or five days during which we traversed its wide belt, the feeling of being drawn more and more into sympathy with the rich and boundless "park" increased. The first thing you notice about the pampa is the extraordinary stillness, broken only by the sound of the wind rushing through the dried liganeous grasses, producing a harsh, rustling sound. There is no bird life, if you except the hawks and falcons circling high in the air, watching for their prey. There are no flowers on the pampa, and in this it differs from the prairies of the northern hemisphere and the veldt of the Cape. I found a few scarlet and purple verbenas growing between the lines, and a little meadowsorrel and larkspur flourishing on the rank grass along the rails, but these were the only sign of the blossoming of spring. Oft we are delighted with constant visions of mirage floating in the distance, when the hot air quivers and dances, picturing blue lakes and green islets with cattle standing knee-deep in water, tantalizing delusion in a "barren and dry land where no water is."

A perpetual source of interest are the vast herds of cattle, sheep and horses, feeding now near the line, or anon appearing as specks in the far distance. One thousand sheep will be counted in a single flock, or five hundred head of cattle in a herd. The horses are

The Camp of Argentina.

always seen to be in groups. They follow the lead of the tingling bell of the maddrina, an ancient mare, who leads and guides the "tropilla" in their aimless wanderings over the plain.

Occasionally some picturesque figure of a galloping gaucho, with flying poncho, lasso in hand, will come in sight, rounding up a tropilla, and sending them flying before him; but generally these vast herds apparently roam where they will.

A melancholy source of interest are the skeletons, thickly strewn through the camp. Where the grass is most arid and parched, there they lie thickest, or in the gulleys where the water should be, and where they have come down to drink, and die for lack of it. Where they die there they lie. In pathetic attitudes, with heads upturned and limbs outstretched, their whitened skeletons are bleaching in the sun. It is terrible to see them in their different stages of decay, with the flesh blackening and entrails protruding; but generally the birds of prey do their work quickly, and nothing but the vertebræ and skull remain after two or three days. Meat is so cheap that the skin only is worth saving from off the carcase. Now we see the skeletons of many sheep. They lie thickest along by the railing which marked the old road, and where the grass is perhaps a little better. The drought has been terrible throughout the country, lasting for three years. Cattle have died by thousands. In many places the ground is quite bare, with not a single blade of grass. The water-gulleys are dried up; only the thistles seem to thrive. They are large and abundant everywhere.

It is true that in the pampa there is little indeed to

be imagined, not even a sense of vastness. Darwin, touching on this point in his "Journal of a Naturalist," truly says: "At sea, a person's eye being six feet above the surface of the water, his horizon is two miles and four-fifths distant. In like manner, the more level the plain, the more nearly does the horizon approach within these narrow limits; and this, in my opinion, entirely destroys the grandeur which one would have imagined that a vast plain would have possessed."

This is so, and yet, though the distance is not great, that clear circumference circling round our little coach, holds a mystery. What is beyond? Whither leads it? A question asked all through life. A question never answered here below. You ascend a mountain—how big the world looks. You descend and travel on the plain—how small it is, circumscribed by this yellow line of grass.

Now and again we pass a solitary graveyard by the line, roughly fenced in, where the gaucho, lonely in life, is left lonely in death. Once we saw a few rough carts, drawn by their untidy mestizzos, standing with drooping heads, while a group of rough gauchos stood gazing into an open grave where a comrade had just been laid to rest. A few weeping women were crouching at the head of the grave. It was a pathetic scene, and a touching theme for a picture, this last act in the wild gaucho's life, this laying to rest amid the pampa where he had roamed at will during life.

We have seen the pampa in the early morning, with the mists rolling away; in the brilliant glare of noonday, when the hot air scintillates with mirage, or obscured by driving clouds of rain. We have seen it at sunrise, noontide, eventide, in the dusk, by moonlight, or with darkness brooding over all. But it is always interesting, always attracting, always silent, always monotonous, yet always pleasing.

The stations are mere brick buildings by the side of the line, placed at equal distances of twelve miles apart, and named after the different Estançias through whose land the line runs. There was no idea of a village or even a collection of "ranchos" when the station was being made, but quickly a little town, or perhaps it would be more correct to say a straggling group of buildings of some sort have grown up around them. A few tents, marked F.C.C.A. (Ferro Carril Central Argentino), are grouped around. They are used by the men employed on the railway. Now we pass the solitary house of the superintendent of the quadrillo or gang who maintain the line in repair, or a few platelayers, who lift their trolley off the rails at the train's approach, and then lie down flat to see how much the line has deflected from the passing of the train.

Occasionally a group of trees attracts attention in the far distance. We know that it indicates an Estançia, for in this shadeless and treeless country the first work of settlement is to plant something that will give a little shade. Generally the Eucalyptus is chosen, on account of its rapid growth, attaining as it does to a good-sized tree in a short time; but the tall poplar is also a favourite. A very pleasant oasis of cool shade around the Estançia these groves make, difficult to appreciate, except on a pampa so utterly scorched, blazing, and unsheltered. The next familiar object is the water wheel, whose fluttering white wheels catch the sunlight whilst supplying water (found generally at fifteen to twenty feet) to the estate.

Fencing is pretty general now, and the old days of the rounding up and cheery gatherings at the neighbouring Estançias are becoming a custom of the past. But such fencing. It is no exaggeration to say that not one iron stanchion is upright; all are crooked, bent, or broken. We liked the railway best when it was not enclosed on either side, and when the line seemed to be running directly across the pampa.

Now and again we pass a cluster of two or three ranchos, the abode of the peon. These rough huts are built of sun-baked mud bricks, or even wattles plastered with mud. They are put down anywhere, without the suggestion of a fence or enclosure, and are typical of the untidiness of the country. Their presence generally indicates a small belt of agricultural land, of wheat or lucerne, where the ploughing is done with a team of four or six oxen. The colonists, as the settlers on an Estançia are called, are mostly Italians. They thrive and do exceedingly well, being hardworking and industrious. More often than not they hire land from the Estançiero, and cultivate it for themselves. We had a proprietor on board through whose territory of 30,000 acres we were running. He intended to sell some of his property, and said that most probably it would be bought by the colonists.

The burrows of the Bizacha or prairie dog, with its attendant watcher, the owl, sitting on guard; a huge waggon with upturned roof, the schooner of the

The Camp of Argentina.

prairie, drawn by a team of ten bullocks, creaking and groaning along; the picturesque figure of a gaucho on the horizon galloping loosely on his mestizzo, followed by an ugly whelping cur; these are the only points of interest during a long, long, hot day. Summer has come with a burst at last. The heat, even tempered by the luxury of the car, was terrific, and the dust was a source of misery. It permeated the air in clouds, obscuring everything in a dim fog, filtered through every aperture, smothered everything. Domingo in vain dusted round. It was useless. Dust covered everything again in five minutes. This result of the long-continued drought was a serious drawback to the delight of prairie travelling.

It takes ten hours to accomplish 190 miles, but at five o'clock we arrived at Rosario, hot and dusty, to be kindly received by Mr. Craik, the Administrator General of the Central Argentine Railway, at his charming house opposite the station.

A welcome storm broke during the night, and we awoke to a downpour of rain, which, however, cleared off too soon to do much permanent good.

Although Rosario is the second town of the Republic, it is utterly dull and unattractive. The city stands on the banks of the Parana, which is here a very wide river, bordered with flat, ugly banks. The Parana and the Uruguay are the two great confluents which, flowing both together into the ocean at Buenos Ayres, form the vast estuary of the River Plate. During the last two years the prosperity of Rosario has declined, but a movement is in progress to make it the capital of the Province of Santa Fé in place of the city of that name, and this would perhaps revive its falling fortunes. There is a large population of English employed in banks and offices and by the Central Argentine Railway, though some of these officials live about eight miles out, at Fishertown.

The Boulevard is the mightiest work of Rosario, and its only "sight," if you except the great towered building of the Palace of Justice, or of Injustice, as the Europeans familiarly call it. This boulevard extends for about two miles out, into the utter flatness of the dead level surrounding the city. It cost the City Improvements Company, or rather the unfortunate British public, no less a sum than 2,500,000*l*., and has a *metalled* way, a very wonderful improvement for a South American road. Double avenues of palms and shrubs, with a promenade walk in the centre hung with electric light, border the entire length. But on either side there are wide open spaces. It was intended that this spacious avenue should be lined with palaces, but it is the old fatal story of the Boom and Baring crash, which extended from the capital into the provinces, and which has tainted Rosario with the universal collapse of national credit. Thus we see half-finished mansions of ambitious design, partially plastered, with unglazed windows and unshuttered doors, memorials of a national folly, and never likely to be tenanted by their projectors.

A little hillock, or mound, at the end of the Boulevard is perhaps intended to teach the natives and children what a hill is like. We see people ascending this miniature elevation as if to see the view from the summit, and in truth, in this tableland,

ROSARIO DE SANTA FÉ.

a few inches of height secures a view of the horizon.

As we reach the outskirts of the town from the Boulevard, we have the usual untidy aspect of a South American city, with its waste spaces, filled with débris, and isolated houses dotted down, without any definite plan, where no road passes, and leading no whither. A curiously unfinished look these houses have, with their one storey of mouldy and decaying plaster, and bright washes in strong green and pink tints. The railway runs on a highway along the centre of the road. But when we return to the town we see that Rosario has some bustling streets and good shops. The Day of Independence is celebrated as usual in the Plaza May 25, where is the Cathedral and Court House, a pretty garden with a marble column and statue in the centre. The façade of the Court House is perforated with bullet holes. There is not a whole square inch, and the Cathedral tower is almost as profusely peppered with shot, fired during the thirty-six hours which the Revolution of the other day lasted, by the insurgents, from a high building at the opposite corner of the Plaza. What was the Revolution about? People scarcely know. Some trivial provincial grievance or other. It is generally the same story in these Republics of Revolution. Some party led by an ambitious man, for his own ends, tries to defeat a Government which is ever unstable and dependent on a popular will and vote.

With a special engine, Mr. Craik ran us down to the great workshops of his central station. Never were works in more beautiful order, from the building sheds, where cars were in process of construction, to the repairing shops; from the foundry and casting forge to the cleaning sheds; from the timber-sawing to the stores, where everything from a needle to a lamp is kept in apple-pie order, on shelves that line from floor to roof an enormous building. The works are so self-contained, that at the stationery office they print and check their own tickets by machinery. The grain elevator of many stories is on a siding over the Parana, and the vats are capable of storing 150,000 tons of grain, after thrice winnowing the wheat by a complicated system of machinery. We have seen many grain elevators in the United States and Canada, but never one equal to this.

We left Rosario at 7 A.M. the following morning in a newly-varnished and yet more sumptuous car. It was to be our travelling home on the pampa for the succeeding four days.

A gorgeously hot morning it was for our visit to Mr. Kemmis' well-known Estançia of Las Rosas. The origin of this pretty name is derived from the emblem of the white and red rose of the York and Lancaster Regiment, in which the owner served in former years. The prairie was covered with clumps of tussock grass, and blazed in the glare of an intense heat. As we alighted at the station, a blast of hot air, as if from a furnace, met us, and driving up to the Estançia, the atmosphere was intensely clear and quivering with heat.

The scintillation was quite painful to the eyes, and a wonderful mirage danced on the distant horizon, depicting the usual derisive water and green trees to the dwellers in a land parched and thirsting with drought.

The Camp of Argentina.

We approached the Estançia by a double row of Persian lilacs in full bloom. The Spanish name of Paraiso or Paradise tree has a pretty simile in this sweet-smelling feathery flower, that so closely resembles our lilac at home. Las Rosas is a typical house, with its deep verandahs and rambling bungalow buildings looking on to a garden in front, and behind on to a great collection of various farm buildings and stables. The garden is dried up, and shows sad signs of the visit of the plague of locusts last year. The green arbour has entirely disappeared, leaving a few bare stalks, and the tops of all the trees are eaten clean away. It is doubtful whether the latter will ever recover. These swarms of locusts appear suddenly, and in a few hours they have swept off all green things. Wonderful stories are told of the havoc they do, of the blackness that darkens the sun as the swarm passes. At Leones, a station we noticed on the line, the train has several times come to a standstill on account of the locusts. The wheels of the carriages had become so lubricated with the oil crushed out from them, that they revolved without progressing.

Life on an Estançia seems to us very pleasant. The learners certainly have a much better time of it than the cowboys on the Ranches of America or Canada. It must be a life with a charm of its own, with wild, lonely rides, galloping over these vast stretches of grass from early morn until dusk. The horn sounds as a signal to begin work at daybreak, and one goes off to the shearing shed, and another to inspect the watering places. This is a most essential and important duty. The troughs have to be filled three or four times daily, and special men are kept for this work. Every part of the Estançia is dotted over with watering troughs. Another will ride north or south, according to orders, to oversee the work being done, and this will involve a daily ride of perhaps forty miles. Thus every part of the Estançia is visited and patrolled twice a day. Luncheon is at twelve, and in the hot weather a siesta is accorded to all, peones included, and the whole Estançia is wrapped in drowsy repose until two o'clock. Tea at four, and dinner at seven, concludes the routine of hours and meals.

In some Estançias, the learners live in a separate building, and mess by themselves. Mr. Kemmis wisely adopts the civilizing influence of keeping them under his own roof, and at his own table.

In due course, the sound of the horn dispersed all to their work. The heat continued tremendous, and was over 90° in the shade, and equal to one of the hottest days in January. It presaged the storm that all are hoping and longing for. This is the usual formula for the weather to pursue during the summer. It grows hotter and hotter, the air becomes more stifling and oppressive, it is working up for a storm, which will break with tremendous lightning and thunder, cooling the air with torrents of rain. I accepted the custom of the country, and retired for a siesta. It was very pleasant to rest, with the drowsy hum of the insects outside the deep verandah, the cooing of the doves, and the whispering of the wind in the poplars, coming in through the wired doors and windows.

Mr. Kemmis has just had his annual sale of yearlings at the Buenos Ayres Tattersall's, so that he had only a few horses to show us, but we saw the famous "Whipper-in," whose progeny are found on every race-course in the Republic. He was the enterprising Estançiero who first treated for the sale of "Ormonde" to this country, offering 20,000*l*., but through some mishap the transaction came to nought. Then we visited the shearing sheds, where shearing was in full operation. The sheep-rearing industry of Australia and the Argentine are about equal. The numbers reared are nearly identical. Scab and burr are the diseases they both have to contend with; certainly these Lincolns, Rambouillets and Negretis are the finest sheep I ever saw, with wool of two inches staple. The process of shearing, if slower, is more carefully done than in Australia, and the shearers are strictly superintended, and not allowed to hack the sheep.

In an adjoining corral were some horses, just driven in fresh from camp, and being haltered for the first time. It was most interesting to watch the operations of the head peon, in flowing chiripa (trousers) and leathern "tirador," bright with silver piastres, throwing a loop over the head, and with great dexterity avoiding the ugly rushes of the frightened animal. This loop was gradually tightened, pressing on the windpipe, whilst two more lassoes attached a hind and fore leg together. These lassoes are made by the peones, of raw hide, with a loop and button, and never break.

It required something strong to resist the wild plungings, and rushing to the corner of the corral that ensued, whilst four peones were required to hold on to the lasso and "give and take." Gradually the horse realizes that it is useless, and allows the man to come slowly nearer and nearer. Very gently and cautiously he approaches near enough to slip the headstall first over one ear, then the other. The nose band is passed around, and with a few more plungings and backings the horse is led out and tied up with some others standing quietly by, who a few minutes before were remonstrating as vehemently as the last captive. These horses seem to use their fore legs, and rear and paw, while Australian walers are more handy with their hind ones and in bucking.

In all Estançias the buildings are of the roughest description, not excepting the stables, and the yards are thoroughly untidy. Utility, and not show, is all that is thought of, and they would scarcely pay if managed on other lines.

The peones, as the farm servants are called, live in a separate building, and are found in everything, rations of meat (which is eaten four times daily), bread, coffee, and maté being served out to them. A large collection of horses are kept in the corral, and the peones catch one and gallop off to their work. A peon would think it a degradation to be asked to walk. The criollo, or native horses, are small, hideous animals, but they present a picturesque appearance when saddled with the high peaked saddle, covered with sheepskin, the clumsy carved wooden stirrups hanging therefrom, and a decoration of leathern strips, studded with silver, dangling over the nose band. The mestizzo, or cross between a native and an English horse, is an improvement on the criollo, but all the fine carriage horses are imported, as the native animals are too small.

The peon has taken the place of the gaucho, who now roams further over the plain. A type quite by itself, the gaucho resembles the Bedouin of the desert, with his flowing costume of the bright coloured poncho, a simplification of the Arabian burnous, the chiripa, or riding trousers, floating like the full pantaloons of a Zouave, fastened at the waist by a raw leathern tirador, scaly with silver piastres, and boots made out of the skin of the hind leg of a calf. The spur is a large circle of blunt points some four inches round, and resembles a star.

This pampean gaucho is very Oriental in aspect and manners. He is full of superstition. His name is derived from an ancient Quicha, or Peruvian word, signifying "orphan, wandering, abandoned." The epithet suits him. He is really a wandering or "lost child" of the social group. Born somewhere in a rancho on the Argentine plain, growing on horseback, learning from childhood to fight and suffer, his first and indelible impressions are those of self-reliance. The immense pampa, without trees or outlined ways, more barren than the sea of old to ancient mariners, unfolds itself to his eyes, mysterious awful, indefinite. It is there that he must live, grieve, fight, love, and die. To overcome distance, to get his food, he has his horse and his lasso.

To find his way on this invariable circular horizon better than by the moving sun and the inconstant stars, he has the smell of certain herbs or bushes, which once seen he will never forget. At night, fifty leagues away from home, after ten years' absence, he will yet find his way, by the peculiar smell or taste of the pasture he is crossing. His senses are sharpened as necessary weapons. His sight is as keen as a hawk's, and his insensibility to pain and hunger belongs to a lower organism. In a far distant galloping he counts the horses, and knows whether they are ridden by soldier, Indian, or comrade. In the trampled grass his Mohican eye follows the track of an animal, distinguishes the footprint of a lost horse among tracks of a numerous group. He recognizes amongst a hundred the running colt that he marked with fire the preceding year. The gaucho's skill with the lasso, a raw hide rope of six yards in length, throwing it with such exactitude as to entangle the feet of any running animal, is simply marvellous. Not less wonderful is the casting of the bolas, or three-balled weights, in the capture of the ostrich. His luxuries are simple as his life. The maté cup, with its long tube or bombillia, is his solace after a long day's ride, and "the carne con cuero," or ox, roasted with the hide on over a fire of hot cinders, is his idea of a sumptuous feast.

We had a lovely drive in the cool of the evening, right out into the midst of the wild pampa, surrounded by it and seeing nothing else. The sun was sinking sullenly, a dull, livid ball of fire, into crimson clouds, whilst a faint indication of mountains in the pointed and peaked clouds indicated a coming storm. A sort of dull twilight was creeping over the wilderness, accompanied by a great stillness and oppression. Before us, stretching to the horizon, was a belt of luscious green. It is a crop of alfalfa, or lucerne, the raising of which is a new introduction by Mr. Kemmis, who first tried the experiment. It is now universal throughout the country, and forms a most valuable crop. Green and succulent, the extremely deep roots prevent the alfalfa being parched by drought. When it is pressed and dried it forms a food as nourishing as hay, and cattle fatten quickly on it.

Over the limitless paddocks we fly—for the paddocks here are boundless in extent—now nearing a herd of bullocks, with enormous branching horns, fattening for export to England, the two-year-olds as big as four; now a flock of 500 lambs, which will be forwarded to Liverpool on December 1st, and sold there for Christmas fare. After all expenses are paid, including those of the shepherds who accompany them, Mr. Kemmis will be able to count a clear profit of 1*l.* 7*s.* 6*d.* per head. Several well-known Estançias, including that of Mr. Dickenson, the great sheep breeder, are visible on the horizon, and the large buildings we see at the station belong to the different estates, each having its separate shed, corral, and lading platform for the forwarding of cattle. We pass some of the wells, where the water wheels are pumped by mules, and then, in a fast gathering dusk, we gallop home up the avenue of Persian lilacs. But suddenly their sweet smell is lost in an awfully pungent and pestiferous odour, that fills the air far and near. It is the trail of the skunk across the road, that most vindictive of animals, who, when attacked, retaliates by squirting over his enemy a fiery juice that burns and scarifies, and smells for ever. It was delightful sitting out after dinner, watching the sheet lightning. A bright star shines amongst the trees, darting backwards and forwards. Several clusters are on the ground. They are fireflies, "nature's night-lights," shining with a pure, brilliant light, very beautiful to behold, paling in their magnificence the lights of the Southern Cross above.

We awoke the next morning with the sound of many waters rushing in our ears. It was a joyful noise, and one full of music to the ears of the Estançiero. "The floods clapped their hands," and the waters gurgled and flowed in rivers off the verandah, and flooded the yard into a lake. The storm has come after a long drought, accompanied by a hurricane of wind that bends the willows and lilacs, waving them wildly to and fro. It is rain that is worth a 100*l.* a minute to the country, for with spring here, and summer heat coming, the parched country was utterly exhausted, and food for the cattle had well nigh given out.

We had a perilous and exciting drive in the break to the station. The wind blew a regular "pampero," or whirlwind. The pair could scarcely face it, although sinch horses, ridden by peones, and drawing from the girth, helped to pull the carriage along. The road was under water, deeply in some parts, the whole way. Rain came down in torrents, and blew through everything. Trees bent double under the gale, whilst the cattle stood looking pitiable objects, with drooping heads and tails, backs against the storm. The cloud effects, with rain hailing along the ground, in black mist, were very strange and beautiful; distant objects appearing twice their natural size, and looking most unearthly. The whole face of the country was under water. The change from yesterday was sudden and startling.

We reached the station, after a final struggle, to find one of the car windows had been blown in. Wet, dishevelled, and bedraggled, we were grateful for the refuge of the car, and felt it was like coming home. A special engine took us to Cañada de Gomez, to join the ordinary train.

A marvellous transformation takes place after rain has fallen over the pampa. We had been told about it, but it is necessary to see it to believe. The same burnt earth, hard as a brick surface, is changed to rich loam; green grass is sprouting up already in tender shoots. Even the brown clumps of tussock growth are a little less harsh and stringy. Abundant pools gather in any little hollow or declivity. The cattle seem to graze more eagerly. And all this gracious change comes after a few hours of rain, so rich and prolific is this pampa soil. It only lacks irrigation to become a smiling country.

It was very pleasant all through that long day, hour after hour, watching from our large airy-windowed coach the endless vista of pampa unfolding before us. The turf mounds, heaped round the telegraph poles, come at last to possess an interest. We jump up to see the distant figure of a solitary gaucho. And the stations, which in the evening are a favourite resort, are as amusing as the appearance of an unexpected special coach on the train is to the native population. Our curiosity is mutual and reciprocated.

In the afternoon, soon after passing Villa Maria, a distinct change comes over the country. We travel through a great grey wilderness of scrub trees, whose bare skeleton branches are composed of thorns. It is a sterile belt of Pampa, a sandy, barren district, whereof the vegetation is harsh and ligneous, and composed principally of thorn bushes or low trees, of which Chañar is the most common. Hence it is called the "Chañar steppe," and is the beginning of the Monte formation, a sterile saline pampa, that reaches up to the salt lake, and encloses Tucuman in the far north. It continues until we reach Cordoba in the evening.

The approach to the city is most pleasing. The sand dunes and hillocks, with their deep watercourses, and the railway cutting through them, is a welcome change, even before the view over the town looking down from the high embankment comes into sight. Cordoba lies in a delicious green valley, a perfect oasis, where the tall poplars flourish abundantly, and the little flat-roofed pink houses peep out from their midst, giving a very Eastern look to the city. It is really the bed of an ancient river, and the barrancas, or ridges, crowned with buildings, surround the town. Then, to the eye's delight and refreshment, rises far away, some twenty-five miles in front of us, the great sierras of the Cordoba range, in a succession of serrated peaks, each one rising regularly above the other in tier-like steps, cool and intensely blue in this crystal atmosphere. Only after two days of continuous travelling on the pampa, and a fortnight of living in a country flat as a rolling board, could we have appreciated the modest charms of Cordoba.

We dined and spent the evening with Mr. Munro,

the manager of the Central Cordoba Railway, and passed the night in our coach on a siding.

The morning following was cold and rainy for our exploration of the old city. We seem to be transported into a different world, for Cordoba is an ancient Spanish town, full of reminiscences of the Jesuits, whose headquarters it was during the sixteenth century, a centre of learning and civilization, and the only place east of the Andes with a printing-press. A walk soon brought us to the Plaza San Martin, with its double promenade of red granite, a favourite resort for the evening stroll of its citizens, who wander round and round the inner and outer circle. It is well shaded by the spidery foliage of the pepper-tree, mingling with the sweet-smelling paraiso.

The cathedral overshadows the Plaza, the only beautiful thing in Cordoba. It is a grand and complicated Moorish building, stained pink, but worn black with age in many places. The turreted towers with their open campaniles and green bronze bells, are crowned by other miniature towers. These are joined by a Moorish archway, whilst a massive dome, rising behind, is flanked by flying buttresses, and crowned by a crucifix enclosed in a halo of iron trellis. The interior is cold and bare, they say, but, as usual, the church was shut. Open very early in the morning only, we always find that, contrary to the custom of Roman Catholic countries, the churches are kept shut all day. It does not give the idea that they are very devout in their religion.

Certainly this cathedral is a striking pile, and one appreciates it the more, in that you soon learn to look for no architectural beauty in a Spanish-

G

American town. We had certainly seen nothing as yet "more picturesque than this grim, battlemented pile, built as if its founders meant it to be a stronghold of historic faith." The Moorish Cabildo adjoins the Plaza.

Not far off is the Jesuit church, where the richly-carved wood ceiling, put together without nail or screw, attests to the skill of the ancient fathers. Tradition has it that the trunks of cedar from which the roof was carved were brought down on rollers from Tucuman. The gold it is decorated with came from Peru. Then we passed the quadrangle of the University, with the Academic Hall where degrees are conferred. The Bull sanctioning this bears the signature of Gregory XV., 1621, and is countersigned by Philip III. of Spain. "The library collected by the Jesuits with infinite toil was scattered at the suppression. The remnants form the bulk of the State library at Buenos Ayres. Grocers and confectioners used the Jesuit books as wrapping-paper for more than forty years, until the late Dr. Gordon, Her Majesty's Vice-Consul, saved many valuable works by buying them." So says Mr. Mulhall in his "Handbook of the Argentine Republic." The University was revived in 1870, and flourishes with a staff of modern professors.

It seems appropriate that the Observatory of the Southern Hemisphere should be found at this seat of learning. We ascend the barranca and see the revolving telescope, contained in a circular building, that follows the course and checks the position of each star by the aid of a clock-like instrument. The sky is so clear at Cordoba that stars of the seventh magnitude can be seen, whereas the tenth degree is the ordinary standard of observation.

In an adjoining building the meteorological observations for the Argentine Republic are registered. The windmills on the housetop cause the pencils to trace in delicate shadings and thin strokes the velocity of the wind for each minute and hour of the day.

In returning, we drove past the Alameda with its reservoir and stone balustrades on the Plaza Sobremonte. But the glory is departed since a great tornado visited the city, tearing up the trees by their roots and leaving the Plaza bare and desolate. The theatre, with its Corinthian columns and façade, is unfinished; the National Bank is lodged in a palatial but half-completed edifice. It is the old story, we tire of hearing, the boom and the collapse of the bubble. Cordoba now, with its 30,000 inhabitants, seems a complete city of the dead. The streets are deserted. Two persons occupy the principal avenue. There are no carts of merchandise, no movement in the roadway. Occasional trams pass half empty. The shops are open, but there are no customers. The Spanish houses, with their barred windows, look mysteriously desolate. We seek in vain, during passing glimpses, for a sign of life in the pretty patios. The city appears as if plague-stricken, a mournful impression, aided by the cold wind of a cheerless day. It is a sarcastic comment on this condition of things when, in an empty street, our coachman is called upon by a policeman to stop, and proceed over the crossing at a walk. This ancient custom survives from a time when the streets were full of life, and crossings frequent. A policeman then, as now, stationed at the cross-roads, was deputed to see this order executed.

We returned to our coach, which was now attached to a goods train of fifteen waggons, to retrace our steps to Villa Maria. It was a slow progression, with long halts at each wayside station. The clouds lay low on the pampa, rain came on, and a cold wind bent the thorn-bush and whistled round our car; whilst the gauchos, huddled together, sitting in groups on their haunches on the platforms, wrapped in dirty brown ponchos, presented a picture of misery.

Arrived at the junction of Villa Maria, after much jerking and shunting in pitch-darkness, we were left quiet for the night, or rather until four in the morning, when we began our journey over the Andine line. This is one of the very few Government lines (all the other railways are English concessions), and in consequence the permanent way is in such a condition as to be almost dangerous. We risked derailment; but partly owing to the splendid construction of our bogie coach, partly to being attached well in the centre of the train, we escaped easily.

This Andine railway runs through a very pretty bit of pampa, and morning found us amid a changing scene of comparatively wonderful variety, bounded by a low line of hills, very soft and blue with distance. Some poplars and a few trees, rather thorny and stunted, it is true, gave a somewhat park-like appearance to the country.

Arrived at Villa Mercedes, another junction, our car is again shunted for a few hours, before being attached to the train on the Great Western Railway. Thus, owing to the courteous combination of three lines, our private coach has been run direct from Buenos Ayres to Mendoza, over the Central Argentine, the Andine, and Great Western systems.

Villa Mercedes is only remarkable for its Indian ranchos, with a swarming population of swarthy women and children, and many mangy curs, and for its enormous avenues of poplars, running in all directions.

We cross the River Secundo on a trellis iron bridge. The rivers north of the Parana to Brazil are numbered consecutively, one, two, three, &c., and thus we know this is the second tributary northwards. It seems quite strange to see a railway cutting and an embankment once more, for the Central Argentine is laid down on a plain so flat and straight, that there is scarcely one such engineering difficulty on the whole system.

It was a lovely summer's afternoon, the sun shining brightly and turning all the pampa into a rustling, waving sea of golden sunshine. Soon the shadows lengthen out, and make a neighbouring hill look large and abnormally out of proportion.

The San Luis range of mountains, the end of the Sierra of Cordoba, now rising out of the great yellow waste, is a forerunner of that other and far mightier range, the Andes. Intensely blue, their crevasses and summits are frosted with half-melted snow. They appear almost unreal, as the phantasy of some dream, but strangely beautiful after the mile upon mile of utterly flat, bronze-green country of the past days.

We are passing over the poorest province of the Argentine, that of San Luis, where all the land is covered with clumps of coarse grass. But we see here a remnant of the ancient pampa days. A puma, of a bright-fawn colour, the size of a large dog, with a short black nose and cunning, furtive eye, is seated beside a dead horse, gnawing away at the carcase. With the advance of cultivation two characteristics disappear—the Indians and real pampa grass, and now neither the one nor the other are seen, unless it is far up in the interior of the country.

The orange-glowing horizon and sumptuous setting of the sun was our last view at night over the prairie. In the morning it is sunrise over the valley of Mendoza, with the foothills of the Andes in the background.

And what a scene of beauty and freshness does the sun shine upon! A green, smiling valley, encircled in the arms of lofty ranges, where the shadows lie long and blue; whilst far, far away, lost amongst the fleecy clouds, are the virgin snow-peaks of the great Sierra of the Andes. It is scarce possible to tell where the snow ends and the clouds begin. Swiftly we pass from the saline desert of sage-brush into the region of the vineyards, with their trellises of pale-green vines, into the valley which is filled with tall poplars, amongst which are the white houses of Mendoza.

Behind us, for league upon league, stretches the boundless prairie. Before us is this happy valley. Mendoza is an oasis, a fair, green resting-place for the traveller, ere once again he plunges into the wild, grim rock recesses of the stern Andes.

CHAPTER V.

ACROSS THE ANDES.

MENDOZA, under the influence of a fresh spring day, looked enchanting. The breeze rustled gaily in the giant Carolina trees that in double and triple rows line the magnificent width of avenues. These trees shoot up a thick grey stem, then branching out overhead, with their large, flat leaves, form beneath a cool, spacious arcade.

Mendoza is a typical up-country town, and one never tires of watching the characteristic peasant types that throng the streets. Now it is the pampa gaucho, with a broad slouch hat and crimson poncho, passing by. The great leathern covering to his stirrup originated as a protection against the pampa grass. Now an ancient country dame, of strongly marked Indian type, with coarse tresses of black hair, a wide straw hat, a brilliant red and yellow petticoat, comes pacing along. Rough country carts, with their comical troika of mixed mules and horses of all colours and size, gallop by with a deafening noise. Their drivers, whilst riding the outside animal, keep the whip extended over the necks of the others like an artilleryman's salute. Horses hobbled with a strap and button passed round the fore-legs stand waiting before the shop doors.

Women, hooded and clothed in sable, rosary and breviary in hand, flit by on their way to mass. We attend the American Methodist Church, where a service is being held for the first time for three years. Constantly, as we turn into some street, the blue grandeur of the foothills of the Andes overshadows us, and lifts us for a moment out of the everyday life of the streets. The snow yet nestles in the crevasses, and though fully ten miles away, we feel that we are dwelling under them; the intensely clear, crisp atmosphere brings them delusively near. And these mountains, which are yet 10,000 feet above the sea-level, are only the foothills of the Andes! They are mighty forerunners of a still mightier barrier.

Our enthusiasm for the prettiness of Mendoza is somewhat damped by the dirt and discomforts of our first experience of a South American hotel, an experience we had been lucky in hitherto escaping. Our two lofty rooms, opening on to a dusty patio full of litter and refuse, are dirty and shabby to a degree. The stained and discoloured wall-paper; the carpet of gaudy pattern, containing the dust of many previous occupants; the dilapidated chairs and sofa, with the horsehair protruding through sundry rents; the beds, which we strip with a shudder over their filthy coloured blankets and smother in "Keating's," are suggestive of all that is horrible. The drawers and cupboards are in such a condition that we determine not to unpack our boxes. The food is so bad as to be scarcely eatable. Soaked and fried in oil, it requires the spur of hunger to be able to swallow it at all. Such is the typical hotel of the country.

The shaded depths of San Martin's Avenue tempted us for a stroll in the evening. The same hooded figures of this morning are now, gorgeously arrayed in bright apparel and displaying their charms, racing up and down the avenue in their carriages. A grand funeral procession, with its attendant following of nearly fifty carriages containing the merest acquaintances of the deceased, has spoilt, they say, the spectacle of the Sunday evening parade on San Martin. The great excitement to-day was the return of the hearse, surmounted by the grim figure of Charon, with his scythe, galloping back for a fresh burden from the living, and accompanied by the carriage containing the wreaths sent in honour of the last departed.

Then we drove to see the ruins of the earthquake of 1861, when nearly the whole city of Mendoza was destroyed. The broken archway of the church of San Domingo and a few other fragments remain amid the most unsavoury surroundings of adobe ranchos, reeking in mud and slime, with grovelling children and dogs.

We made a pleasant expedition the following day, Mr. Villalonga, the kindly and courteous Administrator-General of the Great Western Railway, taking us in a special train a little way into the country to see one of the largest vineyards. The adobe-walled vineyards are suddenly succeeded by the saline desert, where the ground sparkles with the briny deposit; sage-brush flourishes with a few clumps of waving plumes of real pampas grass. It is an apt example of what irrigation will do. Water this same land and it will become as smiling and fruitful as the country encircling Mendoza.

All around the western horizon sweeps that insurmountable barrier, a glorious panorama of snowy peaks, their pure summits mingling with the cloud-flecked sky, and yet just discernible, being faintly outlined by the pale shadows that indicate a peak. It is a splendid vision—a view one never tires of seeking amongst the clouds, for, unless at early morning, they are seldom visible in their naked grandeur, but always veiled by vapour.

The drive to Senor Benyas' vineyard was charming. "Trapiche" is approached by avenues of poplars, hedges of roses, and magnificent weeping willows, sweeping in a green waterfall to the earth. It is almost impossible to picture the graceful beauty of these trees when they attain to the height we see here and are clothed in new spring foliage. We would fain on arrival have lingered in the shady depths of the verandah, shut in by a thick trellis of honeysuckle and roses, perfuming the air, or in the garden, where cabbage-palms and other tropical specimens grew alongside with the wisteria, syringa, fuchsias, verbenas, and arum lilies of an English home garden.

First we passed through a yard where they were making adobe, or bricks of mud. Like the ancient Egyptians, they constructed bricks without straw. Of this material the fourfold vaults are made, and they seemed admirably adapted for keeping the wine cool. In pitch-darkness, candle in hand, we groped our way inside the vault, past enormous barrels containing 1000 litres of new wine. A tram-

Across the Andes.

way runs through an adjoining building, direct from the vineyard, up one incline and down the other. The vats filled with grapes are passed up this line, tilting their contents into one of the eight presses that are employed. The expressed juice then passes into the enormous vats we are shown, and is left to ferment for from four to six days. The wine is then ready for use in due time.

Introduced by the Jesuits in the sixteenth century, Mendoza is well adapted for vine-growing. The whole valley is rich and smiling with their extensive growth. This vineyard is one of the largest in the district, and comprises 500 acres. A drive through the broad road, bordered by vines, showed us how beautifully cleaned and well-kept was each plant. Already branches of tiny green berries give promise of a splendid harvest in February. Irrigation is the great secret of success, and each furrow is filled with water twice daily. It is often difficult and expensive to get the concession for water in a valley where all and everything depends upon such a supply. The vines here are grown in the French fashion, that is, each plant is like a bush, and the tendrils are trained along vertical wires. But some proprietors adopt the Spanish system, which is to prune the vine until there is a wooden stem of four or five feet, and then the leaves grow over a trellis, leaving a cool, shady avenue underneath. A vine takes three years to mature, but if the planter has sufficient capital to wait that time he is amply repaid. The profits are large, and the machinery required is simple.

We drove home under the deep-blue shadows of the mountain range, catching distant glimpses of the yellow pampa. The road was the usual typical sample that we have learned to think nothing of. Now the axle of the wheel is deep in mud with water spurting around, or the carriage in passing over a hillock is tilted at right angles. Now it is a stream that we ford on a few loosely laid, rotten boards, or a gulley, the dried bed of some torrent, that we plunge into and emerge with a struggle on the other side. The horses gallop gaily over all obstacles, heedless of inequalities in the road, and you soon tire of watching for accidents when you find that nothing happens.

We returned to make our final preparations for the morrow's start across the mountains. Our luggage had to be divided up into equal packages, weighing forty kilos each, to allow of their balancing across a mule's back. We confided it all to the care of M. Rosas, the agent for Villalonga's Express Company, and we had good reason to be satisfied with the care he took, for everything arrived, after the perilous crossing, in first-rate condition.

As the time approaches for our start, imaginative friends suggest every new kind of danger and difficulty. We are warned that we shall suffer from the sorocche or mountain sickness, that our breathing in the high altitudes will become oppressed, that our ears and noses will bleed from the same cause, that we ought to take provisions, that it is quite unnecessary, that we have a period varying from five hours to five days' riding on muleback; that the cold will be intense, that storms are raging in the passes, and the summit is impassable. We have ceased to listen to these idle tales. From Buenos Ayres even to Mendoza, from the moment of landing until now, we

Across the Andes.

have never ceased seeking for information and asking advice. The result has been so contradictory and unsatisfactory, so few people from the Argentine side have crossed the Andes, that we determined to believe nothing more, but to rest satisfied that we should soon find out for ourselves. As it turned out, a letter written by Mr. Bagallay, C.E., before we left England, proved the only reliable account, and we wished afterwards that we had followed its advice more closely.

It was a glorious morning for starting on our journey across the Andes, and eleven o'clock found us at the station of the Transandine Railway. A tiny train of one baggage and one passenger coach awaited us, and we are rejoiced to find that there were only two intending passengers beside ourselves, and so little danger of overcrowded inns. The tender of the engine was piled high with wood, which fuel is used in place of coal. The gauge is only one metre, but the bogie carriages, with their one seat to each window on either side, are very comfortable.

The Transandine Railway, crossing the Andes, is being built in combination between the Argentine and Chilian Governments, to connect the two provinces. It now takes ten days to pass the Straits of Magellan, and costs 40*l.* This route can be done in two days and a half from Buenos Ayres, for the sum of 12*l.*, so say at least the advertisements. The cattle trade between Argentina and Chili is very large. The railway will save them the long, toilsome journey of many days' duration, and the subsequent rest and fattening. Freights being cheaper than by the sea route, the railway hope to secure much of the present coast trade. The Argentine section, though it has

108 miles to lay against the forty-four miles of the Chilian side, has by far the easier task. The railway now nearly reaches Punte de las Vacas, and the Tolorzia Valley presents no engineering difficulties. The Chilian section has to be carried through with one extended system of tunnelling, ending in the summit tunnel of the Cumbre. The mountain range of the Chilian side is so complicated and precipitous, that it has been decided that this will be the cheapest and only possible method of constructing the railway.

The giant trees of the avenues of Mendoza waved their farewell to us. The valley smiled joyfully in the sunshine, as we steamed past the green vineyards and the willow-shaded ranchos, with their adobe enclosures.

Very soon we are out among the winding foothills, a series of large hillocks, barren and stony, covered only with a great growth of cacti, just beginning to flower. The small, wax-like petals are just bursting out of their red sheath, atop of their thorny, bristling stems. The mountains that form the outer barrier of the Andes, with the sun just overhead, look intensely blue and deep in morning shadow, and so different to the afternoon aspect, when the slanting sun-rays bathe them in golden sunshine.

At the first halt for water we left the carriage, and by special permission from Mr. Grant Dalton, the administrator of the line, we mounted the engine. Here we found two wooden seats, placed at right angles over the cow-catcher, railed in in front. Away from all dust, heat, and smoke, it was a delightfully commanding position.

Across the Andes.

Our first experience was a wild rush down into a ravine, with several acute curves. The clatter was tremendous, the noise deafening; it fairly took our breath away for the first five minutes. Then we described a sharp circle in turning on to a trestle bridge, where the lines, supported only on cross sleepers, left a widely open lattice, looking immediately over and down beneath into the foaming, muddy torrent of the Mendoza.

This river will be with us all day. We shall see it in every phase of its existence, follow it up to its remotest sources. Here it is a broad, foaming river; now compressed into a rocky channel, and raging angrily; now it is spread out over a wide bed, from which it has shrunk into a succession of smaller channels, percolating over a river-bed much too large for it. And so we pursue its windings, until it is lost amongst the plains of Uspallata.

We are rushing next into a tunnel with a deafening roar, and a firework illumination from the flying sparks of the wood fire. We know what a tunnel feels like from the inside of a railway-carriage, but it is a very different experience to being outside. An arch of black darkness engulfs the engine. We plunge blindly into an abyss of space, and are seemingly lost in it for a few moments, until a glimmering of day slowly dawns at the other end, finishing in an archway of light, and we emerge in clouds of mist and smoke into air and daylight once more.

We have turned up out of the valley by this time, and, entering the defile of mountains, have begun to penetrate the inner range. There are nothing but great barren mountains all round; no level space except the little bit of railway-line coaxed from the bed of the Mendoza, or blasted from out the steep cliff side. Should the straitened valley open out a little now and again, it is only to be filled up by a moraine of rock and *débris* that has rolled down from the heights above. Every quarter of an hour finds us among mountains, growing grander and mightier. Now we see some snow-wreathed summits, with white chasms deep cut into their sides. If we could approach near enough, we know that each is a mighty glacier firmly wedged into a crevasse.

We had occasion again and again to remember that in this intensely clear atmosphere the height of the mountains is extraordinarily deceptive. Perhaps we think these neighbouring giants are not, after all, so very colossal. We shall find that they are from 7000 to 10,000 feet high. Nor must we forget that on the summit of the Andes we shall attain to an altitude not far short of Mont Blanc.

I have heard the Andes spoken of as such a desolate range, so drearily rockbound and monotonous. It is true, but we forget that they are highly volcanic. We see it in the glowing colours all around, and this redeems them from their uniform sterility. Sometimes it is almost like being enclosed in a crater, recently in action, so copper-red are the rocks about. A great deal of ash-coloured scoria mingles with the more vivid shades. A stratum of bright-yellow clay forms a dash of violent chrome on yonder precipice, whilst here on the side of this mountain some beautiful chameleon shades of heliotrope and green subtly intermix. One monster is clothed in vermilion, so deep is its shade of red. It is as if red-hot lava had recently poured over its sides.

Deep shadows, as the sun rose higher above the ravine, caused strange illusions, pinnacles and isolated rocks standing out in strong relief, and resembling men and animals. A serried line of rocks shaped themselves into a battlemented fortress, raised on a sheer wall of the same; whilst a perfect row of little pillars represented soldiers storming the stronghold. From our frontier seats on the engine we had an uninterrupted survey of this grand pass in its solemn loneliness. Not a single house, except the rancho of the quadrillo engaged on the line; not a single human being, save the solitary, picturesque signalman, standing with outstretched flag at the saluting point, did we pass the whole day. The stations are simply a platform and shed by the side of the line, with a watering tank for the engine.

It was a changing scene of grandeur and beauty, differing little except in degree, until in the wane of the afternoon we emerged from the shadow of the narrow defile, left the high chain behind us, and came most suddenly into a widespread upland. It is the beginning of the great valley of the Uspallata. We halt at the station, where a few houses, buried, and low built behind any convenient rising ground, adjoin some stone corrals. These corrals are of frequent recurrence. Built roughly of the stones lying about, the square walls form a pen, with an entrance. The beasts are driven in here for shelter when storms arise. The Uspallata is a valley of rest for the herds of cattle, numbering 40,000 or 50,000, yearly driven across into Chili. They remain a few days eating the rank, brown grass, and seeking the few green weeds that flourish under the shelter of a stone, before beginning anew the labours of the Pass. The herdsmen carry no forage, and again and again we wondered how these poor animals subsisted for a period of eight or ten days on the meagre gatherings of the wayside. It is almost impossible to believe that this wide valley, so open to the north, is in the heart of the Andes, and some 6000 feet above the sea-level.

As we left Uspallata Station there was a most beautiful vision, the effects of a storm: sun and rain in the mountains behind us fought for the mastery, amid banks of massed-up black clouds. A thunderbolt flashed out, a brilliant zigzag of blinding light. The battle raged furiously for some time, then the clouds lightened until merged in clouds of rain, which were drawn heavenwards in gauzy ribbons of pale-grey mist. And whilst this storm was progressing behind us, all the mountains in front were lighted up in glowing sunshine, one leviathan in particular singling itself out by its translucent shades of pale opaline streaks, from against the deeper brown, red, and blue of the remainder of the range.

The Uspallata is left behind, as we enter a narrower defile, where the summits are loftier, the sides more precipitous, the whole scene wilder, grander, and more utterly desolate, The Mendoza is lost to view in a deep gulley. The earth-banks are cut in strata, so clean and neat, as if done with pick and shovel, that it is quite remarkable. A last halt to replenish the ever-thirsty engine, and we reach Rio

Blanco and alight at the station. The progress of the Transandine is well marked, for last year the railway reached only to this point. Now we can continue on the last finished section, but in a baggage car, roughly fitted round with seats. Accompanied by some navvies, with their tools and large flat cakes of bread, we started, crossing the Rio Blanco, a tributary of the Mendoza, on a bridge, and winding round into another defile. Now the mountains are deeply streaked with snow, lying thickly in crevasses. Very grand they appear, in the glimpses we obtain through the sliding doors of our waggon. We pass frequent quadrillos, putting the finishing strokes to the line. Then a graveyard in a sandy waste, with rough black crosses, crooked and tumbling down. Lastly the railway works are reached, with their stores of iron rails, bolts, and nuts, their piles of pot sleepers, zinc wheelbarrows, and enormous dredgers. The quarters of the men appear fearfully rough. The hovel-like houses are made of sheets of galvanized iron, or are merely wattle huts, plastered with mud, but suited perhaps to the requirements of the dirty Indian women standing at their doors. Groups of men in ponchos, who have just finished work, stand round smoking.

We make a little further cautious progress on the line, blasted out of the cliff side, or won from the bed of the Mendoza, which is here a rushing snow torrent, thick with the *débris* of the moraine. It is another phase, for never did river change like the Mendoza, varying so greatly at different points of its progress. A steep ascent. It is the end (for the moment) of the Transandine Railway on the Argentine side. We alight to find ourselves on a rocky incline, while a troop of mules await us and our baggage on a platform below.

The loading of the mules is interesting. The animal is blinded with a poncho tied like a hood over the head, refusing to be laden unless this is done. Even then they kick and squeal at each tightening of the rope, which is a thong of raw hide of enormous length. Our baggage was divided up into packages of equal weight, and balanced on either side, being fastened round and round, over and back, on the wooden saddle, covered with sheepskin. Thus they transport packs of enormous weight and size, 150 kilos., or 300 lbs., being no unusual load for a mule. Spare animals are taken in the caravan, so as to relieve the too exhausted.

When all was ready we mounted our mules, mine being a bright-brown animal, handsome, if obstinate, refusing to move unless the arriero or muleteer was behind, ready to cut it with his lasso. The cruelty of the bits used is awful. A large ring is forced into the jaw over the tongue, with a bar crossing beneath, whilst another ring encompasses the nose. These people are true Spaniards in their cruelty to animals, and jagged and bleeding mouths and sore backs are, with few exceptions, the unvarying rule. The Chilian saddle, with its high pommel, was an instrument of torture. Never shall I forget the weary hours I passed in that saddle, nor the misery I endured from it.

We started over a good road, the track ready made for the line, for the engineers hope to be at Punta de las Vacas by the end of the month. Twilight and

Across the Andes.

fast-falling darkness wrapped in gloom the encompassing mountains, though daylight lingered lovingly in a blush of rosy light on their highmost summits. One huge mountain behind us, filling in the valley, thus lighted our onward path. It was a lonely, gloomy ride of nearly two hours, travelling thus through the deep fastness. We had one nasty place to descend in the dark, on a steep bank, where the cutting for the railway bridge across the river had been commenced. Then the mules shied violently at the light shining on the water inundating the road, and we arrived, none too soon, at Punta de las Vacas. The friendly fire of the muleteers' camp, and the light from the windows shone out to greet us as we stumbled, tired and dazed, into the house.

Punta de las Vacas is a typical " posada " or inn. It is filthy and rough as possible. The sheds and outhouses are built round a mud corral, into which the mules are driven at night. In one of these outhouses, an adobe (or mud) lean-to, thatched with reeds, where many apertures let in light, we passed the night. The earth floor was covered by a filthy mat by the bedside ; one tin basin and a towel completed the furniture of the room. There was neither chair nor table. It was a question of camping on one's bed, sleeping in one's clothes, the bed looking of doubtful cleanliness. By dint of bribery we obtained this apartment to ourselves, else it is usual for the ladies to be herded five and six in one room, and the gentlemen in another. Two smoking lamps lighted us through a very indifferent meal, the *pièce de résistance* of which was tripe, whilst the correspondent of a New York paper did all in his power to alarm us with an account of his day's experience in crossing the Cumbre or summit. He related how the snow lay deep and impassable, described the eight inches that, with a false step from your mule, separated you, on either side, from a bottomless precipice and sudden death. He talked of the horrors of mountain sickness, the springing up of storms and gales of wind, the endurance and physical strength required, and sent us to bed thoroughly uncomfortable and frightened, with his stories ringing in our ears.

To bed, but not to sleep. The great height of 7000 feet affected us. It seemed to excite our nerves until we felt quivering and palpitating all over, whilst our breathing was oppressed by the high altitude. We scarcely closed our eyes all night. It was a bad preparation for the ensuing day, for the crossing of the Andes. We were thankful when, at 3 a.m., the call came to rise. We had been warned, in this keen mountain air, not to wash the face, so we were soon dressed, and turned out on a brilliant starlight night, crossed the corral to eat something at the house. Chunks of burnt toast and execrable chocolate were somewhat untempting fare, but we struggled as well as we could. After groping about in the darkness, we at length found the mules and mounted. The exorbitant charges did not lessen our disgust with the discomforts of this posada, in spite of the smiling landlady.

The rough mountain path led up and down, but in the pitch-darkness we blindly followed our arriero, stumbling along and trusting in the surefootedness of the mules. Nevertheless, it was very uncomfort-

POSADA ON THE ANDES.

able work; but we forgot it in looking at the solemn, silent scene around us. Above was a dark-blue vault, brilliantly spangled with stars. The Southern Cross, more perfect than I have ever seen it before, lay at cross angles just above a great black mountain top; whilst Venus, gleaming large and blue, shone stedfastly above our night's resting-place. In the valley immediately in front of us was a mammoth mountain, its sloping shoulders filling up the space, and visible only to us, because the pale glimmer of dawn was heralding in the grey east.

Now we turn from the stony bridle-path into quite another valley, where the desert space is wide and sandy. It is the Valley of Tolorzia, where Nature has seen fit to perform some marvellous convulsions. We cannot but feel here that we are penetrating into the fastnesses, the deepest recesses of this herculean range, the greatest mountains of Nature's creation, wrapped as they are now in mysterious gloom.

A little grey light glimmers around, showing things in the undue proportion of an uncertain light. We look behind. Dawn is breaking over the range in an opalescent grey. Daylight dawns apace. We hail its advent as a welcome messenger. And then looking up suddenly before us, gleams a glorious mountain, one " of the Andean Kings, with a snowy ermine falling from stately shoulders "—a splendid apparition brought very near to us in the chill, clear light of dawn. Even as we gaze, the rosy pink blushes over the crystal white of the summit. Then the sun rises, reflected in a few shafts of light, thrown up from the disc-like halo, appearing above a hindmost peak. All the mountains around and above us are steeped in golden light. We alone travel in the deep shadow of the valley. Slowly and lovingly caressing their rugged sides, the gladdening light glides down, and with a suddenness too startling to describe, I saw in front on the road the two elongated shadows of ourselves. Looking up, the whole valley is bathed in a full flood of warm sunshine.

It was the herald of a glorious day for the passage of the Cordillera.

How is it possible to bring before anyone the utter barrenness of this Tolorzia Valley, with its narrow tract of sandy wilderness? How describe the awful loneliness of this great barren range? yet withal its stately grandeur, the imposing array of mountain standing behind mountain, in unceasing length, the eye pursuing a line of 15,000 feet from base to summit, or a distance of five miles, in a few seconds. The dazzling perfectness and purity of the eternal snow summits! The long, even-sloping shoulders of snow, or the glaciers fast frozen for ever into their vast crevasses! One such of these would be sufficient to please, but with their never-ending number and height, they are almost overpowering, and one felt almost unable to rise to a sufficiently high level of admiration throughout the day. It is marvellous when we consider that this giant elevation is only after all a continuation of the Rocky range of America and Canada. The system of mountains, with a slight break at the Isthmus of Panama, continues all along the western coasts of North and South America.

The road we are on is a good though stony track across the sand, extending for a distance of thirty

Across the Andes.

kilometres from Punta de las Vacas to Las Cuevras at the base of the summit. A feeling of sadness is induced by the number of carcases strewing the way, and adding to the sensation of loneliness. Now we see the leg of a mule, or the bleaching skull of an ox. Or again, it is the skeleton of a horse or bullock that is lying directly across the centre of the track. Their dying attitudes are pathetic. As they fell, so they died. In one case the head is raised and supported on the point of the horn, which has penetrated the ground. In another the cow has fallen on her knees, and thus expired, although it is difficult to believe that in doing so, the body did not roll over on to the ground. I describe what we saw. Stone corrals for the cattle are frequent. How terrible are their sufferings in this barren vale. It must truly be to many a valley of death. An enormous eagle with outstretched wings soared aloft. King of birds, his dwelling is in a lonely eerie far above the haunts of man. In strange contrast, one tiny bird twittered alone on the ground amongst the thorn scrub. How it came there, and how it lived, was a mystery. It bore us company for many an hour.

We passed one or two round adobe huts, a casucha or post house, to shelter the carriers employed for the mail. They make the passage all through the year, even when the mountains are deep in snow. The mails are frequently lost, and the service is so irregular, that, except in summer, people choose the longer but safer Straits route. Very occasionally, the loneliness is relieved by a train of mules. The arrieros, in their gay-coloured ponchos, are solemn-looking men, who go indifferently on their way, after passing the usual salutation of "Buenos Dias."

At length something white, that is not rock, appears in the distance. The clear atmosphere makes it seem nearer. It is yet a weary way off. On and on we go. At last we ride up a slope, and find ourselves on the plateau of Puente del Inca. We dismount, to see the wonder of the natural bridge overhanging the Mendoza, which is buried far below in the chasm of its own hollowing. The formation of jagged rock is thrown across in a sloping archway. A hot mineral bath is found bubbling up in an adjoining cave, the roof of which is hung with dropping stalactites, glistening with quartz and mica.

This little halt was very welcome, with its few minutes' relief from the discomfort of the saddle. We had ridden ceaselessly for three hours, and already reached an altitude of 10,570 feet. We wanted to have some coffee at the Posada, which bears an even more evil reputation than the other Andean rookeries, but we were urged to hurry on to Las Cuevras, another two hours' riding. Though beginning to weary, we remounted without further delay. A horrible little watercourse, with an alarmingly sheer descent, followed by a rickety wooden bridge over the stream, brought us again on to the road, in the valley of the Inca. Where this valley begins and ends it is impossible to find out. The exploration of the Andes is so recent that the mountains have not been distinguished by names, and we soon found that it was useless inquiring what this or that was called.

For weary, weary miles, for an interminable distance, we could see the road stretching its relentless length before us. I began to feel that my strength was ebbing. Yet the mountain scenery was glorious. Now it is "the rock-bound monastery of the Penitentes, with its procession of pilgrim boulders;" a perfect simile for this crenellated extended length of rock, beneath which in procession are the winding lines of jagged rocks, representing the pilgrim's progress up the mountain side.

But we are getting too weary to look much more. It becomes a ride of physical endurance, a long drawn out agony. The sun is hot. We have ridden breakfastless, save for a few biscuits, since 4 a.m. The provisions we have brought with us in our hand luggage are on a baggage mule far in the rear, a contingency we never foresaw. The stirrup leather had skinned my leg, so I gave that up, and let my foot dangle helplessly. Then the pressing of the high-peaked pommel caused such pain, that at last I removed my leg, and rode just sitting sideways on the saddle. We urged the mules all we could. We dared not linger to rest, for already the sun is high, and we must pass the Cumbre ere noon. We have been warned over and over again that a wind, often rendering the summit quite impassable, springs up in the early afternoon, and this is what we dread. That fear drives us on, forbids us to linger.

Again and again we anxiously inquire of our muleteer as to the distance still before us. "Another hour." Thus has he stolidly answered for the past two or three hours. And hearts begin to lose courage, and strength fail altogether, with ever that relentlessly unending road before us.

We come to some shanties lying in a valley by the Mendoza. A chapel and these few mud houses give us once again an idea of human companionship, even though we only see a solitary figure. Some galleries in the rock have been blasted out, in preparation for the railway tunnel. Winding up a mountain out of the valley, we turn, when half-way up, on to its further side, and find ourselves face to face with a magnificent mountain. It is exactly opposite to us; so near we think to touch it, and yet so unreachable because of the fathomless gulf between. It was a curious feeling, to be hemmed in between these opposing monsters. The little foaming torrent in the abyss below is our old friend the Mendoza, whose windings and turnings we have now nearly followed up to their source in the snow beds of the summit. We seem to penetrate further, as each turn bring us into into a fresh valley higher up, and nearer to the central peaks.

There are many more weary turns in the bridle path, and now I am only able to hold on feebly to the saddle, and long ardently for Las Cuevras. Will it never come? Up and down, round boulders, now mounting, now descending. But a final climb, and beneath us, in the open plain, we hail the shanties of Las Cuevras. Even that last bit of descending road seemed very, very long, and I felt as I reached the Posada, that I could scarcely have held on for another moment.

What a filthy place it was! A low doorway led into a mud shed, surrounded by rickety tables and benches. Well was it that we had been warned not to pass the night here, and though we had settled to leave the question open, the sight of this disgusting hovel was enough. Weary as we were, after riding for seven hours continuously, a distance of thirty kilometres, we determined at all hazards to persevere. Some travellers who had just come over the summit from Chili strongly advised us to hurry on, on account of the wind. We could not tarry, although I was woefully disappointed of a rest. We trusted that food would restore us somewhat. Delusive hope. A chicken sopa of hot water and grease, some orange fish, rancid and strong-smelling, a beefsteak too hard even to cut, proved simply uneatable fare. It must be added that the exhilarating air takes away all inclination to eat. After twenty minutes' halt, we remounted.

The valley in which lies Las Cuevras is extremely beautiful. It forms a large circular plain, around which mountains rise to an altitude of from 15,000 to 20,000 feet, their summits clothed in snow, that extends also in deep streaks down their sides. It is extraordinary to stand there on a perfectly flat space and see these mountains opposite rising up abruptly out of the level valley, without slope or shoulder. Behind the Posada are some large zinc-roofed buildings. They contain the motors for driving the air compressors to be used for drilling the rock, in the great tunnel through the Cumbre. Already 253 metres of this gigantic undertaking have been bored on the Argentine side.

Our attention is rivetted on the earth mountain, which is to take us sheer up the remaining 2000 feet to the Cumbre. The face of the mountain is delineated in long zigzags, and already the path is marked out by the ascending line of laden pack mules, toiling in single file up the terrible incline. The bell of the leader tinkles regularly, answering the musical calls of the muleteers, encouraging the patient progress of these much-enduring animals. Traversing a stony arête, we too find ourselves on the track, and beginning the ascent.

My mule led the caravan, the arriero encouraging him vigorously from behind if he showed signs of halting. A few turns brought us wonderfully quickly on to a level with those mountains opposite I have just described. We wondered to think how unapproachable they had seemed when we were down at Las Cuevras. The end of each zigzag brought us to the edge of the mountain, and it was disagreeable turning the corners sharply overhanging the deep ravines on either side. Soon, indeed, it made one sick to peep down on the plain, so far and directly below was it, and the best way was to look always up to the path above. One false step from the mule, and we should have rolled to the bottom, or bounded down the mountain side.

The precipitous steepness of that path it is difficult to depict. The mule's head rose up before you, whilst his tail was somewhere far below, and you had hard work to lean sufficiently forward to prevent slipping off behind. Still, though an unpleasant and giddy piece of riding, it is not dangerous; moreover, the ascent on the Argentine side is child's play compared to the Chilian descent on the other, with its howling precipices, ugly arêtes, and rocky paths. For this is an earth mountain, giving a good foothold to the mule.

ROAD OVER THE ANDES BETWEEN THE ARGENTINE REPUBLIC AND CHILI.

Across the Andes.

The path is so narrow that it is impossible to pass anything. We overtook an overladen pack mule being cruelly driven by a drunken muleteer, and just as I arrived behind him, his mule slipped, fell, and commenced rolling down the mountain before my eyes. It was sickening to see the frantic efforts of the poor animal to save himself, the scrambling to try and obtain a foothold, whilst the man drove his enormous spurs deep into its flanks. I could not look at what happened, but somehow he was saved. The incident, however, did not tend to make us more comfortable, as the path grew even more precipitous towards the end, and resembled mountain climbing on muleback. An hour and a half brought us to La Cumbre, or the summit. We arrived quite suddenly, with one last curve. To spring off the panting mule was the work of an instant. To look round the next. Great heavens! What a glorious spectacle! It is supreme. You are breathless, you gasp at the marvellous grandeur. It is worth enduring everything to gaze upon this. Fatigue, hunger, weariness, fright, all are forgotten. You feel inclined to pour out one long peon of thankfulness at having ever been permitted to know such a glorious view.

Standing on that little barren summit, among a group of mules and muleteers, we were 13,000 feet above the world. First we look upon the glorious succession of snow mountains belonging to the Argentine range; then turn face about to the Chilian Cordillera, startled to see below a great crater filled with dazzling snow. The long smooth shoulders of the mountains are sparkling and glistening in the brilliant sunshine, with these crystal particles, whilst the great ermine-clad range beyond forms a perfect horizon chain of peak towering above peak, piled up heavenward. It is a stupendous vision. It is scarcely possible to believe that a grander one exists anywhere.

What a glorious day it is. The sun seems to be so near, shining in a sky of deepest ethereal blue. There is not a cloud or suggestion of mist on these heights, varying from 15,000 to 20,000 feet. There is Tupungato towering in solemn silence, the highest peak in this colossal range, looking down from a height of 22,000 feet. Yonder Juncal reveals its ruined crater. "Those silver threads here and there are the beginning of rivers emptying in the Atlantic. Those tangled skeins near the snow beds yonder are the sources of the Aconcagua and rivers flowing into the Atlantic. The gales which sweep over it come from the Atlantic, and, depositing their last drops of moisture in snow, pass on to the rainless seaboard of the Pacific, dry, cool, and balmy. This is the heart of the Andes. It is an earthquake-shattered region, over which the creative mysteries of the past seem to brood."

We were too absorbed in the scene around us to think of the promised sorocche, or mountain sickness, the bleeding of ears and nose, the difficulty of breathing to be experienced on the summit. Nor were the too numerous wraps we had taken necessary. We must not stay long on this wind-swept platform. There is no place to corral the mules, or protection for ourselves. We gaze wistfully, wishing we could linger yet a little. We look reluctantly again, and yet once again, then mount and bidding farewell to Argentina, we turn and set our faces towards Chili.

We entered deep snow directly we commenced the descent. The beaten track was slippery with ice, whilst the snow reached up to the saddle girths on either side. Although my mule was led, it was extremely unpleasant, descending on this path of iced snow down a precipitous mountain side, the animals sliding and slipping along as best they could. There were a few ugly places, where the snow had melted and given way, and where the mules sunk into a crevasse four or five feet deep, floundering, plunging, falling, and recovering. One place was impassable, until stones had been dug out and placed to form some sort of foothold.

But worse was to come. For when the snow and boulders and the last arête were past, we found ourselves on a scarcely discernible track of loose scoria and stones, winding over the side of deep precipices. They yawned below and on either side of us. A false step by the mule, and we should be hurled to certain death. It was blood-curdling work. One tried not to see, but glimpses of these death traps would appear in the windings of the dangerous way. Only a fortnight before a family had come over. One of their pack mules slipped in the snow and was lost with the baggage in a crevasse. The arriero's mule made a false step and rolled over, carrying the man, hanging by his stirrup in the lasso, over a precipice. Fortunately some little obstacle caught them, and with the greatest difficulty they were rescued.

How quickly we descended. The great snow fields were soon left behind us. But the valley was deep and winding, and before we were half-way down I called a halt, and notwithstanding all remonstrances dismounted. The descent threw me against the pommel, causing such pain from the pressure that I could endure it no longer. My nerves, unstrung with excessive fatigue, could stand the strain of riding over these dangerous precipices no more. The sharp stones cut my feet horribly. The loose earth and stones formed a glissade down the steep places, or were sometimes turned into running rivers of liquid mud, ankle deep, and flowing down, as mule after mule churned it up in descending. It was not a moment to consider such trifles as mud and dirt. Heedless of all, I plunged wildly on, down, down, thankful only for every inch of descent accomplished.

The wind sprang up. How thankful we were to have passed the Cumbre in safety. Stumbling, tripping, clinging to rocks, sliding down anyhow; at length, after a very long while, we saw a glad sight— the end of the deep ravine, the valley of rest. A further source of satisfaction was the joy of our luggage passing by safe and sound, for we had suffered many pangs of doubt as to its safety, at various periods of the journey.

Little did we think that this extremely long, steep descent was only the prelude to many other similar ones, ere our arrival at Juncal. All the afternoon we descended from valley to valley, dropped down successive altitudes, each one being reached by an equally terrible descent carved out from the mountain side. I was obliged to remount. It was best to put entire faith in the mule and never attempt to guide him, even when he persistently chose the outer and overhanging edge of the pathway. Twice we stopped to rest under the shelter of a corral. I could scarcely hold on much longer, being utterly exhausted and too weary to think of anything but an arrival at our destination. The mountains might be most beautiful, but I could only cling in a long drawn-out agony to the saddle.

So steep is the Cordillera on the Chilian side, that during the afternoon we descended 5000 feet, still leaving over 8000 feet to be accomplished. The scenery was magnificent, far grander and more varied than that of the morning. As I have before said, the Chilian ascent is much more beautiful, if precipitous, than the Argentine Valley.

Late in the afternoon we found ourselves opposite a mountain, looking down upon a lovely valley. This scene, tired as I was, was of such extreme beauty that it remains imprinted on my memory. "It was the descent of the Caracoles, one of the boldest and most picturesque sections of the Cordillera." Our muleteer then took us over a fearful moraine, turning off the path which would have led us past the black waters of the desolate Inca Lake. It may have been a short cut, but we were sorry afterwards to have missed seeing this mountain sea. At the bottom, at Calavera, on a large open space, were the zinc-roofed buildings of the railway works and the drilling installations for piercing the entrance to the Cumbre summit on this, the Chilian side. The tunnel is to be 5000 metres in length, without ventilation, and will pierce through and under the valleys we have been descending during the afternoon.

Will Juncal never come? Yet another valley to

ride through, yet another descent before us; but in the distance is the wooden house of the Juncal Hotel, lying far away below the hillside, beside the foaming torrent of the Aconcagua, which oozes out of the snow beds of some of the Andean Mountains we have just been passing. The final descent is fortunately over a good road, engineered by the railway for transporting their material to Calavera, for I had come to the final stage of exhaustion.

We arrived at the hotel. I was lifted off the mule and placed on a bed, where for two hours I lay aching and throbbing with pain, unable to move or speak. Then tea was a great refresher, accompanied by a hot bath with arnica, to relieve the weary limbs.

We had ridden between fifty to sixty kilometres, or from 4 a.m. to 4 p.m., with only half an hour's rest, and almost without food. We arrived smothered in mud and dirt, with everything spoilt we had on. But I had saved my face from swelling by means of a linen mask, and a paste of cold cream and vaseline. The mountain air is so dry and keen that several ladies described to me the condition of their faces as being so inflamed and painful that they had to keep their rooms for a week after crossing the Cordillera. Hence my precautions.

During the entire day, the mules had been given nothing to eat or drink. They did not appear over tired, but on a fair road it is always reckoned that a mule can comfortably do from fifty to sixty miles per day.

The Juncal Hotel is a clean wooden structure in a lovely situation at the head of the Aconcagua

Valley, and surrounded by mountain peaks. It is kept by M. Hispa, a Frenchman, who, we are glad to hear, is about to take over the Posada at Las Cuevras, when, let us hope, it will become as clean and comfortable as this pretty little inn. We slept for twelve hours. Awoke refreshed, though still so sore and stiff, we felt we could not face another thirty kilometres of riding after yesterday's experience, so we chartered M. Hispa's carriage for the lovely drive on a spring morning down the valley of the roaring torrent of Aconcagua.

Unwise decision. In a few minutes we wished ourselves back on our mules, for the springless two-wheeled waggonette, with its mixed team, jolted and bumped relentlessly against the stones loosened from the banks, that had fallen on to the road, causing renewed suffering to our bruised and wearied bodies and making us almost seasick.

As we dropped down the valley, it was interesting to watch the various stages of vegetation, beginning with a scrub growth, continuing with evergreen shrubs and hardy trees, then a quantity of pansies and marigolds and wild flowers, and ending in a magnificent growth of cacti, growing in groups of wanton luxuriance on every hill-side, their round, thorny stems crowned by a white, waxy flower, resembling a Eucharis lily. Counted as a troublesome weed in this country, in England what a curiosity we should consider their peculiar and bristling growth.

Salto de Soldato is reached after a three hours' drive, and we rest under an arbour of dried branches, until the arrival of the special engine generously sent for us by the Company. Then M. Hispa insisted upon driving us to the station himself, and it did seem hard lines that after escaping all the perils of crossing the Cordillera, and just when we had, as we thought, arrived safely, that worthy gentleman should all but succeed in sending us over a last precipice by the aid of bad driving and a refractory mule. But so it was, and we had a narrow escape.

The special engine awaited us at this, the end of the Chilian section of the Transandine Railway. It was a funny little machine, being a trolly surmounted by a boiler, with a single seat to hold two passengers behind. It was truly the "machina especial" mentioned on the ticket, and was to run us down to Los Andes over the completed section of the railway. The line here is being merely kept in repair, as since the crisis there has been no money forthcoming in Chili to continue the work. But whilst we were at Santiago, Mr. Matteo Clark was obtaining a fresh concession on new lines from the Government. If successful in securing the assent of Congress, the works should be recommenced immediately.

A few instants after leaving the station we plunged into a tunnel, then out again, and in the second before entering another tunnel we catch a glimpse of the Soldier's Leap, from which the place obtains its name. It is a deep-hewn chasm in a rocky defile, with the Aconcagua rushing below. The legend runs that during the war between Chili and the Argentine a soldier escaped his pursuers by leaping across this gap.

It was a wild, mad rush downwards, lasting over

an hour, on that little trolley. Ever descending into the valley, with the mountains receding rapidly before us. That fertile, smiling valley of vineyards, with its green fields of lucerne and wheat, its teeming habitations, seemed to us like returning to the world once more. This morning we were in the fastnesses of the mountains. This afternoon we are in a well-populated plain. The " Lion of the Andes," a great snow-capped peak, with a summit resembling a square Norman castle keep, rose prominent from the range. Down, down, in a frantic rush, amid clouds of smoke and dust, amid a deafening clamour of rattling wheels. We cling vigorously on, being shaken and rocked from side to side ; it is only another method of battering our aching limbs. A final rush and a spurt of steam, and we draw up at the platform of the station of Los Andes, or Santa Rosa.

Soon we are at rest in the quiet green patio of the Hotel de Commerce, fragrant with roses and lilies, and listening to the gently splashing fountain, whilst good M. and Madame Haler minister to our wants. How grateful we were for that pleasant two hours of repose. What an oasis of refreshing quiet and greenness it seemed after the gaunt grimness of the scenes of the past few days.

I have recorded our experiences in traversing the Cordillera, but I am well aware that many will not agree with my account of the fatigues and discomforts of the journey. I have met several ladies who have thoroughly enjoyed the expedition, while others again will think with us that the trip may be made under pressure of necessity, but certainly *not* for pleasure. I think myself that the question resolves itself into one of physical strength. If a lady is sufficiently strong to ride continuously for twelve hours without undue fatigue, the journey through such grand scenery is enjoyable. If, like myself, she becomes so over-tired that the only question to be thought of is whether strength can hold out until the end of the day, she will probably agree in my account.

The advance of the railway will quickly lessen the amount of riding. Ladies will be warned by the experience of others to take their own saddles. The inns, with the increase of passengers, will improve in food and accommodation.

Los Andes, with its green plaza so well laid out and carefully tended, is a charming little place, but it owes everything to its grand background of the Andes, in all their glory. Now that we have penetrated far into their innermost recesses, and have made such an intimate acquaintance with their ascending heights, it is pleasant to contemplate them from a distance that lends them somewhat of enchantment.

At six in the evening we took the train to Santiago, making our farewell to the Cordillera, under the blush of a rosy sunset that etherealized, while bathing their rock-bound surface in a tender pink. A last look in the twilight revealed them faded into a cold and ghostly grey. The gathering dusk hid from view the thriving farmsteads, the vineyards, gardens, and rows of poplars of this smiling Chilian valley.

Santiago is reached shortly after 10 p.m., and we are soon established in the palatial, if rambling,

Hotel de Françia, giving on to the Plaza. We fully rejoice in a return to civilized quarters once more, while a feeling of thankfulness is not absent that our crossing of the Andes is a feat accomplished.

CHAPTER VI.

CHILI AND THE CHILIANS.

"Toll, toll, toll," the neighbouring bell of the Cathedral of Santiago booms into my awakening ears. Cracked as the bell is, it yet gives forth a sonorous full-toned note, and on looking out of my window, overlooking the vast Plaza, I see crowds of black-robed and hooded women obeying its summons, and hurrying in at the great door, to be joined by a procession of white-robed priests, wearing large black shovel hats.

There is a great commemorative funeral service in progress, for the anniversary of the death of the patriot minister, Portales. You enter the Cathedral to see a most impressive sight. Hundreds of women, all clothed in black, are kneeling on the floor, their faces upturned, listening to an eloquent sermon from the black-gowned curé. His sonorous accents echo through the aisles, accompanied by many eloquent gestures. There are no chairs or *prie-dieus*, but each woman brings in her own mat or handkerchief to kneel on. The catafalque is ablaze with hundreds of lighted tapers, whilst the whole Cathedral is sumptuously draped in black and silver. The choir-stalls are occupied by high Church dignitaries. There is the Archbishop, with an enormous white mitre and spangled gold vestment, whilst below are grouped the lesser lights of the Church—the bishops arrayed in velvet vesture scarcely less gorgeous. The acolytes and surpliced choir complete the picturesque grouping around the High Altar.

We were enjoying this gorgeous spectacle, when I began to find out that the women were staring and whispering about me. I suddenly realized that my hat was the object of comment, and that all the other females were shawled and hooded except myself. Luckily we made an exit before being forcibly ejected, for no woman in Chili or Peru is allowed to enter a church except their heads are covered in this fashion. The idea originated in a good principle. There was to be no difference amongst the worshippers. The hood and draped figure were common alike to the highest in the land and the humblest churchgoer.

The difference in religious fervour between Chili and the Argentine is at once apparent. Here they are ardent devotees. Churches are open all day, bells tolling forth perpetually over the city, and hooded women, kneeling, mat in one hand, rosary and breviary in the other, swarm in the streets in the early morning, hurrying along to mass. Even in this levelling costume, the distinctive mark of the lady will peep out. Now it is discovered by the jewelled hand stealing from under the shawl, or the heavily-chased silver mounting of the breviary. Some daughter of vanity may even try to lessen the severity of the costume by a border of lace, and many contrive to adjust the mantilla in such a coquettish way that it marks out to perfection the shape of the head. But the Spanish ladies need not fear the severe simplicity of the *praya*. It forms the most becoming and effective frame to their beautiful complexions and lustrous black eyes.

Santiago is a most fascinating capital. Of all the places we have seen in South America it pleases us most. To begin with, there is that wonderful setting for the bright little town, formed by the semicircle of the Andes. Look which way you will, their white-crowned summits peep above the brown roof-tops, and glimmer behind the many church towers. Now, as through the whole summer, they appear always wrapped in a golden haze. It imparts to them a transparent delicacy of colour hard to describe. They are thirty miles away, and yet how near they seem, for in this lucid atmosphere distance is a fantasia that deceives greatly.

One of the great charms of Chili is the perfect climate. Rain may fall for three months of the year, but during the other nine months the sun shines without fail, day after day, while the heat is tempered by a fresh breeze. It is an ideal atmosphere, with an air bright, light, and invigorating. The want of water is the only drawback, but the industrious Chilian, by the aid of trenches and miniature canals, brings the mountain stream into the valley, and by a complicated system of irrigation, produces the luxurious vegetation and crops that we see.

Santiago possesses a magnificent boulevard, extending for two miles in the Alameda or Avenida das Delicias. Truly named is this umbrageous avenue of trees and shady promenades. In the evening, when

SANTIAGO DE CHILI.

Page 124.

the band plays, the citizens there stroll in large numbers. Its great length is frequently interrupted by equestrian statues, and other monuments erected to the memory of patriot generals and citizens. The Chilians, of all people in the world, are the most patriotic, and on every plaza and in the park of every city you find these tokens of a grateful people to the heroes who have rendered services to their country. The tramway is accorded a special avenue to itself. The trees of the Alameda, in their rich green foliage, call for much admiration in a country where all becomes burnt up and brown unless carefully watered.

The end of the Alameda is crowned by Santa Lucia, the unique feature of Santiago.

Santa Lucia was a barren rock until the munificence of a citizen, Vicuna Mackenna, transformed it into the fantastic eminence before us. The winding walks that ascend to its summit are fringed with pepper trees. Aloes form a natural prickly hedge, whilst the rocky walls are draped and blazing with scarlet geraniums. There are cool grottoes, with trickling water, a restaurant and theatre. Santa Lucia has its chapel, with the marble statue of a mitred archbishop, with hand upraised in the act of blessing the city from this elevated position. The view from the crowning pavilion, with Santiago spread out at our feet, is magnificent. We see the brown tiled eaves of the houses of its 200,000 citizens, the masses of church spires, the green lines of the Alameda distinctly marked out, and vanishing in the distance, the dry, unsightly bed of the Rio Mapocho, crossed by numerous bridges, the whole encircled by that glorious snow range of the Cordillera.

Our Plaza is the centre of life. The Hôtel de França, with its imposing façade of Ionian columns, occupies the whole of one side, the Cathedral and Archiepiscopal Palace another, and the Post Office a third. The colonnade under our hotel is an open bazaar, with its stalls and goods disposed on counters in the streets. Lovely flowers and fruit, such as strawberries, bananas, pine apples, green figs, and custard apples, are exposed for sale.

The wonderful covered gallery of San Carlos is only equalled by the arcade at Milan. This lofty colonnade is cruciform in shape, meeting in the centre under a lofty arched dome of glass. The shops in it are Parisian, whilst its pavements are a favourite lounge for the *flâneurs* of the capital.

The streets are full of movement. The tram service is frequent, and as they all start from the Plaza on a single line, the block is often great. At night their red lamps proceed in slow procession, forming a complete circle of coloured light around the square. Their conductors are women, the distinguishing uniform consisting in a straw sailor hat. It seems strange to us to see these women seated on the footboard of the open tram, collecting their fares. Knifeboard passengers have to pay before they go up. The Tramway Companies find that the women, whilst working for less wages, are also much more honest. The receipts have materially increased since this change was adopted.

The shrill cries of the ragged street urchins, offering lottery tickets and newspapers, cease not day nor night. Monster bullock waggons creak along the road, the driver walking alongside, to admonish his fourfold team of oxen with the wand-like whip. Gauchos, of even more picturesque type than those in Argentina, pace along. Their ponchos are shorter and of more brilliant and varied stripes, their sombreros are woven in straw of many colours, whilst the huge circular star-shaped spur, which does not prick so sharply as an ordinary one, is more utilized to hold on with than to punish the mule or horse. The saddle is even more decorated than that of the Eastern gaucho. As the most characteristic object to take home from South America, we invested in Santiago in a complete gaucho equipment, consisting of high peaked saddle, lasso, bolas, wooden box stirrups, spurs, and a cruel ring-bit.

We observe a novel form of advertising. A tram is hired, and with a band playing on the top to attract attention, drives round the town in the afternoon, scattering hundreds of handbills, with notices of some evening entertainment. The hackney carriage is so quaint as to deserve special notice. Swung high on C springs, the carriage roof projects over the driver's seat, affording him protection. It gives a curious elongated and somewhat awkward appearance. Badly paved with the usual stone cobbles as are the streets, they are yet an improvement on those of Buenos Ayres. A block away from the Plaza is the Camara de Deputados, or Parliament buildings. The Corinthian columns and pink exterior of this pretty little House of Deputies is indicative of the simple interior. The semi-circular Chamber contains the President's desk, slightly raised on a platform, with rows of desks around. Each desk provides space for two deputies. There are special galleries reserved for the Press, the Diplomatic Corps, and the public. The dining and waiting rooms are small but comfortable. Adjoining the lower Chamber, is the National Library and the Senate House.

One of the sights of Santiago is the Cousiño Park, where between the hours of five and seven the Chilian ladies come out for their daily drive. Avenues of pepper trees and groups of Eucalyptus surround the circular promenade, whilst the eye is refreshed by that most rare growth in South America, green glades of grass. In a country where for so many months of the year no rain falls it is difficult, nay, almost impossible, to keep a lawn from becoming burnt up. The lake in the centre is fringed with water reeds. Clumps of arum lilies cluster on the banks. Hedges of roses surround it, whilst rustic bridges, wreathed in creepers, are thrown across to an island in the centre. Among the groves of trees that surround the lake there is a restaurant, but the fashionable circle is found elsewhere. Here, enthroned in state, the ladies sit in rows, watching the occupants of the other carriages. Some of these equipages amuse us greatly, such as a char-a-banc full of young men, an English tandem, and a high dog-cart. There is even one four-in-hand, but perhaps to us the strangest custom is that of two young men solemnly driving round and round in a close carriage. Doubtless, the ladies are the attraction.

Beautifully dressed, the charms of these ladies are partially concealed by their closed carriages. An open carriage is not considered the proper thing. So soon do we fall into the ways of the country, that a victoria now looks to us quite an outrage on established custom. True it is that the panels of glass, forming the sides of the carriages, display the occupant as much as possible. As in Spain, the Eastern seclusion of women yet lingers in these South American capitals. Their lives are chiefly confined to the patio. The daily drive in the park, varied by much mass-going, is the only amusement and occupation.

We were granted an audience by the Archbishop of Chili at the Palace. An outer lobby, filled with suppliants, admitted us to the corridor overlooking a patio green with palms, and to the crimson upholstered reception-room, with the usual portrait of the Holy Father.

The Archbishop received us in state, in the Hall of Convocation. Advancing over the polished boards, down a long room, attired in purple and scarlet robes, and attended by a group of high ecclesiastics, His Eminence courteously greeted us, and led us to chairs placed at the upper end. The Convocation Hall is a stately chamber, dim with stained glass, reflected in shining colours on the carved oak stalls that line the walls. The ceiling is adorned with a beautifully painted fresco, of an allegorical subject. The light catches the burnished points of a crucifix turned eastwards. The chapel, immediately opposite, is florid in blue and white decoration. Marriages and baptisms of state are performed here.

We gave much greeting from Cardinal Vaughan, and presented the letter of recommendation addressed by His Eminence on our behalf to "Omnibus Ecclesiæ Catholicæ Archiepiscopis, Episcopis, Sacerdotibus, et Fidelibus."

The conversation turned on Cardinal Manning, and our host was much interested when we related the story of our little girl's visit to him, a few days before his death. She wore a scarlet coat and hat. He laughingly asked her how she dared appropriate a cardinal's headgear, and, taking it off, placed it on his own head. He then fetched from his bedroom a sacred picture, which he gave her with his blessing and salute. Monsignor Cazanova is a very able man, of commanding presence and deep-set brows. He asked many intelligent questions respecting Ireland, Mr. Gladstone, and Home Rule.

The Roman Church is all-powerful in Chili, and has enormous political influence. He attributed this to the pure Spanish descent of the population; whilst the Italian element which largely predominates in Argentina, hampers the progress of the Church there. The Catholicism of Italy has never been so fervid as that of Spain. The interview, with the listening group of ecclesiastics, was somewhat formidable, especially as we are not children of his Church, and I was relieved when we found ourselves outside the Archiepiscopal precincts.

An hour later the President of the Republic received us in his crimson-canopied reception chamber, at the "Moneda." These Government buildings of the old Spanish rule are a succession of rambling plaster courts, connected by wooden verandahs and staircases, covering a large space. The interior windows of the Mint are guarded by iron bars.

Characteristic of the simple state observed by the President is the ante-chamber, guarded by a single officer in uniform. President Montt wears the uniform of the navy to which he belongs, and speaks excellent English. He is pleasant and affable. The salary of 1500*l*. does not admit of much ostentation or show. None is needed by this simple and loyal people. Later in the evening, we met the President walking unattended in the Alameda.

A great national and Conservative demonstration was taking place at the Opera House, to celebrate the anniversary of the death of Portales, a former minister, who was assassinated at the early age of forty-four. He died nearly fifty years ago, without achieving any great work, but with the reputation of being an upright and honest minister. The enthusiasm, therefore, his memory arouses is quite extraordinary. His name is to the Conservative party what Beaconsfield's is to ours.

The committee kindly put a box at our disposal. We arrived to find the Opera House crowded from floor to roof with an appreciative audience. Not a place was vacant. The House was festooned with roses, and a bust of Portales occupied the centre of the stage, whilst the ladies of the chorus were grouped around, among the overhanging palms. It was a brilliant spectacle, the lower boxes of the tiers adding to the *coup d'œil*. The President was there in his loge, whilst that of the Municipality, opposite, was occupied by the ladies and gentlemen of the committee.

The interest of the entertainment consisted in the concert, all the music and orchestra being undertaken by amateur performers, many of them being members of well-known families. The music was interspersed by speeches and addresses in praise of the statesman. We found these latter very long and tedious. A lady recited a poem composed by her mother, a daughter of Portales. We were taken during the interval behind the stage, and introduced to some of the leading ladies and gentlemen.

When the allegorical tableaux, with a picture of an angel crowning the laurel-wreathed bust of Portales, wound up the demonstration, we found that it had lasted for four hours and that it was nearly 2 a.m. We escaped the dancing that was to follow in the *foyer*, and hurried home.

The charming Minister of Foreign Affairs—Señor Don Venturo Blanco Riel—came on Sunday afternoon, to drive us out in his carriage to the Quinta Normal, to witness the opening of a picture-gallery by the President.

The Quinta Normal is a species of "living encyclopædia," exhibiting the products of the country, and combining a Botanical and Zoological Garden. There are specimens of the llama, alpaca, guanoco, housed indiscriminately near cages containing partridges, Dorking hens, and species of our common geese. The gardens are shady, and well laid out round a pretty lake. Two military bands were performing. It was pleasant watching the crowds of people strolling about, enjoying the music and the Sunday afternoon rest.

The Quinta Cousiño is one of the sights of Santiago, and thither Señor Osa and Councillor Lopez conducted us one afternoon. This magnificent palace belongs to Madame Cousiño, the proprietress of the Peninsula of Lota, the owner of its rich coal-mines, and almost the wealthiest woman in the world, with a fortune estimated at perhaps 400,000*l.* sterling a year. We have not time to go south and visit Conception and Lota, but everyone tantalizes us by descriptions of the latter spot, with its lovely gardens overhanging the sea.

This beautiful house is well worthy of a visit. We pass through room after room, hung with exquisite and priceless brocades, embroidered by hand. The curtains, wall-panels, and furniture are *en suite*. The ceilings are frescoed with water-nymphs and cherubs; costly cloisonné and exquisite Dresden china adorn the ormolu or Mexican marble mounted tables. The house is a gem, worthy of the Rothschild family of South America. The marble hall, full of beautiful statuary, leads to the spacious staircase, whose wall-panels are decorated by the French artist Clarin with realistic scenes from the life of Paris. One panel represents the Champs Elysées and the Arc de Triomphe, full of gay carriages, and another the course at Longchamps.

I have never seen anything like the sumptuous decorations of the bedrooms. The beds, hung with *vieux* rose satin or pale-green *eau de vie*, are draped in costly lace, the wall-panels and furniture being similarly covered; the blue satin canopied bed in Madame Cousiño's own room being a work of art in itself. A picture gallery possessing a Meissonier, and enormous stables, with accommodation for 120 horses, completed this Palace of Delight. The house at Lota is even more superb, and yet the owner of all these mansions elects by choice to live in a small apartment in Paris; seldom comes here, and, most ironical coincidence of all, is in perpetual ill-health. One daughter is a permanent invalid, another in a convent, and one of the two sons dislikes all pomp and show. Such is life!

We are told that there are several other houses on the Alameda and elsewhere in Santiago almost as magnificent as this Quinta Cousiño; for they are free here from the Baring boom and crash, and are not living in a state of retrenchment and retirement as in Argentina.

Señor Osa (to whom we were indebted for much that was pleasant during our stay at Santiago) gave us a magnificent paseo, or *déjeuner*, at his Quinta in the country, asking a distinguished company to meet us. It was a drive of four miles out, along a typical country road, full of ascents and declivities, hidden in clouds of dust.

The Quinta, with its marble hall and large apartments, was very handsome; the garden charming, with its long walk arched over with trellises of vines, leading through to an avenue of tulip-trees in full bloom. The large yellow flower, with its orange centre, filled the air with perfume. A lake, covered with water-lilies, was beyond. There were orchid-houses, ferneries, and conservatories, and some lawns, though not quite perhaps of the shaven smoothness we are accustomed to in our gardens at home. As for the roses, their luxuriance could not be equalled. On trees over six feet high, masses of white and pink blossoms clustered thickly; others grew in hedges, or climbed over archways; the

BRIDGE ON THE VALPARAISO AND SANTIAGO RAILWAY.

tea-roses being exceptionally fine. South America is, in this spring season, a land of flowers.

The table at *déjeuner* was decorated to form a *parterre* of bloom, being completely covered with floral designs. It was a native repast, with several favourite Chilian dishes, and commenced with "cazuela," a soup of hotch-potch, and was followed by some "empanadas," or pastry pies; the characteristic feature of both being the hot curry flavour, produced by a liberal use of the red chili. Prize horses and bulls were produced afterwards for our inspection; but we were growing impatient to leave, as time pressed. A paseo is an interminably long entertainment; for beginning at 11 a.m. or so, it frequently lasts until dinner-time approaches.

At length we bade farewell to our kind host and hostess, drove with Mr. Kennedy, the British Minister, through the blazing sun on our return to Santiago, packed up, and were ready to leave for Valparaiso in the evening.

The Chilian railway system is a Government enterprise, and the cheapest to travel by in the world. Our journey of 120 miles only cost eight shillings. The setting sun crimsoned the snow summits of the Cordillera, as we wound among the little valleys and low foothills. We judged that the curves and gradients of this line are severe, from the way the carriage shook. Now in the dark we heard the engine puffing and struggling up hill, then again shutting off steam for a downward rush.

Valparaiso looked its best under the beams of a crescent moon, the pale-blue light gleaming and dancing on the foam of the waves, washing into the bay we were skirting. Myriads of lights twinkled in long-drawn-out or arched lines, up and down, over the rocky promontory on which the town has found for itself a foothold. We see the sea once more. We have travelled from ocean to ocean, from the green waves of the Atlantic to the blue waters of the Pacific.

A walk through the solitary and deserted streets brought us to the Hôtel de France. Worn out with the overwhelming hospitality of our friends at Santiago, we rested well and slept soundly.

Valparaiso, most quaint of seafaring ports, is laid out in one long street, on a piece of land that has been rescued from the bay. After the precise chess-board configuration of other South American towns, the windings of the Calle Arturo Prat are a refreshing variety. All around are the great bare hills of yellow earth, sparsely dotted with green scrub and bushes. Their natural conformation is preserved, whilst the houses are terraced a little way up each hill, and divided by deep gulleys. They are reached by winding wooden stairs, or steep roads, carved out in the cliffs. The overhanging wall of rock, that rises above the roof-tops of the central calle, is hung with scarlet geraniums and yellow marigolds.

Valparaiso has its cool, green public gardens, its central Plazas, and national monuments to patriotic countrymen, chief of which is that to Arturo Prat, the hero of the naval battle at Iquique; but save the theatre, no other fine public buildings. English abound in the streets, for somewhere about 2000 reside and are engaged in business here. Mr. Wetherall, the English chaplain, kindly gave up his

THE ESPLANADE, VALPARAISO.

day to us, and from the top of a tram, showed us the little there is to be seen in Chili's chief seaport.

We spent the afternoon in going by train to Viña del Mar, the fashionable watering-place on the sea-shore, celebrated also for the national races that are frequently held on its racecourse. Through the wharves, with piles of merchandise lying before the numerous shipping offices, we go, slipping along the sea-shore, amongst the rocks, where the waves, black with seaweed, come rolling in. In this sheltered and placid bay the Pacific gleams pale and misty in the afternoon sunlight. Far away yonder, hidden under that white cloud, is the snow cone of Aconcagua.

A sad sight is a large steamer wrecked on the rocks quite near the shore. She is one of the steamers belonging to the Sud Americana or Chilian line, and went ashore in a dense fog the night before last. Her captain, an old servant of the company's, mistook the whistle of the train going round the bay, for that of the tug sent out to meet him. The ship is heeling over fast; indeed on our return journey we saw a marked difference in the list to starboard. They fear she will become a total wreck.

We travel through the midst of the pretty quintas and green gardens of Viña del Mar, and alight at the hotel opposite the station. The garden, with its deep, shady groves of casuerina-trees, its terraced walks, lawn-tennis courts and winding paths, is the great attraction to the hotel. Many come and pass the summer here, to enjoy the sea-bathing, though the little wooden houses on the sands look somewhat rough, and the cold current renders the water too icy cold for many to endure. Chili is superior to the

Argentine in possessing this seaside place and several mountain villages for a summer change of residence. At Buenos Ayres they have only one seaside (and shadeless) village, Mara la Plata, to resort to in the hot season.

The racecourse, marked out by a circular row of poplars, is pointed out to us in the distance. A natural hill has been taken advantage of to form a grand-stand. The boxes are dug out in tiers on the hill-side, and pleasant to remember are the open-air picnics which take place in each loge. The climate of Valparaiso, as its chief charm, deserves a passing word. A clear atmosphere, pure as ether, bright sunshine, temperate heat, with a rainfall of only thirteen inches, confined to three months in the year, is a climatic condition hard to find elsewhere.

We left Valparaiso at sundown, embarking from the Plaza, with many regrets that our stay had been so shortened, to go on board the *Maipo*.

The *Maipo* is one of the fleet of the Sud Americana line, which, with a friendly competition, shares with the Pacific Steam Navigation Company the trade along the coast-lines of Chili and Peru. We spent three happy and comfortable weeks on this charming little steamer, with her roomy deck cabins, her splendid promenade decks, and cheerful saloon, gay with paper flowers. Passengers came and went at each port, but we were never crowded. The food was excellent, the Chilian stewards attentive, and Captain Selmer, most pleasant of commanders, did well the honours of his ship as only can a Dane. Above all, it is one of the few calm sea-voyages of the world. Day after day the sea was like an expanse of dark-green glass, varied only by the long, undulating, heavy swell, which *did* sometimes make us roll a little uncomfortably. Not even the latest arrived passenger thought, however, of being ill.

But the *Maipo* had one great drawback. She carried three hundred head of cattle from Valparaiso and other ports to supply food to the towns along the "Rainless Coast." The cattle arrive alongside in flat lighters, to be swung on board. It is a sight to make one miserable, watching these poor bullocks, packed so tightly together in the lighter, that when one falls down, the others crush it by standing or trampling on it. For hours they stand in cramped, uncomfortable positions, horns tightly tied, heaving up and down in the lighter, alongside the vessel. As they are slung up they look meekly round, whilst being bumped and crashed against the ship's side. The chain and pulley go down with a run, and they are given a final plump on the lower deck before scrambling to their feet. Many pause breathlessly, then a pole with a pointed nail is dug into their sides, and the tail is twisted until the crackings are plainly audible. The effluvia arising from the lower hatchways is nauseating, and at times overwhelming ; it pervades the atmosphere and cannot be got rid of. The stench greets you as you open your cabin door in the morning, and is with you all day. The longer the cattle remain on board, naturally the stronger it grows.

The stern of the ship is fitted up with booths, where a regular market of fresh vegetables, fruit, flowers, shrubs, plants, butter, and eggs is held at each stopping port. The saleswomen sit enthroned amongst their household gods, and crowds of boats put off to buy provisions, hovering around until the officer of the port has come on board to receive our papers. Then there is a frantic rush and scramble up the gangway, followed by much chaffering and bargaining. But these stolid ladies are too wise; well they know the worth of their goods in this desert land, where no green thing will grow. They have no competition, they command the market, and will not abate one cent. Thus the coast of Chili is fed daily from the south.

The voyage along the coast brings us in contact with the most wonderful phenomenon. For 2000 miles, for a distance extending from Coquimbo all along the northern coast of Chili, and including the whole coast of Peru, to the Gulf of Guayaquil, we see a zone of rainless desert. Nothing will grow; there is not a tree or tiny blade of grass. It is all sand and rock. Rain is unknown, and drinking-water for the towns can only be obtained from a great distance in the interior of the mountains, whence it is brought down at considerable expense. Some places resort to distilling the sea-water. Fogs at night are frequent, and they impart a little moisture to the thirsty sand. The zone extends inland for a width varying from twenty to eighty miles. At Guayaquil it ends abruptly, with a return to a moister atmosphere.

A scientific explanation of this extraordinary freak of nature is forthcoming. "The trade winds strike Northern Brazil loaded with vapour, and currents of air drift westwards, supplying the Plate and Amazon systems with abundant rainfall. When these currents beat against the ramparts of the Andes, the remaining moisture is wrung from them by the condensing power of low temperatures at extreme altitudes. From the crest of the range, there are no sources of evaporation, until the tranquil levels of the Pacific are reached. The air currents in their passage to the coast are without moisture. The snows on the eastern slopes and central summits of the Andes are final deposits of vapour, which exhaust the water supply of the Atlantic trades. There is nothing in reserve for the strip of sea-board and the intervening mountain slopes." Hence this extraordinary " Rainless Coast."

The only seaport town we landed at in Chili was Coquimbo. It served as a sample for many other smaller and more primitive places. The steep streets of Coquimbo, with a big mountain behind, even the smoking chimney of the large copper-smelting works, looked picturesque under the shining light of a full moon. Coquimbo is the centre of a great copper-mining industry. Some of the great fortunes of Chili have been drawn hence. We find the shops open even at this late hour, as we proceed down the street. The railway runs through it to Sarsena, the principal town, for which Coquimbo is only the port. We find a great crowd at the post-office (where we go to post our letters), eagerly watching the letters of the mail we have brought being pushed, after sorting, into the guichets.

We proceeded to the Plaza, which is the usual green oasis, fringed with pepper-trees. The doors of the cathedral opposite were open, and the sound of music attracted our attention. The sight that greeted us, as we stole up the steps, was very pretty. The altars were ablaze with light, and the church decorated in blue and white, for it is the month of the Blessed Virgin Mary, and every evening, from the 8th of November to the 8th of December, this commemorative service will be held. The floor of the church was massed with black-robed women, whilst the treble, childish voices of the choir chanted a sweet-toned litany. The refrain of the "Ave Maria" echoed again and again, floating out to us on the still, night air, dying away into silence as the black-robed priest, with his sympathetic voice, admonished his flock from the pulpit. Truly this night service is a fresh proof of the religious devotion of the Chilian nation.

Day after day we touch at these little seaport towns. Sometimes two are accomplished in one day. The hauling up and letting go of the anchor grows a very familiar sound. They are desolate little villages, consisting of a few brown-roofed houses, scarcely distinguishable from the surrounding desert of sand. If the place is of sufficient importance, a band-stand occupies a commanding position on the landing-stage. There are no wharves or piers. The surf is heavy and the landing often difficult. The arrival of the mail steamer is the great event. Our variety of merchandise is large, consisting as it does of sacks of flour, maize, or coffee, of trusses of hay, iron castings, steel rods, and barrels of lard. A few passengers leave, a few arrive at each port. The six steam-winches work merrily, and noisily all the time we remain at anchor.

Yet it is an interesting voyage, the outline of the

Chili and the Chilians. 143

coast is so extremely curious and beautiful. Like the desert of Arabia it is indicated in a faint, pale grey, white, or lavender outline. The intense dryness of the atmosphere absorbs all colour, and leaves only these dim monotones.

Yes, it is almost an impossibility to describe this phantom line of coast, designated in pale tints. The mountains are so spectral, so distinct, yet veiled; such delicate pearl-grey ranges meeting such a pellucid sky, with neutral furrows depicting the crevasses on their precipitous slopes. Fleecy banks of cloud float midway along the range, or gather, veiling in mystery their summits. Anon, the white sand of some mount will shine and glisten like a mantle of silver.

Morning, afternoon, and evening, day succeeding day, this transparent, illusive coast is ever with us. Barren and deadly drear as with a near approach it is, the distance enfolds it in this entrancing and transforming haze.

The sunsets of this South Pacific are wondrously beautiful. They are washed in, in full, soft shades. There is nothing gorgeous about them, no orange or blood-red crimson; but delicate tones of cerulean rose, pearl-grey, or apple-green suffuse the sky, dying into a soft, full, glimmering twilight.

Antofagasta, the capital of the province of that name, is situated on the Tropic of Capricorn. The horizontal line of that tropic runs through the town. From the deck we can distinguish the sandy streets, laid out in American squares, set down on this Sahara, this "abomination of desolation." Brown are the houses, brown the streets, brown the shore. There is a small church on a bleak plaza, and many Pulperias, or drinking-saloons. One house is singled out by its frontage, painted in imitation of a brick wall.

Yet Antofagasta boasts of the largest silver-smelting works in the world, and has railway communication to the interior. We can see the puffing engine running along the valley, of the line leading into Bolivia, opening up a connection with La Paz, its capital.

We are now passing along the coast of the great Atacama Desert. Some curious stratified and flat-topped ranges attract our attention one afternoon: they are beds of ancient guano deposits, now worked out.

This utterly barren coast, so forbidding in its rock-bound desolateness, is yet a land teeming with gold. Hidden in the interior is a mine of wealth, possessing an abundance of rich minerals, of gold, silver, copper, tin, and manganese ore. The vast nitrate-fields of Tarapaca are of priceless worth, and the deposits of guano reputed still rich and workable.

CHAPTER VII.

THE NITRATE-FIELDS AND THE DESERT SHORE.

WE approach Iquique, chief town of the Province of Tarapaca, on a cloudy morning. In any other part of the world, we should have thought that these heavy clouds indicated coming rain. There is no fear, however, of that. Rain has scarcely fallen within the memory of man.

The ocean is alive with flapping pelicans. These great black birds are called by the Spaniard "the monk of the ocean," appropriate name for their solemn ways and deliberate floating on the surface. See, one turns a somersault, disappearing under the water as it dives with his huge black beak after a fish, which he promptly deposits, if caught, in his depending pouch, to be consumed when wanted.

The purple-red mountain range comes very near to the shore, seeming to press Iquique down to the water's edge, where the town clusters, low and black, among some ships' rigging. It is hard to believe that this little brown-roofed settlement is the second principal seaport in Chili, contains 20,000 inhabitants, and is the great outlet for the export of the nitrate deposits. We can see the line of the Nitrate Railway ascending the side of the mountain.

Iquique has no port, but the sea is like a lagoon to-day, and we are spared the usual disagreeable landing. A long island forms the only protection, and the boatmen choose their course between the ledges of rock, over which the sea rushes precipitately. The landing-stage is flanked by some bodegas or warehouses, labelled with the familiar names of North and Jewell, and Gibbs and Sons.

Iquique is celebrated in the history of Chili for the great naval battle. As we approach this part of the coast, the history of the great war between Chili and Peru, allied with Bolivia, assumes a more interesting connection. The war, begun upon various pretences, was in reality directed to the possession of the valuable nitrate-beds, then bringing in a great revenue to the Peruvian Government. Iquique, with the possession of the nitrate deposits, passed victorious into the hands of the Chilians in a few months.

The Peruvian ironclads, the *Independencia* and the *Huascar*, encountered the Chilian *Esmeralda* and the little gunboat *Covadanga* in the harbour of Iquique. The commander of the *Esmeralda* was Arturo Prat, and, running his ship alongside the enemy, he endeavoured to capture the *Huascar*. He boarded the latter, calling on his men to follow him, but the vessels separated ere the order could be obeyed. He was instantly shot down, and his ship sunk, with its crew of eighty men. Such is the heroic deed commemorated in the monument at Valparaiso. Round the promontory, on that ledge of rock, we shall presently see the wreck of the *Independencia*. The captain of the *Covadanga* saved his ship by the following stratagem: unable to outstrip the pursuing

Independencia, he sailed with his tiny gunboat close in shore, and lured the fine ironclad on to the neighbouring rocks.

Mr. Griffin, the Administrator-General of the Nitrate Railway, came on board to meet us, and before breakfasting at his house, took us for a drive through Iquique. The green plaza, with its blooming flowers, is of course named after Arturo Prat. The low houses, all built of wood, the general store-shops, and the drinking-saloons, some of which are painted in vivid shades of blue and green, an attempt perhaps to supply the colour of vegetation,—are laid down on this barren desert. Yet the town is not unhealthy. The ozone breezes of the sea sweep over and purify the streets.

The lion of Iquique is the pretty sea-walk of Cavancha, extending for two miles along the beach. The great surf rollers, with their curling crests of pale green, are for ever rolling in and flinging themselves amongst the brown seaweed covering the rocks. The cool sea-breeze is refreshing, and the beautiful tints of the ocean, lose nothing by comparison with the barren desert dust of the interior. We reach the promontory, which is occupied by a few houses and a restaurant, with a balcony overhanging the sea ; the garden is full of flowers and creepers. It is hard to imagine the value these few common nasturtiums and geraniums suddenly acquire in this land where no green thing exists, and where even the soil in which the plants are grown has to be brought from a great distance. Situated though Iquique is in the tropics, the absence of all damp makes the heat temperate ; children thrive and do well, and there is none of the langour and exhaustion of a tropical climate.

We drove back to breakfast, hurrying for our start. The Nitrate Railway Company have most generously given us a special car and engine, to run over the great nitrate-fields of Tarapaca. We shall cross the pampa of Tamarugal, sleep at one of the oficinas, and rejoin the steamer at Pisagua on the morrow.

Away over the desert we started on our journey, passing first the bright-blue buildings of the hospital, and then the cemetery with its many black crosses half buried in the sand. The ascent commenced at once as we ran on to a long V. Here the engine was reversed, and we commenced puffing up the mountain side. We see a Fairlie engine for the first time; it is a double locomotive with a funnel at either end, and quadruple boilers, possessing the necessary power to draw the heavy trucks of nitrate up the steep gradients of this railway, a gradient occasionally rising to one in five. This V helps us greatly in our upward progress; we have already risen rapidly above the town. Iquique, on its little black promontory, is even now growing small, whilst the long, serpent trails of foam marked out the blue ocean along the shore. We pass the three large water-tanks, used for the storage of the water supply of the city. Brought down from Pica, far in the interior of the desert, we are constantly tracing the black line of the water-pipes in our journey across the pampa.

Now we see a wonderful phenomenon. The ocean is lost to sight behind a great sandhill, 800 feet high. When we are opposite to this mountain it has a most peculiar appearance, derived from the perfectly even, smooth surface of sand, slightly crinkled in places with the ruffling of the wind. The narrow edge at the top is perfectly built up on either side, to the finest apex. There is an idea that this mountain, now about six miles distant, is slowly but surely travelling towards Iquique. The southerly breeze is always driving up the particles of sand over the summit to fall on the further side, and thus visibly the mound is shifting northward.

The range of the sea-coast has been climbed; we have reached the summit and find ourselves on a large plain, surrounded by other mountains, and broken up by low foothills, amidst which we are continually winding. It is extremely curious to look upon this vast tract of country, composed of nothing but sand, dust, and rock. There is not a herb or a blade of grass; it is a dreary, monotonous desert, and yet this barren land is teeming with mineral deposits; it is "a vast chemical laboratory," highly charged with saline matter. The earth in places is white and shining with these crystals of salt. Again, the district is intensely volcanic, and in many places assumes the conformation of a crater, streaks of red and carmine giving to it the appearance of a recent eruption.

There is little to vary the monotony. An occasional black cross, marking the lonely spot where some traveller lay down and died; the bones and skeletons of many beasts of burden; the empty bottles or sardine-tins thrown away by the passing caravan, are the only signs of civilization. The long lines of telephone and telegraph poles bear us company, now running along by the line, or anon taking a short cut over some hilltop, forming a connecting link with the outer world.

Indications of the ancient sea-level, in the deep depressions and curious strata, are perpetually present. We imagine that the conformation of the bottom of the sea, resembles our strange surroundings.

How were these great nitrate deposits formed? There are several theories brought forward, the most popular being that these fields were the bed of the ocean, and that the mineral deposits were formed chiefly by decayed animal vegetation, seaweed, and shells, mingled with salt deposits left exposed by the receding of the water. This theory is borne out in some measure by the constant finding of petrified shells, fishes, and seaweed as the caliche is dug out. Others again formulate elaborate calculations, based upon the wind currents and rainfall of the Andes. The guano is thought to be the deposit formed in the passage of vast flights of birds.

Whichever supposition is right, it is quite certain that these deposits could only be possible in this Tarapaca desert, where rain is unknown and where the intense dryness of the atmosphere has evaporated all moisture, leaving the caliche, slightly covered by a fine dust, in a high state of preservation. If rain fell, this wilderness would blossom with fruitful vegetation ; but it is perhaps the one spot on the face of the earth where rain is not prayed for. Damp or moisture would injure this field of wealth.

The central station provides us with the anomaly of a quaint, wooden Norwegian house, alongside the platform. Hearing that the nitrate-fields were in

The Nitrate Fields and the Desert Shore. 151

high altitudes, some one thought that for mountain heights this would be a suitable building.

The "pampa" of Tamarugal is extraordinary. We are accustomed to think of a pampa as suggesting wide plains of grass, but here there is nothing but bare earth, crisp and saline. Each railway siding is full of trucks containing sacks of nitrate. Every sack weighs 300 lbs., and some 120 trains pass daily over the line, bringing down to the seaports the output of the numerous oficinas. The first oficina we see is that of Sevastopol. It forms the commencement from this side of a continuous series of works, oficina after oficina, for the next hundred miles succeeding each other at quick intervals. To Sevastopol attaches the interest of having been the oficina visited and described by Darwin in his "Voyage of the *Beagle*." He thus speaks of his impressions: "The appearance of the country was remarkable from being covered by a thick crust of salt, and of a stratified, saliferous alluvium, which seems to have been deposited as the land slowly rose above the level of the sea. The salt is hard and compact; it occurs in water-worn modules, projecting from the agglutinated sand, and is associated with much gypsum. This superficial mass very closely resembles that of a country after snow, and before the last dirty patches have thawed. The existence of this crust of soluble substance over the whole face of the country, shows how extraordinarily dry the climate must have been for a long period."

Of the forty or more oficinas, over thirty are in the hands of English companies, whilst ten millions of British capital is laid down on this Chilian desert.

Colonel North, the nitrate king, is the head of a syndicate owning many of the best oficinas. The railway touches at each of these establishments, connecting them by separate sidings leading into the works. Unfortunately the railway has fallen out with some of the companies, who object to the heavy charge for freightage. Three rival lines are in process of construction, and it is feared that they will injure and absorb a substantial share of the profits. The combination to limit the output ceases on March 1st of next year. When that time arrives, a great scramble will begin for the yet untouched fields.

For miles and miles the entire face of the country is delved and dug up, in the search for caliche. The friable earth, light and saline, is turned over into heaps, leaving deep holes, which have been blasted out. The appearance of all the oficinas is the same: a row of smoking chimneys, some lines of black tanks, piles of brown, dark-looking refuse, and shining heaps of the snow-white nitrate lying beneath the cancha. A powder-magazine, enclosed in a stone corral, a water-wheel, and the ranchos for the workpeople completes the establishment. One well-known oficina after another comes into sight. A few are deserted, as the deposits on their section have been worked out. Others are only producing a small output.

How long will these deposits last? That is a question no one can answer. Some estimate their duration for a hundred years. But certain it is that long ere that period arrives, the machinery of many of the present oficinas will be useless, unless moved

The Nitrate Fields and the Desert Shore. 153

into the interior, where, they say, rich deposits still remain unexplored.

We come on to a plain where, eighteen years ago, a freshet descended from the far-away snow mountains. The furrowed earth yet shows signs of the receding waters, and, wonder of wonders, a few thorn-bushes manage to eke out a barren existence, and to burst into flower with a yellow bloom. Strange that, they say, this wild child of the desert cannot be induced to grow on a cultivated soil. The saline, parching dust, penetrating every part of the carriage, was overpowering. It obscured the smoke of the mills. A single dog racing the train raised a white storm, whilst the solitary rider could be traced miles away on the plain by the trail of dust that he raised. The dust is the great curse of this nitrate pampa, whilst the exhilarating climate, obtained by the height of 3000 feet above the sea-level, is its great attraction. The intensely dry air is only tempered by the fogs which descend at night, and cling over the plain in the early morning.

We now pass the great battle-field of Pozo Almonte, and see the heights where the artillery were posted. The little heaps of stones raised by the Peruvian soldiers, as shelters to shoot from, yet line the hillsides of the plain where the engagement took place. Their brave commander, Pozo Almonte, was wounded at the commencement of the battle, but he returned to the combat, only to have his horse shot under him, and to be wounded again, mortally. He was carried to the shelter of the railway-station, where he died. The station-master entertained us with a description of how he provided for the safety of the women and children by digging a large hole in the earth, where he buried them with his family. The war raged fiercely all over this ground, the Peruvians fighting to retain possession of the valuable country that provided them with a revenue.

A conical hill shows a perpendicular path to its summit. It is an ancient Indian burial-place, where, from the distant village, they bore their dead to be interred on a height, towards the rising sun. The tumuli are doubtless full of archæological remains, and as interesting as the stones we have already passed, covered with hieroglyphics, but already broken in pieces by the vandals employed in repairing the railway or telephone lines. It is curious to distinguish the Indian trail, with its arrow-like directness, from the hundreds of winding tracks formed by the European, which are always in sight, traversing with a patchwork design the mountain sides.

At length we reach our destination, the Primativa oficina. The carriage runs into a siding under a railway bridge, where the cutting is supported on hundreds of sacks filled with earth, making a splendidly solid embankment. We directed our steps to the flat-roofed wooden bungalow, standing on a slight eminence, the residence of the administrator, Mr. Hawes. He had unfortunately met with a terrible accident a short time since, falling into one of the tanks of boiling nitrate, and barely escaping with his life. His deputy, however, Mr. Nines, showed us over the works, but not before their pressing hospitality had made us partake of a dinner we scarcely wanted.

The Primativa, belonging to the group of Colonel

The Nitrate Fields and the Desert Shore. 155

North's undertakings, is one of the largest establishments on the pampa, but all the oficinas are carried on on similar lines. All have similarly excellent houses with European furniture. The manager and his family live in separate apartments, but the secretary, bookkeepers, and clerks reside also under this roof, and meals are taken together. They live well, too, although all provisions and every necessary of life has to be brought from a great distance by the steamer and railway. Perhaps the comforts of their daily existence reconcile them to the loneliness of the pampa life. Some houses have billiard-tables, others lawn-tennis courts. Cricket matches are frequent, and even balls not unheard of. The oficinas are sufficiently near together to allow of social intercourse. The telephone forms a connecting chain between each establishment, linking them also with the railway and the outer world. The hospitality of the oficinas, as we had good occasion to know, is unbounded, and extended to any passing strangers. The guest-rooms are always in readiness, and a traveller chancing by, is most cordially welcomed.

We started off to visit the works, and to inspect the various processes. The caliche in the rough conglomerate is shot down from the cart into the crusher beneath, where it is ground into powder. Passing into waggons waiting below, it is thrown into the tanks. Here we see a mass of yellow, brown matter, seething and boiling fiercely, in a succession of large vats. During the boiling process the insoluble matter, dirt, &c., called ripio, falls to the bottom, leaving the nitrate of soda in a liquid state. The boiling process continues for from eight to ten hours, or until the whole charge of caliche is held in suspension; it is then run off into the cooling or settling tanks. The boiling tanks are now cleared by allowing the ripio to fall out through traps, which form the bottom. When all the refuse is removed the tanks are sealed up, and re-charged with the drainage from the settling tanks, fresh water, and caliche. The process is always in progress, when in "full make," day and night. The boiling tanks are worked in pairs or sets, so that whilst some of the tanks are employed boiling, others are being cleaned.

The steaming liquid having been carried by gravitation to the bateas (precipitating tanks), cools, and forms a dense mass of granulated crystals, not unlike a somewhat coarse snow. In this state it is allowed to stand from twenty-four hours to four or five days. After the crystals are precipitated, steps are taken to carry off all excess of moisture in the form of liquid (agua vieja), which is collected and pumped up to the boiling tank to be re-boiled, or used in the manufacture of iodine. The iodine from this agua vieja, or mother liquid, is produced by steam impregnated with fumes of sulphur being passed through it at high pressure. During the process, which only lasts from twelve to fifteen minutes, the dull-yellow liquid changes colour to dark cobalt. At a certain stage in the process, only known to the chemist, the high-pressure steam is shut off; floating on the surface of the liquid appears six to eight inches of a bluish, soapsud-looking matter, which is removed. The process of subliming, to obtain crystals, has then to follow. The fumes of the shed used in the manufac-

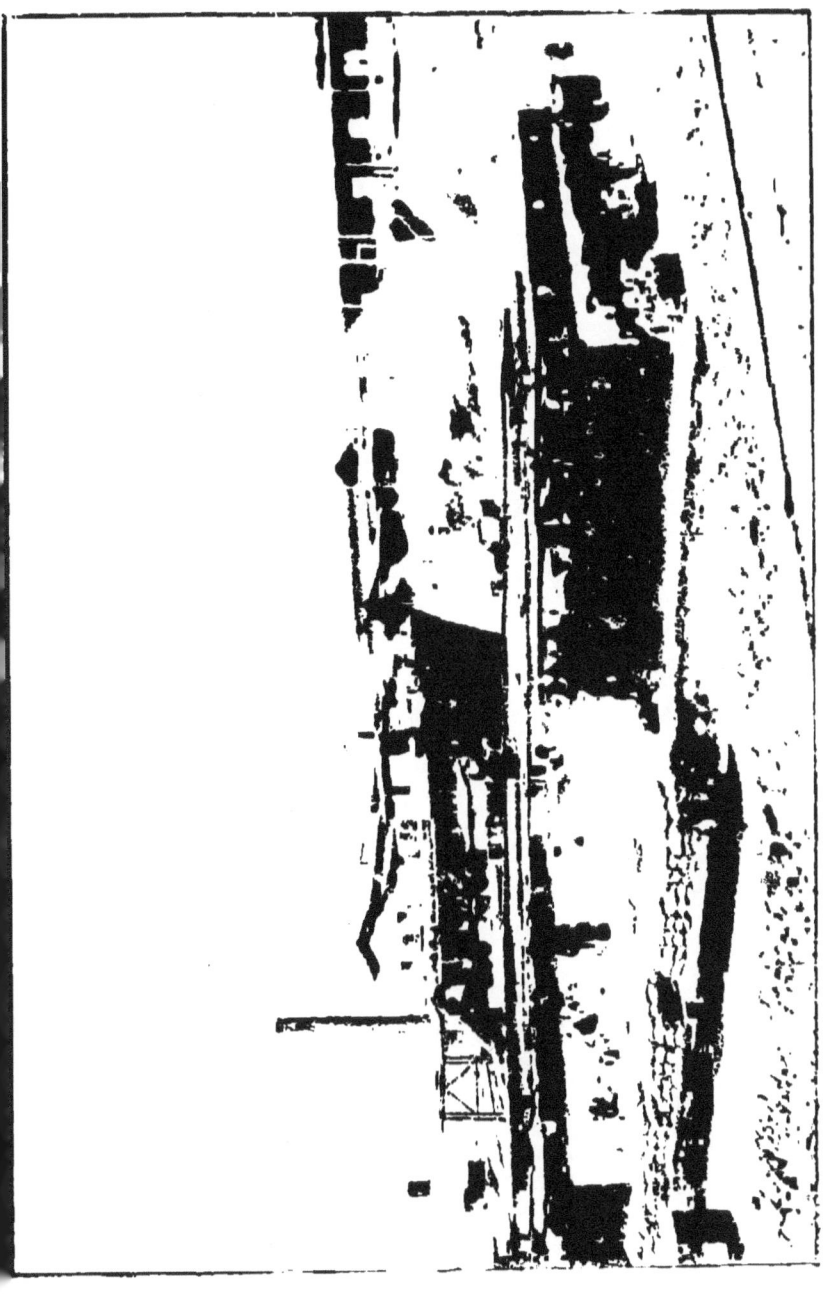

NITRATE WORKS.

ture of iodine were overpowering. The ripio, when run off from the tanks, gradually accumulates until it forms a high hill on one side of the oficina. I am indebted for the foregoing description of the process of the nitrate manufacture, to a small pamphlet ·published in 1887 by Captain Castle, of the Royal Navy.

The roads surrounding the oficinas are alive with carts drawn by mules, bringing in the caliche. A mule in these parts is a more valuable animal than a horse, costing about 16*l*., but they are very fine large beasts for that price. An engine drawing some little trucks, connects the distant beds with the works. The caliche is found buried in the earth, at a distance of from 4 to 30 feet, and at a level never less than 2000 feet above the sea. It never exists in the mountains, but always lies on the lower slopes, or on the surrounding plain. A favourable place is selected, a shaft is driven through the upper crust of friable earth, and a small hole is excavated, sufficiently large to allow of a boy being lowered into it. He prepares a funnel-shaped hole, where the charge of gunpowder is inserted, the explosive being manufactured on the oficina, from the saltpetre extracted from the caliche. The bed being thus exposed, it only remains for the pickaxe and shovel to work away and fill the carts.

There is great difficulty in obtaining sufficient workmen; competition for labourers runs high between the different oficinas, and a system of bribery, by an increase of wages, is in many cases resorted to. Even then, there are generally from 200 to 300 workmen tramping across the pampa from one oficina to another, seeking work on better terms. They will leave at a day's notice and on the most trivial pretext. The work is done on the "piece" system; the men, working day and night by electric light, earn the enormous wages of 15*l*. to 18*l*. per month.

Yet how they live! We drove through the quarters where reside the 1500 employees, to see hovels, with mud floors, made out of a few old sacks or decayed strips of matting, hung on poles. Pieces of zinc, old packing-cases, biscuit-tins, anything is utilized to form the walls. There are no windows, so the door is generally open to give a glimpse of the squalid interior. The centre of these slummy lines is occupied by decaying refuse, composed of old rags, iron, vegetable parings, or filth of every description, whilst for some distance around the plain is strewn with the refuse cast forth from this odoriferous camp. Many of the workmen are Bolivians, and can be recognized by their squat faces, swarthy complexions, lank hair, and for their peculiarly revolting and dirty habits. The remainder of the population show marked signs of their Indian descent. The women, in gaudy petticoats of magenta, yellow, and blue, indicate the liking of their race for a bright touch of colour, whilst their hair, depending in two coarse plaits of hair, is covered by a wide-brimmed Panama straw hat. The import of these must be enormous, as men and women alike wear them throughout the country. Pigs, dogs, and goats and children roll indiscriminately in the dust together; the donkey alone seems cared for, but he is a treasured beast of burden, bringing into camp, as he does, contraband stores and liquors.

All supplies and provisions must be bought from

The Nitrate Fields and the Desert Shore. 159

the store belonging to the oficina, the amount of goods taken weekly being subtracted from the wages of the peon, the residue being handed to him. It partakes of the hardship of the " truck system," but the " salitreros " have found by experience that it is the only practicable way of preventing drunkenness, and works for the good of the people : it is a source of profit, too, to the establishment, for the store at Primativa earns a large income yearly. How do the men spend their high wages, hedged round by these salutary regulations, and living in this squalid manner? They go on " the spree," throwing their money recklessly away in buying silk dresses for their wives, in drinking, and rioting. It is only the pure air of this healthy and exposed pampa that prevents an epidemic from sweeping through these fœtid slums, where no attempt at sanitation is essayed, and where morality is at its lowest ebb.

Returning to the car, the sunset transfigured the whole face of this barren pampa; it glowed and palpitated in crimson light, and was flooded with a delicious warmth. Then the sky was suffused in saffron light, then apple-green, finally dying away into a soft heliotrope twilight. It was succeeded by a brilliant moonlight, making the night as day, bringing out in startling relief the shadow of each wayside rock, silvering over the mud walls of the workmen's hovels.

The electric beacons of the oficinas flashed far out over the plain, and the fitful flames of the furnaces gleamed brightly as we sped past. We sat at the carriage window watching this strange, weird country with the caliche-beds shining brightly as if frosted on a starlit night.

We passed the bungalow of the doctor opposite a station. Several are employed in the district, and are attached to a group of oficinas. It is a hard life, and the distances to be covered, on horseback or on a hand-car on the line, are very great. Many a wild and lonely ride across the pampa does this hardworked official perform, when summoned, as he constantly is, for urgent accidents. We had a good example of this, for at the oficina where we passed the night, the doctor had paid his visit and just returned home, when a boy, thrown from a mule, was brought in unconscious, and he had to be telephoned for again.

At this moment the brakesman came in to say that a car was on the single track in front of us. We whistled loud and often, but to no purpose, and, pushing the waggon in front of us, we deposited it in the next siding; it was being employed for the illicit transport of caliche, dug out from under the line under cover of night. A horseman set to watch, galloped after our special to give the alarm, and thus saved a disagreeable accident.

Immediately after this startling incident we arrived at the oficina of Jazpampa, Mr. Erichsen, the courteous administrator, entertaining us most hospitably for the night in his pretty verandahed house.

In the early morning the pampa, with its dim shadows and pale tints, looked perfectly lovely. The camanchaca, the white mist of the Indians, rolled away over the plain, resembling in the distance the undulating waves of the ocean. A great white bed

The Nitrate Fields and the Desert Shore. 161

of nitrate, glistening snow-white in the morning sun, lay at my feet; whilst descending deep into the ravine on the opposite side of the line, but lying half way up was the black group of works belonging to the Paccha Oficina.

We commenced the descent to Pisagua; dropping down 3700 feet in two hours. It was a wonderful journey, described in steep declines and broad zig-zags, on a gradient often as much as one in five. Cautiously, with a detaining ballast of three carloads of nitrate, we descended over these steep gradients and sharper curves; constantly we had only an embankment, bounded on either hand by deep rock-bound ravines, just wide enough for the train to pass over. We found ourselves frequently wondering how these banks, built out of the loose sand, could support the weight of a succession of heavy truckloads of nitrate. Fortunately the phenomenon of the total absence of rain secures them from the danger of a wash out, which would certainly be fatal to the engineering feats in many parts of the line.

The final descent into Pisagua, and the manner in which the line finds a foothold, blasted out of the mountain side of the successive coast ranges, is magnificent. We found ourselves shooting over an abyss into the Pacific, which suddenly came into sight between two great yellow mountains; but no, just on the edge of the precipice we are saved, and bellowing through some deep cuttings, we turn round the corner of the mountain but a little way below its summit. A projecting peak is blasted through, and emerging from its precipitous crags a full view of the ocean is before us, the hamlet of Pisagua at our feet, the *Maipo*, a tiny speck on the blue waters, anchored in the bay. Two ranges must be climbed down before we find ourselves on the seashore; the first is accomplished by the line clinging on to the mountain side, whilst running down a steep hill and describing a wide circle round the valley to the head of the succeeding ridge.

We stopped on the site of an ancient encampment to inspect the breaks; so great had been the strain and friction of the dangerous descent that the wooden blocks were on fire. All were charred and smoking, although water had been freely poured on the axles by the breaksman of each car. The Nitrate Railway use only a hand-break, which necessitates an enormous staff, as each truck has to have its breaksman manipulating the restraining wheel.

The relics of the encampment of the allied army of Peru and Bolivia are still visible in collections of old rags, bottles, ammunition boxes, wheels, and broken equipage. An unexploded shell, weighing 150 lbs., is set on end under the zinc roof of some temporary barracks, whilst scrawled across the mountain side by the victorious Chilian troops is the motto yet visible, "Viva Chili." We cannot understand how the invading army can have scrambled up the sides of the steep mountain below, and attacked and dislodged the Peruvian forces, encamped in a position so strong that they should have been able to repel any enemy.

The descent of the second and even more acutely precipitous range is quickly and easily accomplished, by the help of three boldly described V's. It was alarming to see the steep gradient of the railway in two lines, one below the other; but as each was reached, we descended as before, imperceptibly and gently, until a last run down brought us opposite the platform of the station. Mr. Clark, the superintendent of this section, awaited us; we had a minute to spare to go over to his house opposite and be greeted by Mrs. Clark, and then we hurried on board. The captain had received orders at Valparaiso to detain the steamer until eleven o'clock, but we had promised to be punctual.

From the deck of the steamer, as we traced the triple lines of railway tracking the mountain side, and watched the trains cautiously creeping down in quick succession, we realized, even more than when we were on it, the engineering wonders of this Nitrate Railway.

The malodorous cattle have gone, the market is finished, the coaling at Iquique we have escaped, and now the *Maipo* is undergoing a much-needed process of cleaning.

Arica, the last Chilian seaport, is reached in the evening; it is the capital of the rich province of Tacna, and was one of the three ports (Iquique and Antofagasta being the other two) that were lost in the war by Peru. The province is temporarily occupied by the Chilians, pending a popular vote to be decided next year as to whether Tacna shall remain Chilian or Peruvian; the party who loses is to be paid a large indemnity by the winner. Opinions vary greatly as to the result, which is becoming urgent and interesting.

It is our farewell to Chili, for Arica is the frontier post of the Republic, on a coast that extends from the boundary of Peru to Cape Horn—on a sea-board of 2500 miles in length, comprising forty degrees of latitude and an area of nearly 300,000 square miles. The Chilian flag waves from on high, on the great natural rock fortress, the final stronghold of a defeated nation. It is celebrated for an heroic defence, and the still more heroic death of its defenders. During the progress of the war, the Chilian forces surrounded and entrapped some Peruvian troops on the position. Sooner than surrender, each and all cast themselves down on the rocks beneath, and thus perished gloriously.

It would be impossible to imagine a place more suited to be remembered in the annals of history than this fortress as we see it now, glowing crimson under the rays of the setting sun, towering as it does to a great height, full of deep crevasses and rising abruptly from the ocean, with its rampart of rocks beneath, covered with a dashing foam. The little town of Arica, in a pleasant oasis of vivid green, nestles below. We can hear the hollow sound of the waves, booming on the seashore in the moonlight.

Farewell to this prosperous, industrious and thriving people. Like the Swiss, they are a hardy mountaineering race, but above all, like them, a most patriotic nation. The Chilian flag, was the first object to greet us as we descended from the Andes into her well cultivated valleys. It is the last to bid us farewell, as we leave her sea-coast territories. Well has one of her writers said about her ensign: "Look at the star of Chili, white on a blue ground, as if placed in a reserved corner of the sky; she spreads her four points towards the four cardinal

The Nitrate Fields and the Desert Shore. 165

points of the compass, with a fifth which is specially reserved to point us the road to glory."

Mollendo, lying on its exposed table-land at the foot of the mountains, introduces us to our first Peruvian port. The rocks around are covered with gleaming white guano, whilst the coast, from its rock-bound appearance, forbids a landing. But see, the boats come out to us from behind a great rock, under that little red house. It is the only shelter for a landing place that they can find along this surf-beaten coast, and even then the foam of the swell and breaking billows often catches the returning boats. Mollendo is the terminus of the long railway, joining Peru to Bolivia. "The line illustrates at once the folly and the genius of Mr. Meiggs. Begun at a coast village with no harbour, and ending 327 miles away in a lake settlement of Indians, 12,500 feet above the sea," this railway is of little practical use.

At our next port we embark some more cattle. The Peruvian mode of boarding them is cruel in the extreme. Slinging is apparently too slow and humane a process, and so, passing a rope over the horns, the steam winch raises the bullock bodily, bumping his helpless body against the iron side of the ship. The strain of the entire weight being placed on the neck is fearful, and is shown by the eyes starting out of the head. Very pathetic is the look of wondering surprise that these animals give, as they are landed heavily on the deck. Twice during the day, two escaped and jumped overboard from the crowded barge. To no purpose, for a curious attraction to their fellow-companions in misery forbade them to go far away, and swimming round and round the ship, they were easily recaptured.

A not less cruel and curious sight are twelve bullocks, brought out from the shore to the ship swimming in couples, and attached to the poles projecting from a frail "dug out" canoe. Their horns are upheld so that their mouths are kept well above the water, and they cannot drown. Poor brutes. Their bodies are swollen and distended from the salt water they have involuntarily swallowed. They struggle vainly, but they cannot sink. The chain of the crane is attached to their horns, and they are drawn up wet and dripping. The mystery remains, how the light canoe does not turn over, as one after the other is hoisted up until only one is left; we think his weight will sink the bark, but nothing happens.

We are having a very pleasant voyage in these southern tropics. What surprises us is the total absence of heat. Coming along by the Brazilian ports, on the parallel line of coast on the other side of South America, how intensely we suffered, how we groaned and endured on the deck of the *Thames*. But here, day after day we have the same cool, dry, yet sunny atmosphere. This pleasant condition of things is attributed to the cooling influence of the Humboldt current, or the Arctic wave that flows from the South Pole all down this coast of the Pacific. The absence of all damp and moisture is due to the effect of the rainless desert. Pottering along the coast, calling at every little port, we enjoy the sunny days as they roll quickly by, unmarked by any incident.

CHAPTER VIII.

PERU, AND FIVE MILES TOWARDS HEAVEN.

ON a cold, foggy morning we cast anchor before Callao, the port of call for the Peruvian capital of Lima.

Callao has a large sea-faring population of some 25,000 inhabitants, but it is a dirty, unwholesome-looking town. The train soon bore us along the eight miles, that separate the capital from the port. The line at first ran through the centre of the streets of Callao, the stations being merely a house in the street, opposite to which the train stopped to take up or set down passengers. Although within the radius of the rainless zone, the valley of the Rimac, in which lies Lima, is not without a certain vegetation, dusty, brown, and burnt up, it is true, and obtained by industrious irrigation. The fields were surrounded by walls of adobe, laid in enormous blocks, and the road following the line was inches deep in dust.

A short drive from the station brought us to the Hôtel de França e Inglaterra. It is the usual dilapidated and shabby hotel, with spacious apartments smothered in dirt, the redeeming feature being the courtyard, converted into a summer dining-room, shaded by green blinds and adorned with flowering plants.

Peru recalls to our mind the picturesque history of the Inca kings, the fabulous wealth of cities paved in gold, the gorgeous temples, the tropical forests, and the brave exploits of that great pirate chief, Pizarro, as related in those graphic pages of Prescott's "History of the Conquest of Peru." The glamour of those ancient days lingers around the capital of Lima, at its near approach. The illusion disappears but too quickly with a glimpse of the Spanish capital, its narrow streets paved with round cobble stones, its shops full of second-rate French goods, its numerous stucco churches, gaudy with coloured plaster and florid carvings.

The only curious feature of domestic architecture are the "miradores," or covered wooden balconies, projecting over the street from the second storey of the houses. Their lattice woodwork resembles the Egyptian moosherayabeah, and adds to the Eastern appearance. From the propriety of this seclusion, seeing, yet not being seen, the Spanish ladies watch the life in the street below. Their use is even more apparent in Carnival week, when for three days water rains in torrents from bucket, jug, or basin on the heads of the unfortunate passers-by. High-born dames only smile grimly as a shower descends on their lace mantillas, whilst the street urchin revels in squirts and other abominable tricks. Lima is given up to a wild revelry for three days. Ash Wednesday sees the churches filled with black-robed women.

The only attraction of Lima is found in the Cathedral Plaza. Here the Gothic cathedral, with its façade of innumerable pillars and carved figures of saints, stands raised on a wide platform. Deeply mellow are the sonorous tollings from the great bronze bells hung in either tower. But typical of the decay prevailing over all things in Peru, the cathedral cannot be entered because the roof is in momentary danger of falling in. Bankrupt Peru has no money even wherewith to repair this, the chief edifice of the faithful. The deep chocolate-coloured buildings of the Moneda occupy another entire side of the Plaza, and the buildings of the municipality are over the arcade filled with shops.

It is in these cool piazzas, the fashionable resort, that we can study the reputed beauty of the ladies of Lima. The old full-pleated petticoat of the national costume has been discarded, but the transparency of the lace mantilla displays to advantage the soft liquid eyes, the brilliant complexions of these Peruvian beauties. Peru was chiefly peopled from the Spanish province of Castille. The blue blood and the handsome features and carriage of the Castillian *noblesse* is distinctly traceable in these ladies of ancient descent, whilst the pure Spanish of their speech attests further their origin in the ancient province. Under the protection of a black-hooded duenna, and eyed admiringly by the men, the lovely senorita strolls demurely through the arcades.

It is too early for the bathing at Chorillos, the fashionable watering-place a few miles out of Lima. Thither every afternoon during the summer the train bears car after car, crowded with these beauties, going for their daily plunge. The water, influenced by the Humboldt current, is icy cold, but it is recommended by the doctors as a bracing tonic, to counteract the effects of the relaxing climate.

Passing along the streets, you are besieged by the vendors of lottery tickets. Every dirty boy in the Plaza is hawking, with shrill cries, strips of pink or yellow paper bearing a number. We missed seeing the lottery drawn. But at Callao our attention was attracted by an open theatre in full view of the street, with a table on a platform supporting three large rotatory balls. The weekly lotteries are drawn here, the tickets being placed inside the balls, and the successful numbers announced on a board fixed above the building. It is a favourite form of gambling with the people. Not discouraged by a permanent non-success, they continue cheerfully buying tickets week after week. One wonders, whilst admiring their perseverance.

We soon found our way to Mr. Jacobi's well-known shop round the corner from the Plaza. Mr. Jacobi has the enviable reputation of being one of the few honest men in Peru, and you can spend hours in turning over his old hoards of silver treasures. Many heirlooms of jewellery have found their way here during these days of poverty; even the Church is so impoverished that the priests have had to part with their valuables, and there are vestments, chalices, crucifixes, holy doves, and silver images for sale. In a museum behind the counter you can see the unbaked earthenware relics assuming the form of quaintly carved faces found in the old Inca tombs. The silver is sold by weight. A pile of sols (a silver dollar now worth about two shillings) is placed in the scale opposite the object. When the scales are equal the sols are taken out and counted, and, with a small percentage for the work, the price is arrived at under your own superintendence.

A drive round Lima only shows how small is the city, every transverse street revealing the mountains at their extremity, and the peaked foothills that fill the plain around the city. Flagstaffs and crosses are the national emblems. The former are used for decorating the streets with flags on Sundays and festivals, whilst the latter satisfy the superstitious inclinations of the people, who imagine that the shadow of a cross protects and blesses the household. Wherever you look in Lima it is adobe, the mud brick of the country. It is used in the construction of the houses, the public buildings, and the churches. Plastered over, it presents the appearance of a whitewashed wall left in its natural state. It is simply a wall of mud. Of the same material are constructed those tawdry and startlingly coloured fronts of the churches, hideous in rococo decoration and carved figures. The interiors, with their velveteen hangings, glass chandeliers, and gaudy paper flowers, are worthy of the exterior; although a peep in at the door, in the absence of a mantilla, has to satisfy my curiosity. They are even more strict in Peru, as to the regulation forbidding women to enter a church otherwise covered.

Amid miserable surroundings of one-storied adobe dwellings is found the Column of Victory, with its handsome bas-reliefs surrounding the base, and commemorating the repulsed invasion of the Spaniards in 1866. The Chilians proposed to remove this national trophy after the war and the sack of Lima, but fortunately the united Legations interfered to prevent such a disgrace to the nation.

A drive past some barracks, where every pane of glass had been broken, probably during some popular revolution, brought us on to one of the many bridges across the Rimac, with a far reaching view up and down the valley.

The Alameda of Statues, lying under the shadow of Mount Christabel, and in this distant corner of the town, is a strange freak on the part of the citizens. It is a narrow alley, railed in, planted thickly with plants and flowers, and bordered with a double row of plaster statues. These represent Roman priests in togas and flowing robes, Greek sages crowned with laurel wreaths, the graceful archer, the laughing faun. Its strange beauties, situated in this deserted quarter, and surrounded by squalid adobe dwellings and a wretchedly poor population, appear to be somewhat wasted.

A dusty road, leading past the crumbling gateway on the outskirts of the old town, brings us to the Ring, where every alternate Sunday a bull fight takes place. It is the fashionable amusement of the cruel Spaniard, who gloats over the shedding of blood, and laughs at the rage and pain of a wounded animal. The returning drive brings us, as always, to the central point of the Cathedral Plaza.

Lima is a saddened city. An air of decadence hangs over it. Depression is rife. It was left a city of mourning, after the days of the disastrous war. Chili, in the possession of the nitrate fields and guano deposits, has sucked the life blood of the

Republic. Peru is moneyless. Private fortunes have disappeared. Rich men have become poor. Commerce is ruined and declining. Her railways are nearly all in the hands of the foreign bondholders, represented by the Peruvian Corporation. What is to be the ultimate end of this nation? Will Chili complete her conquest by absorbing Peru? Santiago would be too distant a capital, from whence to govern such an extended seaboard. Yet Peru should do well, for in her semi-tropical latitudes rich crops of coffee, cocoa, and sugar, and other valuable exports can be grown. It is not in any case likely that Peru can continue long as she now is.

The climate of Lima leaves much to be desired. We have grown so accustomed to days of unfailing sunshine that we feel quite aggrieved at a cold, sunless morning. We have forgotten to question what the weather will be like for this or that occasion. Here for four or five months in the year this damp fog is peculiar to the capital. A mile or two outside the city it may be clear and sunny, whilst here a dull and cheerless atmosphere prevails. It never rains. Umbrellas are an unnecessary encumbrance, in fact an old inhabitant laughed at our carrying one. But this damp fog supplies a certain moisture, falling around in a heavy dew, and foreigners complain of the mildew and damp it leaves behind.

Mr. and Mrs. Clinton Dawkins gave us a sumptuous *déjeuner* at the Exhibition Gardens. It is a fashionable Peruvian custom on Sunday morning, and the gardens, with their collection of animals and masses of flowers, are very pretty. Once again we notice the most tropically acclimatized flowers growing side by side with our familiar blossoms. The geranium, considered almost a weed here, flourishes alongside of a bouganivillea, and cabbage roses bloom beside daturas and magnolias. There are lawn tennis courts, and a croquet ground started by the English colony, but the Spanish ladies would not take kindly to the English game, and were too lazy to take the trouble to put the ball through the hoop!

In the afternoon, Senr. Quesada, the editor of the *El Commercio*, took us to his private house to introduce us to his charming wife and daughter. It gave us a glimpse of a characteristic Peruvian home. Sala led into sala, all built round a bare patio, containing a staircase branching off from the centre landing. The furniture was gaudy with plush, and the decorations in French rococo style, but it accords with the taste of the country, and we learned that it was considered a very richly furnished house.

We finished up this day of many callers and entertainments by a dinner, given us at the British Legation by Sir Charles and Miss Mansfield.

The Oroya Railway, built by the great Californian contractor, Mr. Henry Meiggs, starts from Callao, and passing Lima, ascends 15,665 feet, or to the height of Mont Blanc, and to the summit of the Cordillera of the Andes, passing through a mountain district with no commerce and population save a few Indian villages. To serve what purpose was the Oroya line, and the railway from Mollendo to Arequipa constructed? I fear it was for the personal enrichment of the parties concerned. These concessions were granted by the Government to Mr. Meiggs, during the halcyon days of Peru's prosperity. A larger sum than would be actually required for the construction of the line was demanded from the public. English shareholders invested largely. The surplus balance was divided between Mr. Meiggs, the Government of the day, and any opposing parties. Thus successive Governments and individuals were bought and silenced, whilst the result was seen in these wild railway projects. To draw a line straight up the highest mountain range, and say a railway shall go there, was the triumph of engineering which Mr. Meiggs set before himself to accomplish—and succeeded. The result is an encumbrance to the Peruvian Corporation of Bondholders.

"Between 1869 and 1872 Peru contracted foreign loans for the total capital amount of nearly 32,000,000*l.*, principally for the purposes of railway construction, guaranteed upon the guano customs' duties and all the real property in revenue of the country. In 1876 Peru made default upon her loans. In 1880 the war with Chili further complicated her financial bankruptcy. Owing largely to the exertions of Mr. Grace, a fresh contract was signed in 1890, placing the bondholders in possession of the guano beds, guaranteeing them a sum of 80,000*l.* a year from the Customs' revenue, conceding them 2,000,000 hectares of land for purposes of planting and colonization, and handing over the railways for sixty-six years to be administered and extended by the Corporation under certain conditions."

There are two remarkable things about the Oroya Line. It is the highest railway in the world; it is the greatest of engineering triumphs. The railway cost 5,000,000*l*. It is a common question whether the construction of the Central Railway to Chicla was the more wonderful feat, or the success of the contractor in getting 40,000*l*. a mile for the line. In 120 miles it mounts to a height of five miles above the earth, and accomplishes the usual distance of a balloon ascent.

Mr. Dawkins, the Administrator of the Corporation of Bondholders, despatched us at 6.15 from the station in a special train up the Oroya Railway. The "Favorita," a pretty little coach combining an engine and a compartment, stood awaiting us on the line. The fuel used is the refuse of refined petroleum oil, which is found in the petroleum beds that penetrate under the sea along the coast. A large tank supplies the boiler with oil, which amounts to about half the expense of coal. There is no foul smoke proceeding from the funnel, only an imperceptible cloud of steam, except when the pipes are cleaned out with sand, then a great black cloud is expelled, floating away behind us.

We ran at first through the broad valley, full of the bright green reed of the sugar cane plantations. This is the valley of the Rimac, and it is strange to think that notwithstanding the immense height we are to ascend, we shall be always more or less in this valley, until we reach the dividing watershed of the summit. Estaçion Chosica is soon reached, and we supplement our hurried preliminary breakfast with delicious coffee and rolls, after the departure of the returning train. The trains only run three times a week, and break the ascent by a stopping for the night at Matucama, nearly 8000 feet up. It has the advantage of accustoming the lungs to the rarefied atmosphere, and helps to avoid the inconvenience of sirocche.

A run uphill brought us to Perugas, and the commencement of the engineering difficulties. The engine was placed on a turn-table and reversed. During the construction of this part of the line, all the labourers suffered from a dangerous fever. Its origin is unknown, and the only possible explanation was that some poison was emitted by the excavation of the earth. A well-known doctor at Lima studied the disease, and experimented on himself by inoculation. He died from its effects.

We commenced our upward progress by describing a circular curve on a low mountain, a deep cutting bringing us through the summit. We looked down on a little green village, full of tropical vegetation of camphor, banyan, and sumach trees, a curious surprise in this desolate country of rock and sand. But strange to say we constantly notice all through the day, that the higher we mounted the greener it became. It is contrary to all the ordinary rules of mountain vegetation, where the higher latitudes are generally bare of any growth. But the peculiarities of the rainless coast upset the usual laws of nature. It may dominate the lower districts of Peru, but as we rise we get beyond its power and within reach of the rainfall from the clouds, where it grows greener with every ascending valley.

The mule path follows the railway. We see it generally on the other side of the Rimac, with frequently passing caravans of mules and donkeys laden with merchandise. These beasts of burden are dangerous rivals to the railway, and by their cheap transport, detract from the freight receipts of the line. The ever-thirsty engine has constantly to be drinking from the wayside butts of water.

Now comes a bridge built by Eiffel. Lightest of metal structures, it has the appearance of a filigree of ironwork thrown across a great chasm. The central stanchion only reaches to the bottom of the ravine, whilst the others find a foothold on its sides. The great engineer came out to erect this bridge himself. We experience a peculiar sensation of balancing in space for a few minutes, between two black engulphing tunnels, which are joined by a short lever bridge. This must have proved a very difficult bit of engineering, as there was no foothold to pierce the entrance of the tunnel from the side, and one wonders how it was accomplished under such difficulties. All the bridges are of the same light structure, and occupy the most hazardous points of the line; indeed, they are generally made use of to overcome some stupendous obstacle, such as the crossing of an entire valley, or the passage from one mountain to another.

But to describe the marvellous feats of the Oroya Railway is impossible. It is a *tour de force* as regards the engineering impossibilities that it accomplishes. It is the triumph of the engineer over every artifice employed by nature to daunt him. Things quite impossible, and that would not be even contemplated in any other railway in the world, have been successfully carried out on this adventurous line. A mountain is no barrier. You tunnel clean through it. A valley is made light of, you bridge that over. The

SCENE ON THE OROYA RAILROAD. Page 178.

steepest ascent is nothing. A succession of V.'s will bring you up any height with lightning rapidity. The river is an impediment in your way. You divert its course by blasting a beautiful natural arch in the rock, a glimpse of the river foaming through it, round the precipices of the ravine, being obtained in a momentary vision between the exit from one tunnel and the ingress into another.

Our upward progress on the highest mountains, is marked out by an ascending succession of black tunnel mouths. We look up, to count perhaps three or four of these tunnel mouths heading in various directions. We cannot guess how we are ever going to reach them. For first the train enters a tunnel facing this way, then the line turns on itself in some mysterious manœuvre, and we find ourselves entering another tunnel, but in an exactly transverse direction. We grow at last to wonder where next the railway can be going, but we learn to be surprised at nothing. We find words are not enough wherewith to express our admiration. We are perfectly astounded, never imagining that the line, much as we had heard of its wonders, could be anything like this.

Another remarkable feature is the terraced cultivation of the old Inca days. Up the steepest mountain sides, graduating to the summits, is a network of tiny embankments, running first this way and then that until the mountain has the curious appearance of being pieced out like a patchwork quilt. It is an enduring testimony to the industry of the ancient Indian Incas, and attests to their acumen in choosing this rich warm soil, which, without doubt, is in many places the bed of an ancient river. Standing out against the sky we see the black outlines of many a cross. The Indian, in his dire superstition, thinks the outstretched shadows of the arms will bring a blessing on his crops, and a defence from the mountain storm.

We pass many an Indian village hidden deep in the mountain valleys, and constantly find ourselves looking down on the roofs of these settlements. They lie always on the banks of the river, with a church and graveyard, and green corrals full of lucerne, and wandering flocks of goats and donkeys. Their population is of pronounced Indian type, and all the women wear their hair hanging down in two plaits. The Rimac is always with us, foaming below in the ravine.

It is after the first fifty miles have been passed, that we come into the grandest scenery. The ramparts of rocks, enclosing us into narrow defiles, are magnificent. Their walls are perfectly precipitous; their height overpowering. Withal there is great variety, as we constantly turn around and amongst them. We are equal with their feet, then rise, until we may measure their midway distance. Leaving them behind us, we pass into another range, entering the narrowest possible valley, filled with gloom from the shelving precipices above. And here is the Bridge of Hell, of which we can catch but the merest glimpse from between the intervening tunnels.

We pass the centre of the mountain through a tunnel, emerge on to a trestle bridge, to find that the Rimac, in a torrent of stormy waves, has pierced a course for itself round the mountain we have just travelled through. It foams beneath our bridge and passes round a further mountain base, obliging us to avoid the valley, for there is no room for both line and stream, and to tunnel through this other mountain passage. It is a particularly precipitous and magnificent bit of scenery, and the culminating marvel of the Oroya line. The scenery in crossing the Andes by the Uspallata Pass, pales into insignificance beside it. We had seen nothing at all like this, nothing half so stupendously grand. A little green vegetation and a thriving growth of cacti on the slopes relieve the intense barrenness of the rock-bound walls.

Exclamations of surprise are over and over again involuntarily forced from us. One place in particular calls forth our admiration. No less than five lines of the railway are here visible. There is first the rail we are on, then there are three in successive rows beneath, cut out in V-shaped gashes on the mountain side, whilst the remaining line is espied far below, on the other side of the Rimac, which we had here crossed on a low bridge. This feat alone describes the wonders of the engineering work seen on the Oroya. There are fifty-seven tunnels in the run of 120 miles. We constantly see the beginning of a heading partially blasted out and then abandoned. During the building of the line they were perpetually repulsed by some insuperable difficulty, and had to re-survey many portions of the route to find fresh means of progress. It is said that 7000 men lost their lives during the construction of this railway. Looking at the result, it is easily believed.

We are now getting into the heights ranging above

10,000 feet. For some time we have all complained of a singing in our ears and increasing deafness. Now we feel an oppression in breathing and pains in the chest. These are the premonitory symptoms of the "sorocche," or mountain sickness. I think we all felt a little nervous at the prospect of a further rise of 5000 feet, with the air increasing in rarefaction with each ascending curve.

The "sorocche" is felt in this rapid and high ascent more or less by everybody. It is rare for a party to go up to the summit, and for one or other of its members not to suffer from its nauseating effects. Our chances are increased a hundredfold, because it is not usual to accomplish the ascent in one day, the train halting for travellers to pass the night about half-way up. The symptoms of sorocche are sickness, retching, profuse bleeding from the ears and nose, accompanied often by intense suffering, attributable to the rarefaction of the air.

We arrived at Chicla, where breakfast awaited us. The railway ended here until 1889, when the Peruvian Corporation entered into possession, and continued the line over the summit and thirty miles beyond, down to Oroya. Directly we moved and descended from the train we experienced the dreaded sorocche, in a feeling of being intoxicated, swaying, shortness of breath, and an interior sinking and discomfort. We toiled up the stairway leading to the hotel very slowly, feeling sick and giddy. The only prevention and precaution is to keep quiet and move as little as possible. The rarefied air supplied us with sufficient nourishment. We were not hungry, and speedily recovered from our feelings of discomfort.

We soon started for the summit again. Only another 1000 feet of ascent and we shall be at the tunnel of the Galera. We encouraged the one sick member of our party with this good news.

The first station, Casalpaca, brings us to a last formidable series of V's. We rise now by leaps and bounds, and the last 1000 feet is accomplished in a very short space of time. There are large silver mines at Casalpaca, tunnelling into the interior of the mountain for over a mile. We can see the tramway up the side of the mountains, leading to the shaft at the top. The mine pays 1000*l.* per week in freightage to the railway. In descending we stayed here for a hurried inspection of the smelting furnaces, to see the great bars of smoking silver ore, fresh from the crucible, and the machinery driven by oil that was here drilling into the interior of the mine at a distance of over a mile away.

This village is full of troops of llamas, arriving and departing along the mountain road. We see them now feeding on all the slopes, and the caravans of pack mules and donkeys are replaced by troops of llamas, employed in transporting merchandise. They are such pretty, soft-eyed looking creatures, with shaggy coats, long necks, crowned by a small head, and the ears adorned with gay ribbons. They resemble the ostrich in colour and size, and have with their long legs the same swinging and cautious tread.

It is very strange, but as we near the summit the views become comparatively tame. The mountains appear as if exhausted. Around us are some green hills, with gentle slopes and feeding flocks of goats. And when the last grand sweeps and curves of the line have carried us up to the supreme point of the summit, we find an open plain. The earth is swampy and covered in places with bright green moss. It is a regular bog. There are one or two lakes lying in the hollows, from off which rises a fog of condensing moisture. Vegetation has grown with every ascending mile, and here it breaks out in a green, damp plain. The Rimac is a babbling stream, coursing down over that green slope, and finding its source in the neighbouring fields of ice.

It does not feel in the least as if we had reached the summit. It seems too utterly poor a conclusion for the preceding grandeur of the journey. We experienced rather a chill of disappointment. A single shoulder of snow on this side is the only ice we see.

Monte Meiggs, a small mountain standing by itself, and surmounted by a flagstaff, is before us. Beneath it, and to the left of the base, is the Tunel del Paso de Galera—the summit tunnel, and the great divide of the Oroya railway. We enter the tunnel. We reach the summit of the pass inside. We emerge and find ourselves looking towards the great Amazonian country. The little stream rising inside the tunnel, points out significantly the dividing watershed. It runs downward into the valley of the Rimac on the other side, whilst on this the water is coursing towards the tributaries of the Amazon.

Oroya is some thirteen miles further on, and the end of the railway for the present. But it is hoped to continue the work some day and accomplish the

MONTE MEIGGS, SUMMIT OF OROYA RAILWAY. Page 184.

great purpose of its originator, which was to open up communication with the plains of the Amazon, and form, with the waterway of that great river, a through route to the Atlantic Ocean. Once again then would these great oceans meet, through the medium of the iron rail. What has been so nearly accomplished by Argentine and Chili in the Transandean Railway would be done likewise by Peru and Brazil with the aid of the Oroya Line.

A little panorama, giving a far-away glimpse of a beautiful snow range, is before us. To our left, a lovely blue glacier, lying under a snow-topped mountain; half its frozen surface has thawed and fallen away, exposing a cavity of intensely cerulean blue, from under a fringe of long hanging icicles. A few more partially covered snow peaks. This is all we see. We wonder at the absence of much snow, for we remember that we are in this tunnel on a level with Mont Blanc, or 15,665 feet above the sea level. We think of the dome of snow, and the eternal fields of ice and snow surrounding that King of the Alps. We compare it with this summit, with its peaty soil of green moss and damp vegetation. The contrast is surprising, but is easily explained. Here the nearness of the tropics and the corresponding heat of the sun influences the temperature, even at this enormous altitude. With few exceptions, the snow and ice melt with successive summers' heat.

It was cold and damp at the summit. We dared scarcely move from fear of sorocche. We got down from the car, looked around, stood, and shivered. Then the clouds rolled down and obscured all in mist. We re-entered the coach, steamed the few uphill yards into the centre of the Galera Tunnel, and began the long downward descent.

Steam was shut off, and for the entire distance of 120 miles we ran down hill from point to point, without steam, and only restrained from a runaway career by the application of the strong breaks. The engineer kept his hand always on the lever. His hold never relaxed. Our lives hung on his gentle pressure of that shining steel handle, the slightest application being promptly obeyed by the engine. Fiz, fiz, fiz, we heard all the way down; it was the noise of the break restraining the wheels. It scarcely ceased, for only very rarely could we take a gradient without the restraining break.

The clouds enveloped us. We had marvellous luck in reaching the summit just in time. A few minutes afterwards we looked down on a sea of fog, which continued all the way down for the first part of the descent, ending in a storm of hail and rain in the lower regions. Then the sun burst through the mist, and at Matucama we found a lovely summer's evening.

We go down very rapidly, falling quickly to succeeding levels and from one V incline to another. We "breathe more freely" in every sense of the expression, because all fear of sorocche is past, and respiration is momentarily growing easier. Gliding quickly down the steep gradients, noiselessly and rapidly, is pleasant work, especially as the car is now running face downwards with the engine behind, until we reverse at a siding. We have thus a full view of the line in front, when, horror-struck, a few yards in front of us I see a large stone has fallen down, projecting over the line. The engineer does not see it. It is too late to speak. A momentary suspense, followed by a crash and a bump. The danger is past. The car has not been derailed, the cow-catcher has saved us, and is bent and dented with the shock. It was rather a scare and a strain on our nerves. After this we descended more cautiously and at a slower pace. A little further on there is a similar occurrence, another stone has fallen, but this time the engine driver perceives it in time, and the power of the break is satisfactorily proved by an instant pull up. Both these masses of rock had become detached and had fallen, in the hour or two that had elapsed since our ascent.

There are some startling sensations in the descent of the Oroya line, the least of which is a feeling that the train is running away down hill. There are plenty of places where, holding your breath, you look over into space. There are many moments when if the light car were to jump the rails, we should be plunged into eternity. We hang over abysses whose depths we cannot fathom, and we turn giddy as we peep over the side of many a precipice.

A favourite way, now wisely discouraged by the management, is to descend the line on a hand trolley. Fifty miles an hour, even with a strong break, is a madcap ride, dangerous but exhilarating. Think of the consequences, if an obstacle such as we have just passed should be encountered.

We are slipping down rapidly, dropping from one valley into another, getting down deeper and deeper amongst the endless tangle of ravines. We begin to wonder how much further down we *can* travel. We think the end of the descent *must* soon come now.

Yet after dropping down before some mighty range until we are equal with the bottom, it is only to find ourselves on a lower level, perhaps, but surrounded by equally high mountain passes.

A very awkward incident occurs. Entering a tunnel, about half-way through we feel a concussion, and hear a thud against the side of the car. Looking back, in the dim light admitted from the entrance of the tunnel, we see the outline of the figure of a horse turning a somersault, and falling suddenly as if shot. At the same moment an Indian appeared running through and after the train from the further end. We supposed that the man had been walking through the tunnel, leading his horse. Hearing the train he ran back to save himself, leaving the horse loose in the tunnel. Doubtless we killed the poor animal, but if it had been a hand car the consequences to the occupants would have been serious. The car would have been thrown with force off the rails, and the passengers injured against the jagged crags inside the tunnel. We stopped at the next station to warn an ascending freight train, whilst the station master was sent in search of the man to procure his arrest. We congratulated ourselves upon a further escape. Mr. Mackay, who was doing the honours of the railway on Mr. Dawkins' behalf, assured us that such a series of escapades was a thing previously unheard of, and I must in justice add that they have never yet had a single serious accident or lost a life since the Corporation have been running the Oroya line.

Our engine driver was anxious that we should accomplish the steepest gradients ere nightfall, and asked permission to hurry on and run faster.

We descended below the clouds, and left the rain and mist behind us. The sun burst out, warming in a pink glow the shoulders of the mountains, descending into the dusk of the valleys. A glorious sunset succeeded, seen in all its majesty of flaming orange and dusky crimson, framed in between the ramparts of two granite fortresses. How reluctantly it faded, lingering in a halo of rosy light, and dying into the soft transparent lilac of the tropical twilight. It left with us a worthy memory, framed in gorgeous colours, of our last view of the Andes. Dusk and gloom overtook us, and descended with us to the bottom of the valley. The light just lasted until at San Bartolomé we ran over our last V. Thenceforward it was a long weary run in the dark, through the broad valley, until the lights of Lima shone out upon the darkness.

Fifteen hours of constant travelling, coupled with the excitement and fatigue of perpetual admiration, and the influence of sorocche, had well nigh exhausted us.

One day had been sufficient for us to ascend to the height of Mont Blanc and to descend again. One day had enabled us to penetrate for the second time into the heart of the Andes, and to traverse once more to the highest passes of the Cordillera.

A last excitement though awaited us. Walking from the station at Lima we enter from a side street upon the Plaza des Armas. The electric lights shine brilliantly, the fountains play as usual, but it is strange that it is absolutely deserted. The arcades, usually so full of life in the evening, are empty, the shops are shut, there is not a sign of life. It is easy to see that something is wrong. Picquets occupy each corner of the plaza. The prefect passes by, handsomely mounted, his orderlies behind, hand on pistol. At the corner of the Moneda, or old Spanish Government House, a cavalry soldier draws his sword and bars our passage. But an officer comes up and orders him "to let the English senorita go by." We proceed past the entrance to the Moneda, and see that the courtyard is full of soldiers. Passers-by are turned back at the crossing. The square is kept clear. But see, under those trees there is a scuffle between three or four men going on. It is an arrest. The political culprit is resisting the emissaries of the law; an officer comes up and a soldier gallops on to the pavement to aid in the struggle. We dare not linger to witness the result. The streets are full of excited groups, shop shutters have been hastily put up, and the great entrance gate of our hotel is barricaded.

There has been an *émeute* during the afternoon. What was it all about? A few citizens, as the troops were marching back from a presidential review, or rather a political harangue, much elated by a "lunch á la criolla," have ventured to shout "Viva Pierrola," the popular democratic candidate for the presidency vacant next June. The army (and the Government) is for General Caceres. The town is at once placed under martial law. "Viva la libertad," may be the motto of a Spanish Republic. But what is the practice?

Farewell calls occupied the morning until it was time to return to Callao and re-embark on the

Maipo. We returned to the ship laden with floral tokens of an untoward size. Precluded from entertaining, it is the Spanish way of acknowledging and showing courtesy. Large sums, ranging from five pounds and upwards, are spent upon elaborate designs, such as a huge butterfly of varied hues, or a crescent erected on a pillar of flowers.

A few days more of steaming along the coast of the rainless desert and we reached Payta, where we landed for an hour. As Coquimbo had been a good specimen of a Chilian seaport town, so Payta served to show us a typical Peruvian port.

Anything like the filth and dilapidation of the deserted streets can scarcely be imagined. The tumble-down houses are all built of bamboo plastered with mud, large portions of which have dissolved into the original element of dust, leaving gaping holes in the walls. The floors are of mud. There are no windows or chimneys, yet in strange contrast to the poverty-stricken appearance of the houses are the elaborate attempts at carving exhibited on the overhanging miradores or balconies. The squalor of the interior corresponds to the dilapidation of the exterior. Large families of Indian type lie huddled together amid the filth and dirt, or are seen squatting on the floor engaged in some domestic operation. The streets are full of decaying garbage, being investigated by the troops of mongrel curs that infest the streets.

We proceeded to see the single (apology for a) tree on the Plaza of Payta. It is a small thorn tree, guiltless of green leaf, and bears company to the dead palms waving their withered and dust-laden branches. The seashore is strewn with offal, and the gulls coming up from the beach are pecking at the refuse in the streets. There are a few little shops, containing a wonderful jumble of commodities. Yet the English Consul, who has been here for forty years, went home to England and returned again, declaring that there was no place like Payta, and the English clerk employed at the telegraph office did not seem to dislike the place. This decidedly uninteresting town is yet an important shipping port for vast inland cotton fields, and for the petroleum oil found in the beds reaching beneath the sea and along the coast.

We wasted a great deal of valuable time at Payta transferring the cargo intended for Guayaquil off the *Mapocho*, sister ship of the *Maipo*, to save her calling at that fever-stricken port and so avoid quarantine at the other places of call. This delay cost us the loss of the tide at Guayaquil.

This morning we perceive something dark on the low hills of the coast. So long accustomed to the grey line of sand, it awakens our curiosity. It is the beginning of vegetation on the shores of the Gulf of Guayaquil. The rainless zone is past, and the dense vapour-laden atmosphere of this great gulf brings it abruptly to a close. Now we labour in tropical heat, suffering severely as we anchor for the night at the mouth of the river Guayaquil and opposite to the wooded Island of Pumà, where history relates that Pizarro first landed on his invasion of Peru.

Steaming up the broad river, the approach to Guayaquil is very pleasing. The banks are fringed with forests of tall grey-stemmed trees, twined with flowering creepers. Banyan and cocoa palms wave their feathery arms. Ferns and bright-green mosses form a tangled undergrowth of tropical luxuriance. But these mangrove swamps, beautiful as they appear to us by comparison with the great desert tract of the coast we have so long sailed past, are full of deadly miasma. We wind among the broad stretches of the river, and anchor in the wide reach of water before the quays of Guayaquil.

Guayaquil is the chief port of the Republic of Ecuador. It is the great outlet for the trade of the whole province, a trade consisting largely of cocoa exported to France and Spain. Ecuador provides two-thirds of the production of cocoa to the whole world, and 25,000 to 30,000 bags are frequently shipped on a single vessel. The banks are lined with quays, sloping to the water's edge. Two or three unwieldy-looking river steamers lie at anchor. There are also many bathing establishments.

Guayaquil, with its red-tiled roofs, standing out from the hills of rich green, its cool promenades of arcades, formed by the overhanging miradores of the houses, its waving groups of cocoa palms, appears a picturesque town. Thirty-five thousand people dwell in the houses concealed behind the quay frontage, but we do not venture to land, and sleep with hermetically closed windows, against the miasma rising from this unhealthy port.

Guayaquil is only 4° removed from the equator, and enjoys a reputation for perpetual yellow fever and small-pox. The rainy season, the most unhealthy period of the year, has just commenced, and Yellow Jack has begun to claim his victims with renewed vigour. The steamer, lying out there in the river, has lost four of its crew from yellow fever. Two gentlemen residing at the hotel died of the same disease. The Englishman who died this day week in the room opposite ours at Lima, had been residing in this hotel, and had left Guayaquil but a few days before, happy in having secured for his Manchester house orders for 18,000*l.* worth of goods. The hotel is a plague-spot, and contains now more than one sufferer.

We land one or two passengers for the distant capital of Quito, lying under Cotopaxi's great shadow, and reached only by muleback. We ought to be able to see the loftiest peak of South America, the great cone of Chimborazo, from the steamer's deck, but it is swathed in clouds. The difference in the productions of these tropical latitudes is readily perceived. Now great lighters full of oranges and mangoes and bags of cocoa come alongside, and the ship is besieged by sellers of green love-birds, parrots, alligators, and monkeys. We have to discharge a double allowance of goods. The noise of the six steam-winches, working together and at once, is terrific. Oppressed with the tropical heat, haunted by the breath of the pestilence-stricken town, we lie sweltering before Guayaquil for twenty-four hours.

The monotony is varied by witnessing a popular demonstration, bordering on a revolution. The quays were lined with excited crowds. The boys of Lima had stormed the Ecuadorian legation. The Peruvian minister was expected by our boat, and they intend to mob him on landing. Disappointed in this, they carried shoulder-high an Ecuadorian senator who came up with us. Then they marched backwards and forwards, trailing in the dirt the Peruvian flag, while handbills were issued calling upon all patriots to enrol themselves as volunteers to march against Peru. A meeting was held, and "The dismissal of every Peruvian from Ecuadorian employ, the repatriation of every Ecuadorian from Peru, the recall from exile of revolutionary generals to lead the hosts of Ecuador," was resolved upon. A telegram was sent to the President at the distant and (happily for him) inaccessible capital of Quito. He replied with much emphasis, on the dignity and honour of national and individual security.

This petty ebullition of national feelings completed our typical experience of the revolutions always proceeding or ready to break forth in the Republics of South America. In Brazil, Rio was in the midst of a serious and lasting revolution; at Buenos Ayres we found a state of siege proclaimed for a certain number of weeks; at Lima in Peru we witnessed the result of a few harmless shouts from the populace. Chili, industrious, honest, and prosperous, was alone free from these petty revolutions, fatal to the credit and stability of all good government.

At length the cargo is all on board: the steam-winches are at rest. We long for the refreshing breezes of the ocean. Then it is discovered that a dozen firemen have run away. They have to be sought for, collected together, and brought off in a boat, much the worse for liquor. Further lingering. This time it is the fault of the Ecuadorian postmaster. The mails tarry. For hours we wait. The tide has turned, we fear to lose the whole day. At length they arrive, but only to be nearly lost as they come on board. The stream was racing down, five miles an hour. The steersman of the boat made fast to the gangway, and the tide swung round her head. A second more and the bags and treasure were at the bottom of the river, the boat capsized, and the two sailors drowning in the strong current. "Let go, let go!" came the order, just in the nick of time. The boat was carried far astern, but saved. With a fearful struggle, the sailors beat back against the stream and were hauled up on deck. It ended our chapter of accidents: we caught the tide, and were out and away to sea ere evening closed.

But we have lost much valuable time. Due at Panama on December 5th, the *Maipo* cannot now arrive before December 8th. Quarantine, or some hours' "observation," after touching at Guayaquil, is sure to be imposed. The steamer of the Royal Mail is advertised to sail from Colon on December 8th. Shall we make the connection? We fear the worst and are anxious.

We pass the Island of La Plata, where Sir Francis Drake stored all his provisions on his return to England after his first voyage from the West Indies to South America. From Cape San Francisco we leave Ecuador and stand out to sea, steaming across the crescent indentation that the coast assumes, along the shores of the Republic of Colombia.

It takes us two days to steam this stretch of 800 miles. We anchor soon after midnight of the second day in the Gulf of Panama, but at a distance of six miles from the shore. Our captain advances in the early morning inside the anchorage, but getting frightened at his boldness in defying the harbour rules, soon retreats. Meanwhile no doctor comes off. Just as we had given up hope, a boat appears with the longed-for functionary. He passes us in solemn review in the saloon, and, after scanning our healthy appearance, decrees a twenty-four hours' observation. We despair of catching our steamer. All we can do is to send off petitioning letters to the Governor, the Consul, and the shipping agents, begging that our quarantine may be if possible shortened and the steamer delayed. We spend the day in restless anxiety.

Detained prisoners, we look longingly towards the low, wooded hills of such brilliant green, surrounding the red roofs of Panama, and espy the entrance to the canal hidden round another wooded promontory. We are haunted by visions of the Royal Mail steamer *Para* sailing away this afternoon at five from Colon, on the other side of the Isthmus.

Tropical downpours of rain, with a general cleaning of the decks and saloon, add to our uncomfortable frame of mind. The long day of anxiety and worrying at length draws to a close.

CHAPTER IX.

TO THE ARCHIPELAGO OF OCCIDENT.

At six the next morning they awoke us with the joyful intelligence that the doctor was seen in his launch, coming to let us out of quarantine before the appointed time. To get up, dress, and finish packing, was the work of a quarter of an hour. Another quarter of an hour saw us and our luggage safely aboard the steam-launch. We had no time for breakfast, but what mattered that, so long as we caught the steamer and saved a fortnight's stay on the Isthmus? Our letters had been successful. Mr. Mallet, the zealous English Consul, had kindly moved all the powers that be, to get our quarantine shortened, petitioning the governor and the doctor on our behalf, and detaining the steamer at Colon.

We steamed across the Gulf of Panama. The dense mist lying over the land at the back of the Isthmus indicated the line of the canal. It is to this poisonous exhalation that the Isthmus owes much of its alleged unhealthiness. To the right, some miles away on the beach, are the ruins of the old town, sacked and destroyed by Morgan.

The only landmark now seen of the old city is the crumbling tower of the church, "where Pizarro offered his prayers and vows to the Virgin, before sailing southward for the conquest of Peru." Ancient Panama was founded by the old navigators after their first view from thence of the Pacific. It was a Spanish stronghold, whence Peru was subjugated, and the whole continent of South America overrun.

The early morning cast a halo of beauty around Panama, tinging with sunlight the mouldy, green walls of the battery, ever washed by the waves of the Pacific, and lighting up the deep-red tone of the tiled roofs. Tales of the fever-laden atmosphere fade into the distance with this view of the town. It is low tide, so we have to leave the launch and take to the row-boats. Worse still, the luggage can only be landed on the reefs, from thence put into carts, and brought across the town. The ordinary train is on the point of leaving. A special train, costing 2*l*., must now take us the forty-eight miles across the Isthmus.

A drive through Panama revealed a succession of hilly streets, with low, ugly houses, where damp, mouldy walls are stained and discoloured with excessive wet, and overhung with hibiscus and tropical creepers. The shops seem to consist chiefly of low drinking-booths and barbers' salons, but have a deserted and depressed appearance. The population is made up of tall negroes and negresses, clothed in a single brilliant-coloured cotton chemise, exposing to full view the necks and arms, with a plentiful sprinkling of pale-faced Europeans. The pretty little plaza, with its croton-bordered walks, contains all of Panama's public buildings. Here is the cathedral with its double towers, inlaid with oyster-shells, a mother-of-pearl decoration of quaint but effective style. Here, too, the bishop's palace, the canal offices, the bank, and the hotel, whose doubtful reputation has been noised abroad in our ears recently and frequently. The governor's palace, guarded by a few baggy-trousered soldiers, is round the corner, facing seawards.

Everybody looks depressed, miserable, and anæmic. The damp heat and enervating atmosphere are but too apparent now we have landed. It is a vapour bath, laden with unwholesome exhalations, breeding fever and its attendant evils. Yet some assert that directly the canal works stopped, Panama ceased to be unhealthy. It was the exudation from the newly turned over earth that caused the fever and ague, that made Panama the graveyard for thousands, that filled the splendid hospital on yonder eminence, with its red roofs joining the separate wards, and capable of accommodating 600 or 700 patients. During the canal working it was always full of the sick, the dying, and the dead.

Panama, with its air of decay and crumbling, looks very different now to what it did in the days of its prosperity, when work on the canal was in full swing. Then it was a town with a population given up to reckless debauchery and revelry of speculation. Then it was a hell of vice and gambling. Now it awaits eagerly the renewed confidence of some nation or syndicate, who will recommence afresh the construction of the much-needed waterway.

The mail steamer has only agreed to wait until 10.30. Time presses. Yet the "special" is not

PANAMA CANAL COMPANY'S HOSPITAL.

Page 200.

forthcoming, as the line is blocked by another train. We grow anxious and impatient, our tempers not improved by a further exorbitant charge of three cents on every pound of luggage by this American railway company. After enduring so many and repeated delays, what would our feelings be should we after all miss the steamer! At length, after weary waiting, the train arrives, and we commence our journey across the Isthmus.

I don't know if others have imagined, as I had, that the Isthmus of Panama is, like that of Suez, a desert with much sand.

It is in reality the most beautiful peninsula, designated by vegetation of an extraordinary luxuriance. I have seen tropical growth in almost all parts of the world, but nothing comes up to the vegetation on this Isthmus of Panama. The trees are twined and draped with curtains of creepers, which flower along the branches. Palms grow to an abnormal size, the banyan-trees do likewise. Tall cocoa-palms stand aloft in solitary grandeur, whilst peach and fig trees, sugar-canes and banana-trees rise from the midst of an undergrowth so dense and tangled as to be quite impenetrable. It is a journey prolonged through a vast palmery, or proceeding through a long-continued heated conservatory. But occasionally from below comes a gleam of water, fœtid, stagnant water, covered with green slime, emitting the most poisonous vapours. Nearly the whole of this beautiful forest covers a marsh of standing water. Can we wonder at the brilliant green, the abundant growth, the glowing colours of this truly ultra-tropical forest?

We constantly pass groups of wooden houses, raised on piles, above the standing water. The company erected over 5000 of these wooden huts. Many are locked and empty, but others are tenanted chiefly by negroes and negresses, the former being employed to watch and keep the works and machinery in order.

From side to side of the railway we watch the sinuous course of the canal, "the unfinished ditch, the most startling memorial of human miscalculation and credulity that modern civilization has known." We see the muddy channel frequently blocked up by shifting earth, or lost amidst the dense growth, where lie buried the 50,000,000*l*. already spent. One grieves to think of the many hard-earned savings of the industrious French artisan, that have thus been swallowed up with a result now before our eyes. The banks are strewn with valuable machinery, lines of railway waggons on an embankment, standing idle, piles of sleepers, dredgers of all descriptions, floating in the river or standing on the sidings. Further on there are some sheds full of engines, but for the most part this costly machinery is rotting in the air, becoming rusty in the moist-laden atmosphere. To fulfil the conditions, about to expire, of the Canal Company with the Colombian Government, men are employed to keep the machinery in order and the canal open as far as possible; but how can a handful of men cope with the ravages of an all-destroying climate?

Now the canal crosses the railway to be engulphed in the half-finished excavations of the celebrated Culebra Mountain. It is only a low eminence to look at, but a cutting of 375 feet will be necessary to pierce it for the canal. Large sums of money were expended, and a big machine half-way up the mountain side speaks to the half-finished work. I suppose the banks when first made were clean embankments of earth. Now a rank vegetation clothes not only their sides, but encroaches over the bed of the narrow ditch until it is scarcely discernible.

As we approach Colon we have constantly in view the broad, swift-flowing river of the Chagres. The original idea was to use this river as the base of the canal by widening and dredging its bed. But then a difficulty arose. The Chagres is subject to freshets, and the stream has sudden rises and falls occurring in the space of a few hours. It daunted the engineers, and upset the original plans. Still, part of the river bed is utilized, and it is difficult sometimes to tell where the canal and river merge together, and where they separate.

We pass several stations where a collection of wooden houses, shaded by broad verandahs, mark some important point in the canal works. The street facing the line is largely composed of drinking-booths, posted with advertisements of the great "Loteria de Panama." The population is made up of "darkies" well adapted to work in this tropical heat, whilst their mulatto wives, huge, and lightly clothed, are splendid specimens of that dusky race. The ubiquitous Chinaman is present, too, and we decipher their hieroglyphical signs over many a door.

In an hour and a half the special train has run across the Isthmus, with its dense vegetation, its muddy canal, and broad, flowing river. We have left the Pacific in the Gulf of Panama, and here at Colon we find the Atlantic in the Gulf of Darien, soon to be merged in the waters of the Caribbean Sea. Colon was called Aspinwall in early days, after the name of the railway contractor, but was changed to Colon, the Spanish name for Columbus. Nevertheless, the railway officials are true to its earlier name, and label the luggage Aspinwall.

Colon is a small place, with an even worse reputation for healthiness than Panama. It is, perhaps, more densely shut in and surrounded by trees and heavy growth than the larger town, although more exposed to the refreshing ocean breezes. The Europeans live in the little bay inside yonder point, in houses that face the beach and the seashore. It is a great relief to see the *Para*, blue Peter flying at her mast-head, and steam up, ready to bear us away. Two boats were waiting, in charge of the ship's officers, to take passengers and luggage on board. Thankful were we, after all doubts and delays, to be at last safe on board the steamer.

A last sad impression of the fatal canal is left on our minds as we leave Colon. There is the picturesque châlet-house on the sea point, standing amid waving palms, and with the statue of Columbus presented by the Empress Eugenie in the garden of M. de Lesseps' former residence. We think of the poor old man far away in Paris, unconscious in the last days of old age, of the blasphemies and curses being heaped upon his head by the thousands of ruined speculators, by thousands of sufferers from cupidity and credulousness.

What is to be the future of the canal? Next year must decide. The time allowed by the Colombian Government will soon be over, and they can seize the plant unless work is recommenced. Perhaps a fresh syndicate may be formed in France; but they have been badly caught, and will be shy to bite again. Let us hope rather that an influential company may be formed of English capitalists to carry out and complete the canal. The South American Republics of Central America might well contribute a fixed sum, as it is of every importance to their commerce for them to have through communication with Europe. "Quien sabe?" (Who knows?), the favourite dilatory expression of the Spanish South American. It is a suitable exclamation wherewith to take farewell of this great southern continent of America.

The *Para* steamed out along the well-wooded shores of the gulf of Darien into the open and distressful ocean, bearing us on our homeward way, towards some of those spice-laden islands of the West Indies.

Sunrise over Port Royal; this is what we see on the second day of our voyage out from Colon. The white guardship, lying across the entrance to the wonderful natural inlet which forms the wide shores of Kingston Harbour, and the few buildings of Port Royal on the flat, thin green line of the jutting isthmus, stand out against the crimson sky. The houses of Kingston, hidden amongst tropical groves, cluster thickly down to the black wharves on the water's edge. Golden mists, opaque and dusky, enshroud the higher ranges of the Blue Mountains.

What a wonderful and pleasing variety is found in the great backbone of bristling mountains running through this beautiful island! The serrated tiers of little peaks, whose turret-shaped elevations face all ways, whose descending slopes give such infinite change, are gleaming with brilliant green; yet over all is that wonderful azure haze that imparts to them a bright-blue tone, plainly indicating the origin of their name.

We anchor at the wharf of Kingston, where all is obscured to view by an enormous stack of coal, whilst the air is thick with dust arising therefrom as the baskets are filled with coal. The coaling of the ship is performed by women: with their short petticoats and heads swathed in bandanna handkerchiefs they make strange coal-heavers. With their swinging gait they bear the enormous weight of these coal baskets on their heads. Merrily they go at it all day, laughing gaily as they troop up the gangway in going and returning streams.

Jamaica is the largest island of our West Indian possessions, and alone contains an area exceeding all the other islands of this tropical group. It is also distinguished for being the only British possession that bestows a title upon the Queen, who is here styled the "Lady of the Island"—a title originating in the time of Charles I., in whose reign Jamaica passed into the hands of Great Britain, and who was then designated the "Lord of the Island."

Kingston is disappointing and uninteresting. The two main and far-reaching arteries of North and Duke Streets, with their one-storied houses, offer no attractions. The shops are scrubby little stores, open to the street, and with their goods exposed on the floor, or hung around the wooden pillars that support the rough piazzas raised above the street. Coloured Manchester cotton goods and gaudy bandannas of red and yellow, with coarse glazed earthenware and cheap tin goods, seem to be the favourite native emporiums. The open sewers are unsavoury ditches running generally down the centre of the road, forming a formidable canal at the crossings, which requires careful negotiation on the part of the buggy driver.

But the population, at least to a newcomer, provides endless sources of amusement. The negresses, in their green, red, and blue cotton dresses, frilled and flounced, waddle aggressively along, whilst a little straw sailor-hat, perched aloft on their crisp, woolly head, gives a perky appearance to the general turnout. This jaunty little hat is most generally favoured, but others are partial to a large straw hat covered with nodding plumes of uncurled ostrich feathers. What bright colours, too, they love! Pink and yellow ribbons contrast with their black, polished faces, whilst the protruding lips are on a level with the straw brims of their hats.

The common women swathe their heads and bind them up in gay bandannas, tied behind in a most artistic knot, with the ends standing erect. How splendidly they move and walk, these women with their supple figures, accustomed from childhood to walk with head erect, bearing some great weight. It seems curious to our chivalrous natures to see the woman carrying the heaviest loads, such as a huge box on their heads, whilst beside her walks the husband, bearing a parcel in his hand; but the custom of the country requires it. Men labour in the fields and do all the hard manual work—they are not effeminate; but woman carries the load, and a man relieving her of it would be considered a fit object for scorn amongst his companions.

How strangely alike seem to us these black negroes and negresses, with their crisp, woolly heads, their complexions varying in sable intensity from mahogany and copper-colour to ebony, their thick, protruding lips, and flat, wide nostrils. *We* can see no distinguishing difference in their all-pervading ugliness. But I suppose amongst themselves they find such, and varying degrees of beauty, largely determined by the size and rotundity of the lady.

One of the well-appointed buggies in general use, drawn by a native horse of small but wiry proportions, took us out five miles to the Governor's residence, called King's House. "Manchester Square," a sharp corner, leading into a short street, brought us out of the town proper. A row of open booths, containing a medley of shops, surrounded the approach to the race-course, where some races are to be held on the morrow. The course is open to the public and there is no gate-money, except for the small stand belonging to a company.

As we drive out into the country we might almost imagine ourselves in an English lane, so green are the wayside hedges, so grass-grown are the bordering ditches; but then some great tropical growth—a giant cactus or a trailing alamander bush—recalls us to the fact that we are in an island of the West Indies. We pass many pretty homelike houses, enclosed in fields and surrounded by luxuriant gardens; they belong to the judges and well-known planters of the Island. Always, as a magnificent background to everything we see, is that lovely changing range of deep-blue mountains.

The road is excellent: to us, after our late experience of South American high-ways, it seems a "path of pleasantness" indeed. But the roads all over the Island are in equally good condition, and during his Governorship, Sir Henry Blake has been instrumental in making some 400 miles of communication.

The lodge at the gate entrance to King's House is hidden under the purple bloom of a buganvillea, whilst the long carriage-approach is flaming with orange and yellow crotons, crimson hibiscus, and such gorgeous trees of poinsettias, the scarlet-pointed blossom lying at the end of each leafless grey branch.

The Governor and Lady Blake kindly insist upon our spending the night at King's House, and the hermetically sealed ship in this tropical latitude, dusted over with black coal-grit, combined with the smell of the harbour, which absorbs the surface drainage of the town, combines to render a night on board out of the question.

Kingston may be small and dirty, but the Island of Jamaica is a gem among her rival sisters, enthroned on this West Indian ocean. Little as we can see of the island in our short stay, we see enough to convince us of this.

We set to work to see all that is possible, and commenced by a drive to Gordon Town. The road winds through a deep glen, hemmed in between mountain peaks, and with a stream turning round and about in the narrow ravine below. It was a lovely drive, the charm increased by a perfect morning of bright sun, pleasant breeze, and tempered heat. The tropical vegetation was exceptionally lovely on account of its multitudinous variety, and although the trees and palms mingled together and formed a massive growth, still it was not a tangle of jungle, but each plant had room to grow to its full stature without being too cramped and dwarfed by its surroundings.

We pass some of the soldiers of the Native West India Regiment being exercised in outpost duty, whilst a fatigue party in an adjoining field are encamped by a fire preparing the midday dinner over a fire. There is a large college standing in a park removed from the road: and from it two large waggonettes are bearing the pupils home after their morning studies.

We penetrate deeper into the ravine up the steep mountain way. It is a lovely road, crossing the river on bridges, giving glimpses up fresh valleys, and made picturesque by the figures of negresses carrying perhaps a large pommeloe on the head, or a basket full of oranges; whilst donkeys, laden with paniers of fresh grass or other marketable produce, are constantly driven on one side to let us pass. There are frequent picket-houses and guard-rooms for the soldiers quartered at Newcastle, and yet more frequent drinking-shops, licensed to "sell rum, beer, and brandy," where Tommy Atkins' temptations to refresh himself on his long upward tramp are very great.

Gordon Town is a small collection of roofs, but the carriage-drive ends here, and there is only a bridle-path from this point up the mountain side to Newcastle. Newcastle is represented to us by a number of white houses terraced on to the sloping shoulder of the higher range of the Blue Mountains, almost enveloped in clouds, and two thousand feet immediately above us. This elevated station, some 4000 feet high, is the depôt for the English regiment quartered at Kingston. Cool and healthy, the officers and men quartered on this distant and inaccessible mountain height must often wish themselves nearer to the dubitable charms of Kingston. The drive to Gordon Town is very beautiful, and we are told that it is the loveliest in the Island. We returned home through the Hope Gardens, where the lawns of grass thrive under much careful irrigation, and the ferns grow under the shade of a conservatory made of palm-branches.

A hurried luncheon at King's House and we drove back to Kingston to take the train to Bog Walk, another place famed for its beautiful scenery. The line is managed by an American company, and the coal-dust from the engine smothers the passengers in dirt. The heat was intense, although old residents were indignant at the suggestion, and impressed upon us that it was their winter. Summer must be unbearable, judging by the heat of December. It is a very pretty journey, the line being won out of the mountain side, and in places tunnelling through it. We arrived at Bog Walk Station, where a carriage was in waiting to drive us through the valley to Spanish Town.

Bog Walk is a lovely ravine, filled with banyan groves, overshadowed by overhanging rocks, whose nooks and crannies are filled by maidenhair and other hothouse ferns.

The River Cobra rushes along a rocky bed, hidden deep in the mountain cleft; whilst the mountains, heavily laden with tropical growth of brilliant hues, rise around to a considerable height. Strange fruits hang from many an unfamiliar tree, whilst the cloudy-grey lichen, called the old man's beard, depends from the branches of the trees ; over there, a large spreading one by the water's edge is covered with a trailing creeper that forms an umbrella shade of giant proportions.

Bog Walk is a lovely drive of some five miles long, and worthy of a prettier name. We cross the Cobra on a rough, unrailed bridge, and soon emerge from the ravine into an open, park-like space, where hedges of cacti form a thorny enclosure to many little encampments of thatched hovels. In one clearing is a little brick church, with the neighbouring house of the pastor raised on wooden piles. A few farms and houses placed nearer together warn us of the approach to the old-world capital and quaint little city of Spanish Town. The old plaza is surrounded by the Government House, looking closed and deserted with shuttered windows, although really a finer residence than that of King's House, on the one side, while on the other are the Colonial Secretary's offices, the Government Savings Bank, with a statue of Rodney, bearing a Latin inscription, under an open portico. Spanish Town, with its groves of banyan-trees, and many pretty villas and gardens on the outskirts of the city, is a favourite place of residence.

We just caught the train on our return to Kingston, and paid a hurried visit to the ship to pack our bags for the night, escaping from the smells, heat and dirt as quickly as possible. Then, lighted by the brilliant fire of the glow-worms, dancing hither and thither, we drove out to join a dinner party, and sleep at King's House.

Refreshed by the cool and quiet of a night in the country, and at an altitude of 400 feet above the harbour, we drove back into Kingston and further explored the dirty, unattractive streets. Then, overcome by the tropical heat of their winter sun, we returned on board, glad to stand out to sea past Port Royal, keeping the amethyst range of the Blue Mountains with their graceful peaks running across the island, in sight until sundown.

The following morning we approach quite close to the bright-green shores of Hayti, that most fruitful but independent island, given up under the domination of the two Republics of Hayti and Domingo to savage rule and rude cultivation. We cast anchor in the sheltered cove before the port of Jacmel, whilst a few clumsily manœuvred lighters come alongside to receive the cargo. The shores of Hayti bear us company for the whole day, somewhat breaking the force of a head-wind.

During the succeeding days we are exposed to the full fury of this gale. All suffer, all are miserable. It is only a question of the degree of discomfort everyone on board is enduring, for the following four days.

Relief is brought to all with the anchoring of the *Para* in the open roadstead before the Island of Barbados, and opposite to Bridgetown, early one morning. The green spit of land, sweeping round a half-formed bay, and running out to sea, is crowned by a lighthouse and signal-staff flying many flags. The great, green-crested breakers come sweeping in, curling over to dash themselves on to the shining white beach, recalling many a description of these South Sea Islands. Bridgetown presents itself to us in a medley of buildings and houses, buried amongst much green vegetation.

Barbados is the central point of departure for several of the other islands of the Leeward group—for St. Vincent, Tobago, Grenada, Trinidad, also for Caracas and Venezuela. Seven other Royal Mail steamers, engaged in performing the intercolonial service, lie in the roadstead whilst we are preparing to take on a collection of passengers from these neighbouring islands. Barbados is the most thickly populated island of the West Indies, and supplies coolie labour to other less favoured spots.

Bridgetown, with its glaring white roads, its Broad Street full of general emporiums, narrow streets, and rough, untidy houses, is singularly unattractive. There is nothing to please or interest in this typical little West Indian capital. The bridge spanning the river, filled with shipping, and the green enclosure where the post-office is lodged in a building ornamented with a beautiful Moorish arch, and the neighbouring church tower *might* be called pretty.

Out of the town we drive in one of the abominably bad native carriages, each one worse horsed than the other, past numerous little wooden bungalows. These tiny wooden houses, raised above the roadway, are curious habitations. They have no surrounding gardens, no glazed windows, but only wooden shutters that open on to a passage leading round the house. They appear very small and very public dwelling-places, exposed to the full view of the passers-by. How black and coarse-featured are the negresses, gnawing sticks of sugar-cane; how lazy and insolent in demeanour the negroes we meet as we drive along.

Barbados would be nothing without "the garrison." The military quarters, the mess-rooms, and barracks of the English regiments quartered here are a great feature. There is the park-like space of the Savannah, bordered around by trees, with an officer all dressed in white, taking a morning gallop across the brown turf. A pretty drive of two miles brings us out to the Marine Hotel at Hastings. The sea-breezes sweep around this favoured point, whilst a band-stand ornaments a cool sea walk.

We return to Bridgetown by another road, circling the Savannah again, and passing many pretty stone houses, surrounded by gardens rich in tropical blossoms, where doubtless reside the principal residents of the island. On our way back we call at Government House, a charming residence, so suitably planned as to be open to the draught of the trade wind, blowing through the house for six months of the year. General Paton is in charge as acting Governor during Sir John Hay's absence, and he and Mrs. Paton kindly insist upon Colonel Vincent staying with them until the succeeding steamer takes him to

Trinidad, St. Vincent, Grenada, and Venezuela, whilst I continue on my homeward voyage in the *Para*.

The interior of Barbados, stretching far away in undulating reaches, looks ugly and uninteresting, and is clothed throughout with bright-green sugar-canes. A curio-hunt in Bridgetown convinces us that the shops are only full of native rubbish, consisting chiefly of fans made from the gossamer tissue of a tree-bark, shells, polished tortoiseshell, and carved cocoa-nuts; nor are we greatly impressed with the exterior of the ice-house, the fashionable restaurant, situated in a dirty street, where a breakfast of flying-fish is considered a delectable entertainment for passing *voyageurs*, and where anything from a frying-pan to a dining-room table may be purchased.

The *Para* weighs anchor at sundown to pass out into the stormy ocean.

What a terrible voyage that was! For twelve days we had ceaseless head-winds with a very "big" sea. The ship was battened down, all the skylights and port-holes permanently closed. The water poured over the lower deck, and occasionally overflowed and flooded the passages leading to the cabins.

There was no rest day nor night; nearly all the passengers were sick or sorry—some never appeared at all; vacant places at table were the rule and not the exception. All were worn out and utterly weary of day succeeding day of this wearisome monotony of misery.

Any liquid comestible was looked upon with suspicion at meal-time; a passenger bold enough to venture on soup was a terror to his next-door neighbour. Cups of tea were landed in the lap, and soda-water bottles rolled and crashed on the floor of the saloon.

One wretched Sunday will long be remembered. The *Para* varied her frolicsome dancing on the crest of the billows, and took instead to rolling heavily in their troughs. A sleepless night spent in being pitched out of our berths, or in trying to wedge every movable article, rolling heavily up and down the cabin, found us heavy-eyed and ill-tempered at breakfast-time. Fiddles were useless with such rolling. Spoons, forks, knives, and glasses crashed up and down against their sides, with each awful roll, and overbalanced on to the floor. Life-lines were stretched along the deck, and those of us who were bold enough to venture up, were requested to cling on to the ropes.

Summer skies had long ere this faded into a memory. Deck-awnings had been stowed away, and extra blankets for the berths requisitioned. Deck-chairs lay unused in stacks. Cold and gloomy was our approach to England's shores.

At 10 p.m. on the night of December 27th, small groups of shivering passengers were standing on the deck, gazing on the two brilliant meteors of the Lizard lights. Through the deep darkness shone out these electric beacons, welcoming home many a weary, worn exile. An hour later the gleam of the Eddystone Lighthouse is on our starboard bow.

We anchor off the lights of Plymouth to land the mails and some passengers. The mail contract has been saved by half an hour.

We awake the next morning to find ourselves in the calm waters of Southampton Bay, and passing the white chalk points of the Needles and the green downs of the Isle of Wight. The leafless trees, and the cold white fog give us but a cheerless impression.

The dirty steam-tug, the long delay at the Custom House, and the arrival at Waterloo to the first dense, black fog of the season, complete the regrets that a third long journey, in another world than ours, must now be reckoned only a thing of the past.

APPENDIX

By COLONEL HOWARD VINCENT, C.B., M.P.

THE following letters appeared in *The Globe*, *The Sheffield Telegraph*, and other papers.

TO THE LAND OF REVOLUTIONS.

Island of St. Vincent, September 30th, 1893.

Friends at home thought the present time ridiculous for a tour in South America. For the past month and more every day has brought cablegrams to Europe of fresh revolutions in Brazil or Argentina. We settled, therefore, to come and see what they were about, and whither they were leading the British millions so lavishly sent over the South Atlantic. The crowd on board the Royal Mail steamer *Thames* shows that there is little danger to be apprehended. Brazilians, Argentines, and Chilians are returning after a summer in Europe with their wives and children, and Englishmen, also long resident on the Spanish main. The revolutions are nothing; the revolutions are local; all will be over in a day or two; it is only a tournament between lawyers who are "out" and lawyers who are "in." The country is safe enough, and foreigners are never interfered with. Such is the universal opinion. We shall see how far it is justified. But here we are at St. Vincent, in the direct trade route between the United Kingdom and the rich markets of the River Plate. The total distance is between 6000 and 7000 miles. It is too far for any man-of-war or well-laden vessel to steam without coaling.

The whole policy of the statesmen who founded the Empire was to make it independent of foreign nations. It was the great aim of Pitt, who realized more than anyone, before or since, that the Empire was trade. England holds the route to the great East by well-placed fortresses, and by having the coaling stations in her own hands. The French can barely reach their Eastern possessions, even through the Suez Canal, without the leave of England. They cannot do so at all by the Cape of Good Hope. The Germans, the Dutch, and the Portuguese are in like case. It is a great power in our hands. Hamstring the fleetest runner and he is powerless. Deprive the most formidable ship of war of coal and it is of no account. For the security of our trade, for its economical maintenance in peace, it is essential that sufficient coal should be obtainable on every road of commerce under the British flag. For the protection of our trade, in war, for the safe arrival of those food supplies our neglected land at home compels us to seek abroad, British coaling stations are of paramount importance.

The Eastern trade route has been well secured. But the Western trade route has been neglected. It is of nearly as great value as the former, and, better still, it is only in its childhood. If South American politicians will but cease to revolutionize, and give pledges for security, its limit is not in sight, its volume cannot be ciphered. How comes it that there is no harbour and no coaling station under the Union Jack from the English Channel to the further seaboard of the South Atlantic? Lisbon, Madeira, and the Cape de Verd Islands are Portuguese. Teneriffe and the Canaries are Spanish. Ascension and St. Helena are out of the way and otherwise unsuitable. It may not be too late to repair the error by awaiting the opportunity. Skilful negotiations and the payment of a fair price should be the weapons. Take the map, follow the track of trade, and for a centre point in the South Atlantic you fix on the Island of St. Vincent. We are there to-day. The magnificent harbour of Porto Grande is full of British shipping—colliers discharging coal from England, merchantmen taking in coal. The only foreign flag is on a little Portuguese gunboat. English money is alone current in practice. On shore there are about 40,000 tons of British coal—170,000 tons were imported by English houses last year for English steamers. Every ton is charged a duty of 1s. 4d. to the Portuguese Government. It augments by so much the cost to the shipping. There are 150 Englishmen on the island—the able staff of the Brazilian Submarine Cable, directed for nineteen years by Mr. Lloyd—too valuable a public servant to remove to a more temperate region for toil, and others. They pay to the Portuguese authorities a duty of about 75 per cent. on the goods they import for daily existence. It is a heavy charge. These duties, all paid by England, constitute the only revenue of the colonial Government, and it can but ill-suffice for the officials maintained. It is, moreover, a declining income. Favourable as is St. Vincent for coaling, every effort is being made to escape the Portuguese exactions. The Spaniards have made " Las Palmas " free. The consequence is that its trade has quadrupled in the last five years, while St. Vincent has retrograded 30 per cent. But the Grand Canary is too near England, too far from South America, not sufficiently equidistant, and without a harbour, to compare with Porto Grande. What, then, should be done?

St. Vincent should become British. By force of arms? Assuredly not, for we desire nothing better than peace and amity with Portugal—our old ally—and her safe riding through her pressing financial troubles. But what could be fairer than, if Portugal were willing to sell, and she could well do so without loss of dignity and prestige, that we should buy, or give something in exchange in East Africa? It would be money well spent by us. Of the island itself we could not make much more than the Portuguese. It is arid. But to us as a coaling station, a harbour, and a pivot of cable communication, it would be invaluable. True, St. Vincent could but ill stand alone. Within gunshot is San Antonio, fertile and blessed by nature. The one to feed the other. Let Portugal keep the other seven islands of the Cape de Verd group, including her seat of government at St. Jago, and the valuable salt deposits at Ilha de Sal; but let the British Foreign Office watch for the opportunity of acquiring St. Vincent and San Antonio. The Administration which succeeds in this task—and it should not be a very difficult one—will do a mighty service to British trade, and do much to secure and extend it.

Rio de Janeiro, October 12th, 1893.

" Order and Progress " is the motto of the United States of Brazil. It was adopted on the 15th of November, 1889, when the Imperial House surrendered to two battalions of raw soldiers and a company of cadets, unprovided with ammunition. The aged Emperor had had a long and beneficent reign; but by frequent absences in Europe he had accustomed his people to believe that they could do perfectly well without him. His unostentatious life at Petropolis, his shabby appearance in public, and the scientific, rather than political, bent of his mind, prevented him arousing any enthusiasm even in Court circles. Suffering from softening of the brain, dazed by the suddenness of the blow, the aged sovereign gave up the throne without the slightest effort to retain it. The acquiescence of the Crown Princess and her Orleans husband, the Condé d'Eu, is more difficult to understand. But the people were completely indifferent. One hour they were contented with and loyal to the Imperial House, and gave not a thought to expelling it. The next they joyfully accepted the Baby Republic. Marshal Deodoro da Fonseca was called from a bed of sickness to lead the movement. He had been overwhelmed with favours by the Imperial hand, but no consideration of gratitude restrained him.

The triumph was short-lived. Martial law had to be proclaimed in a month, and it has been enforced repeatedly ever since. The civic liberty and the freedom of the Press enjoyed under the Monarchy have been abrogated. "Disorder and Retrogression" is the practice of the Republic.

A provisional constitution was proclaimed on June 22, 1890, but it was not until the 24th of February, 1891, that it was finally accepted by the Congress, notwithstanding the employment of every electoral device to secure the servility to the Executive of the Senate and the House of Representatives. The American Constitution was practically translated into Portuguese. In one respect Marshal Deodoro da Fonseca disappointed his friends. He was only brought out as "a galvanized corpse," and he showed far too much vitality. A process of harassing him was forthwith commenced. His election to the Presidency was only effected by 129 votes to 97 cast for Dr. Prudente de Moraes, President of the Senate, who will probably stand again with every chance of success.[1] The two Houses passed an Act setting forth the grounds upon which the President could be impeached. Deodoro fell well within

[1] He has since been elected.

them, and trial by a hostile Senate was inevitable if the
Bill passed. It was therefore vetoed. Again it was
brought forward in Congress, and only missed enactment
by a single vote. Forthwith Marshal Deodoro da Fonseca
dissolved Congress and proclaimed martial law. He was
assured of the support of the army. But the great
southern province of Rio Grande do Sul revolted (as it
now has again) and 20,000 men were organized over the
Uruguayan frontier. The Military President had also not
reckoned with the navy. Admirals Wandelkolk and Custodio de Mello took an opposite line. The arrest of the
former was effected, but the latter escaped to his fleet, and
persuaded the officers to join him. On November 23, 1891,
he brought three vessels into line of action in the Bay and
threatened to bombard Rio de Janeiro. Unsupported by
his colleagues, undermined by his Vice-President, the
founder of the Republic surrendered as quietly as the
Emperor had done to himself two years before, and soon,
like his former master, he passed away from terrestrial
ambitions. In accordance with the terms of the constitution, the Vice-President, General Floriano Peixoto,
became without further election the chief of the Executive.
He has himself been a candidate for the Presidency, but
only secured two votes. The people were, as before, absolutely indifferent. Nor do they appear the least to appreciate that the present Chief of the State has continued
annually to draw only the Vice-Presidential salary and to
content himself with a modest abode instead of occupying
the Executive mansion. There can be little doubt that
the first revolt of Admiral Custodio de Mello was supported
by General Floriano Peixoto. It is also practically certain,
although not announced, that an agreement was arrived at
that he should have, on his own behalf and on that of the
navy, the reversion of the Presidency. This is the only
reasonable explanation of the present position of affairs.
Admiral Custodio de Mello became Minister of Marine.
He resigned in April last on a bill being vetoed precluding
a Vice-President from becoming President. In this action
he probably saw that General Floriano Peixoto had no
intention of abiding by the secret understanding, and
that although nominally in favour of a civilian President
supported by the army, he was by no means adverse
to being himself duly elected as President. This opens

Chapter II.—that of the present, or third, Republican Revolution.

What Admiral Custodio de Mello had successfully done in November, 1891, against the President, Deodoro da Fonseca, with the connivance, if not at the actual instigation of the Vice-President, General Floriano Peixoto, it was highly probable he would do again. His movements were watched and the Government placed in possession of full details concerning an extensive naval conspiracy. But with that extraordinary apathy and indifference which is as characteristic of the Brazilian authorities as of the people, no steps were taken to frustrate it. As midnight was striking on the 5th of September last, Admiral Custodio de Mello, although at that time holding no naval commission, went with a score of friends on board the *Aquidaban*, the principal vessel of the squadron, and assumed command. The captains of the fleet were all on shore, of course, by pre-arrangement. The *Republica*, the *Trajano*, and the *Marcillio Dias* surrendered as quietly as the flagship. A landing party was at once organized, and a quantity of ammunition and stores removed from the Nictheroy Arsenal and from the Island des Cobras. The Brazilian vessels in the harbour were also required to give up their cargoes in exchange for receipts in the name of Admiral de Mello. By ten o'clock on the 6th of September the insurgent forces numbered 12 ships of war, 5 torpedo-boats, 5 coasting steamers, and 2 steam-launches—24 vessels in all.

A clear narrative of subsequent events is not easy to obtain. The Government habitually suppresses all information. The Brazilian newspapers, in hourly dread of suppression under the state of siege, only refer in the most guarded terms to the revolution, and some of them—notably the leading newspaper—the *Journal of Commerce*, makes no mention of it at all. The only reliable source of information is the weekly issue of the *Rio News*, owned and edited by an American gentleman of singular ability and fairness.

Consider the position of the Brazilian capital at the present time, and you will see how serious and yet how comical it is, how dangerous and yet how amusing. The beautiful harbour is only broken in its vast circumference by the narrow entrance. On one side of the gateway is the Fortress of Santa Cruz, on the other are the guns of the San Juan Fort. The island casemates of Lage complete the defensive triangle in the hands of the Government. In the bay are 24 vessels, and the powerful fort on the Island of Villegaignon—2½ miles on the town side from Santa Cruz, 1¾ miles from Lage, and 1.9 miles from San Juan, flying the white flag of the insurgents. In the centre of all on another island is the Naval School under Admiral Saldanha de Gama, the most accomplished officer in the Brazilian service. He has succeeded in preserving an attitude of neutrality, as did also Fort Villegaignon, until a few days ago. The adhesion of the latter brought the insurgent forces up to about 1200 men. On shore the Government disposes of as many thousands; but they are ill-equipped, ill-officered and undisciplined—a greater danger to peace and order, most people think, than the rebel cannon. On October 10 two battalions of the National Guard settled a regimental difference with Maxim guns. The normal population of the town is about 400,000, including 16,000 Italians, 14,000 Portuguese, 2000 English, and 1000 Germans. In the hands of the English and the Germans is nearly all the foreign trade, and at all times half the vessels in the harbour are British. To protect these vast interests Her Majesty's Minister, Mr. Wyndham, has the assistance of Captain Lang and Her Majesty's ships *Sirius*, *Beagle*, and *Racer*. Mr. Wyndham is able to bring the experience of 35 years in the diplomatic service to bear on the situation, which is one of great delicacy and difficulty. It is fortunate that he has a Naval coadjutor so capable as Captain Lang. This officer, whose services were lent for some time to the Emperor of China, succeeded in raising within a few years a Chinese fleet of the first rank, and by his devotion, courage, and self-abnegation made a name for himself on the Yellow Sea, second only to that of Chinese Gordon on land. His personality and judgment have been of the greatest service at this crisis. The foreign squadron is completed by 1 French, 2 Italian, 2 German, 2 American, and 1 Portuguese cruisers, disposing of about 700 men. Admiral Sibron of the French Navy is the senior officer, but the guiding mind is that of Captain Lang. On shore Mr. Wyndham is the "doyen" of the diplomatic body. Between the foreign legations and between the ships of the foreign squadron there is complete accord and harmony of action with one unfortunate and notable exception. The German Chargé d'Affaires and the senior officer of the German vessels have severed themselves from their colleagues, and especially from the English. The seniority of the courteous French Admiral may have something to do with the matter. But it would be interesting to know if this independent German action is in pursuance of orders from Berlin, for it constitutes a serious divergence from that harmonious action throughout the world of England and of Germany which is the centre point of the far-seeing policy of the Emperor William II.

Admiral Mello found himself no sooner in possession of the fleet than he issued a manifesto to the nation. He therein declared that his grounds of revolt were—

(a) "Because the head of the Executive (Vice-President Floriano Peixoto) had arbitrarily mobilized the National Army and placed it on a war footing over the unfortunate states of Santa Catharina and Rio Grande do Sul.

(b) "Because he had armed Brazilians against Brazilians, spreading mourning, want, and desolation in every nook and corner of the Republic.

(c) "Because he had perjured himself, deceived the nation, and opened with sacrilegious hand the coffers of the public exchequer to a policy of bribery and corruption.

(d) "Because bankruptcy was knocking at the door with a long train of horrible misfortunes and disasters."

Although the last statement is, at any rate, undeniable, Custodio de Mello failed to explain how such a condition of affairs was to be remedied by his ruinous revolutionary action. A like omission was apparent in the simultaneous manifesto of the four Deputies supporting him. They affirmed that "the seconding of the brave Admiral Custodio de Mello would be the means of restoring the sway of peace under the constitution and laws, and of preserving the sacred principles of Republicanism."

These "sacred principles" appear in Brazil and, indeed, elsewhere, to be a perpetual state of siege and civil war.

The campaign of the Navy against the Army opened badly for the latter, not only in the loss of stores, but also by one of the battalions having fired upon the launch of the Italian cruiser bearing the Consul. A sailor was killed, and a full apology had to be made, a public funeral accorded, and an indemnity of 100,000 milreis promptly paid. To follow the "French duel" through all its ridiculous stages would be absurd. Suffice it to say that on September 11th and 12th the insurgents attacked the provincial capital of Nictheroy, practically securing it; that on September 13th they bombarded Santa Cruz from 10 a.m. to nightfall, being hotly answered; that on September 17th the *Republica*, a first-class cruiser of modern type, ran out of the harbour right under the guns of the fortress, which on September 22nd and 23rd was again playfully bombarded for three hours—an expenditure of powder and shot highly diverting to the inhabitants, who lined the heights, opera-glasses in hand, to witness it.

But on the 25th of September a new phase was entered upon. The Government made ostensible preparations to take possession of the Ilha des Cobras, on which was the Naval Hospital. Two batteries of useless guns were mounted on shore, and under their cover it was sought to embark some troops. The Insurgent Fleet began forthwith to bombard the business quarter of the city, and a panic resulted. On the following day the attempt was renewed, and one of the first victims to the naval fire was Mr. Watmough, a much esteemed clerk in the London and Brazilian Bank, who was having luncheon in a restaurant, and went out on to the balcony to see what was going on. A fragment of shell took off the back of his head and killed him instantly. Again the Government was forced to desist. The seizure of the Harbour Island was abandoned in face of the declaration of the fleet that the bombardment of the city would be continued. The shore batteries were, however, directed to fire on every vessel coming within range. This opened up a very serious condition of affairs. The Government artillery was powerless to do any real damage to the insurgents from the too-distant City Heights. But its existence in position justified Custodio de Mello in treating Rio as a fortified place, and in bombarding it as such at any time and without notice.

The British Minister thereupon ordered the English community "to seek places of safety without delay, and in the event of the town being given up to anarchy and pillage, assemble in the Palace Square, where, upon pre-arranged signal, they would be protected by the joint forces of the squadron." The Government organs were exceedingly indignant at the suggestion that the town might be given up "to anarchy and pillage," and tried to incite an anti-foreign feeling. The Vice-President also issued a proclamation that "the Government was provided with all the means for maintaining order, and that it would direct every one to be immediately shot who attempted to commit a crime against private property."

The efforts of Mr. Wyndham and his colleagues of France, Italy, and Portugal were next directed to obtaining the dismantlement of the useless shore batteries, so as to leave no excuse for further bombardment. These endeavours were eventually successful, and have been rewarded by the officially expressed thanks of the Vice-President, notwithstanding the marked and extraordinary abstention of Germany, as also of the representatives of the other South American Republics.

The representations of the Powers were much aided by the prompt authorization of Lord Rosebery that Admiral Mello should be notified that the British vessels would join those of the Concordat in preventing by force the bombardment of an undefended city, and also by visible preparations for effective action on board H.M.S. *Sirius*.

But, before this could be settled, renewed interchanges of iron compliments took place, on the afternoon of September 30th, between the insurgent fleet and Santa Cruz. The former fired 196 shots, the latter about twice as many, at an average price of from 8*l*. to 10*l*. per shot, but still without apparent result.

On the next day, what might have proved a serious incident occurred. In the afternoon Admiral Mello notified the senior British Naval Officer that a steam launch flying the Union Jack was cruising around the *Aquidaban* under suspicious circumstances. Captain Lang went to inquire into the facts, and found that an American—one Captain Boynton, who is believed to have fixed a dummy torpedo on an American man-of-war one night in New York Harbour —was endeavouring, under cover of the British flag, to tow a torpedo by a submarine wire under the rebel flagship. He was promptly arrested and handed over to the American commander, while his British companions, for whom he denied all complicity, were detained on the English ship. It is said that Boynton was to receive 20,000*l.* if he succeeded in blowing up the *Aquidaban*, and had been given 10,000 milreis on account.

On the 4th of October, the Government, notwithstanding the agreement arrived at, placed a new battery on the San Bento hill, behind the Sandé water front. An English, a French, and an American officer were told off to verify the fact and breach of agreement, which, being done, it was decided that no action could be taken by the foreign squadron to prevent retaliation by the insurgent fleet. The next day, at 7 a.m., the latter commenced the bombardment afresh, and Mr. (now Sir Hugh) Wyndham advised " British subjects to close their establishments, and retire to places of safety," adding " no time should be lost."

Admiral Mello must be credited with an effort to avoid doing serious damage to the city, and comparatively little was done. On the 6th of October, on renewed diplomatic representation, the San Bento battery was dismantled, and confidence thus greatly restored.

We arrived at Rio in the Royal Mail steamer *Thames*, commanded by that prince of mariners, Captain Hicks, on Tuesday, the 10th of October, just after Fort Villegaignon, with its garrison of 700 men, had declared itself no longer neutral, but for the insurgents. The Government is said to have forced this position by cutting off both the pay of the men and their water. In the harbour were between 80 and 100 vessels flying the Union Jack—an eloquent testimony to the magnitude of the British interests involved. Our landing at the Naval Arsenal showed at once the inadequacy of the shore arrangements. There was a sentry, certainly, but his functions seemed doubtful. The town gave little appearance of being in a state of siege. The only interest of the remaining inhabitants crowding the tram-cars seemed to be to get a good place to see the bombardment, which was announced for 4 o'clock. An English schooner, laden with coal from Cardiff, sailed over the bar just before that hour, all unconscious of the arrangements it was disturbing. The spectators were almost impatient at the delay in pulling up the curtain. The autocrat " Democracy " replaced the Emperor Nero. At length, at 4.30, the fight began, and for an hour and three-quarters Fort Villegaignon and the insurgent fleet on the one side, and Santa Cruz, Lage, and San Juan on the other blazed away, "de part et l'autre." So far as could be seen, the result was nil. Although the distances were well known, and the objects stationary, nearly every shot fell far short. It was impossible to believe that there was any desire for them to do otherwise. One shell exploded well over Santa Cruz, and an imperfectly fastened breech-piece in Villegaignon cut one man into three pieces, and wounded six others, but neither the vessels nor the forts were seriously damaged. It was a most absurd performance, and showed that neither side is really in earnest. If it were otherwise, the forts would surely give the rebel vessels no peace, and the insurgents, on the other hand, knowing the inadequacy of the Government forces, would effect a landing at any sacrifice.

This morning certainly a little more energy was shown by the insurgents, and they are said to have inflicted serious loss on the Government troops near Nictheroy. The Marine Arsenal Wharf, too, shows apprehension of danger. An iron revetment has been run up, and quick-firing guns peer through a parapet of hay and sandbags on to the landing-stage. Great events may not be far distant, and the narrow tortuous streets of Rio may be soon writing history with scarlet hands. Admiral Custodio de Mello is also apparently far from dissatisfied with his progress. This is evidenced by his Flag-Lieutenant boarding the *Thames* and endeavouring by force to remove certain fresh passengers in civilian attire. The opportune arrival of Her Majesty's Minister and Senior Naval Officer soon proved to him, however, that the deck of a British ship is the free land of England. But as the Royal Mail steamer steamed slowly out to the South Atlantic under the stern of the *Aquidaban* the Queen's sailors—who are having a hard time of it, all shore leave having been necessarily stopped for many weeks past—stood ready to run to quarters if need arose. Happily such was not the case, or grave complications would have arisen. The Green Flag and the Red Ensign saluted each other, and again presently in passing Santa Cruz, the password of the day being duly exhibited on the bridge to port.

But how is it going to end? That is what everyone

asks. But no Brazilian seems to know or care. Popular sympathy is apparently with Admiral Mello; but on what ground nobody is able to explain. The naval officers are said to be better educated and of a superior class to those of the army, whose appearance is not more calculated than that of their subordinates to inspire confidence. But it is strange that the admiral who is responsible for the discipline and obedience of the Fleet to constituted authority, but who has twice within twenty-four months organized a mutiny and used Brazilian ships and Brazilian money against the Brazilian Government and Brazilian capital, should excite much enthusiasm in the minds of those who have the melancholy duty of paying for both sides in the struggle.

The probability is that the revolution will drag on for some few weeks more, Santa Cruz and Lage being, as now, provisioned under the eyes of the insurgent fleet, the rebel officers coming not infrequently ashore unhampered. Then after immense sums have been thrown away, the present heavy deficit being enormously increased, by the intermediation of Admiral Saldanha de Gama, or other neutral authority, peace will be temporarily restored and an amnesty proclaimed.[1] In the meantime the elections for the new Congress are announced for October 30th, and preparations will soon commence for the election in March next of a new president to come into office in the following November. Under the present condition of affairs the outlook before the United States of Brazil is most gloomy, but gloomiest of all for the unfortunate Englishmen who have advanced some 100,000,000/. for the development of the riches of the country by "Order and Progress." Although it is true that the people are saying openly that the condition of affairs which has distinguished the four-year-old Republic never occurred under the Monarchy, that then order was assured, and Brazilians did not war with Brazilians, that then living was cheaper and employment more abundant, the present revolution cannot be described as one in any sense for the restoration of the Imperial House. It might indeed be otherwise, if there were a pos-

[1] Saldanha de Gama subsequently joined the insurgents and took command of their ships at Rio, surrendering to the Government in March, 1894.

sible and spirited candidate for the throne. The Crown Princess, although capable and energetic, is said to be fatally priest-ridden. Her husband never became popular, and her children are too young, while the sons of her late sister, who married the Duke of Saxe-Coburg Gotha, are from other causes ineligible. The influence of the revolution is, however, fatal to the country, and is likely prejudicially to affect and excite the other Republics of the South American continent.

II.

BRITISH SOUTH AMERICA WON AND LOST.

Buenos Ayres, October 26th, 1893.
The Calle de la Reconquista, the principal street in Buenos Ayres, holds an eloquent pen in British story. It traces deeds on which the English historian is very reserved, and of which the majority of students are ignorant. It recalls acts of valour and heroism from the glory of which a century of time cannot detract. It speaks of the humiliating defeat of a powerful British army, and the probable loss to the British flag of the colossal continent of South America, and its priceless wealth. It is worth while to disinter these memories from General Mitre's admirable history. They should serve as teachings to the present, as warnings to the future.

It was in the spring of 1806. General Baird was in command at the Cape of Good Hope. Captain Sir Home Popham was Principal Naval Officer. Pitt had honoured the latter with a private interview before he left England. The great Prime Minister, whose motto was "British markets for British hands," had given him clearly to understand how glad he would be to see the loss of the United States repaired by the acquisition of the far greater and far richer South America. The overtures of the Venezuelan General, Miranda, and his associates for throwing off the Spanish yoke under British protection had opened up great possibilities. But it was necessary to proceed with caution and without warning to any other nation. Popham understood, and was willing to accept the responsibility of independent action and disavowal by the Home Government if need be. He talked over General Baird soon after the conquest of Cape Town, who gave him the 71st Highlanders, fittingly led by William Carr Beresford. They sailed for the Spanish main. The little fleet consisted of three frigates, three corvettes, and five transports. No telegraph or special correspondent was at Cape Town to betray the British rovers. Popham put in at St. Helena, and obtained a battalion of Marines and a few artillerymen.

On the 10th of June anchor was cast in the River Plate. The Spaniards were taken entirely by surprise. On the 15th of June the news came up to Buenos Ayres. The Andalusian viceroy completely lost his head and fled. Ten days later, at one p.m., the English landed—60 officers, 62 sergeants, 22 drummers, and 1466 rank and file. The 71st Highlanders led the way, supported by the battalion of Royal Marines and three companies of sailors. The whole were under the command of General William C. Beresford. On the 26th, the little column advanced to the assault of the city, then of 60,000 inhabitants. The defending force of 1000 horse and 16 pieces of artillery fled as soon as the Highland skirmishers opened fire. The next day the British marched through the narrow streets, drums beating and colours flying, and occupied the citadel. It was a brilliant performance, and well seconded would have brought the best part of South America under the British Crown.

A proclamation was issued forthwith guaranteeing public justice, the security of private property, and the free exercise of the Catholic religion, as well as an unfettered commerce like other English colonies. A considerable, but not excessive, indemnity was exacted, and, after provision for the expenses of the force, the greater part was sent to England with an urgent request for reinforcements. The good news was received with the greatest enthusiasm. The treasure was drawn through London in a triumphal procession. Merchant fleets were immediately equipped for this new El Dorado. Seven thousand troops were ordered to be despatched at once, and another force destined for the conquest of Chili, under General Crawford, was instructed to give assistance in the River Plate if necessary.

Meanwhile things had gone ill with Beresford. Dissension apparently broke out between him and Popham. When the Spanish thousands saw by what an insignificant force they had been defeated, they felt ashamed. Conspiracy was rife. The citadel was mined. Beresford was short of ammunition, and much troubled by desertions. His forces included a few Roman Catholic Irishmen, and the Spanish priests were apparently successful in seducing some of them. One in particular, Michael Skemnor, went over to the enemy, and gave effective help. Beresford got wind of what was in progress. From the citadel he saw the hostile forces being organized and massed. On the 1st of August he made a sortie with 500 Scotchmen and completely routed the enemy. One man alone stood to the Castilian guns—Michael Skemnor, the Irish deserter. He was tried by court-martial and sentenced to death. But Beresford, most generous of victors, allowed the Bishop of Buenos Ayres to give him extreme unction, and himself received the prelate with military honours. The victory was only transient in its results. The straits of Beresford were too apparent. Liniers, a French soldier of fortune, organized a still larger force to expel the invader from the secure ground of Monte Video.

On the 11th of August it embarked from the bank of the lower estuary under cover of a fog, and in spite of Popham. The next day Liniers led 4000 men to the attack. Beresford did all that was possible, valiantly seconded by the 71st and the Royal Marine battalion. They were hopelessly outnumbered, and the ammunition gave out. The King's colour and the regimental ensign of the Highlanders were taken by the victors. With a standard bearing the cipher "R.M.B.," and three more British flags, subsequently taken, they are to day hanging under glass in massive gold frames on the six pillars in the nave of the great church of San Domingo. Well may the trophies be prized. They are unique. In neither palace nor cathedral elsewhere are like records of British defeat. In the tower above lie still embedded the British cannon balls. Well may the Argentines be proud of their "Victoria," their "Reconquista." But in their hour of triumph under Liniers they were as magnanimous as their opponent. It is a distinguished trait of the national character. "Death to the man who insults the British troops"—now 300 short—went the order, and Liniers received Beresford in his arms for his valiant defence. He wished to let them embark for England, but this was too much for popular sentiment. They were kept as prisoners until the relief expedition reached the River Plate. Before then Beresford escaped, but, faithful to his parole, refused to bear further arms against his victors.

His valour and his conduct were worthy of his name and race. But with him ends the bright page of British martial story in Argentina.

The attitude of Popham towards Beresford is inexplicable. He was brought to trial, and superseded by Admiral Stirling. On the 11th of October, 1806, the British reinforcements for the River Plate sailed from Falmouth, under Sir Samuel Auchmuty. They were followed a month later by the Chilian Expeditionary Force, under General Craufurd. It was May, 1807, before the whole force was massed on the River Plate, and ready to open operations, under the leisurely direction of Lieutenant-General Whitelocke.[1] This British Commander-in-Chief is described as a great parade soldier, who by marriage—some say Royal paternity—obtained powerful influence at the War Office. To his general misfeasance posthumous rumour adds venality. Let us hope it lies.

The whole force numbered 11,771 men. It was divided into four brigades, under Craufurd, Auchmuty, Lumley, and Mahon. The Argentines had been able to muster 8600 bayonets, but they were ill-armed, ill-disciplined, ill-equipped, and badly led. The powder had to be obtained from Chili, to be carried 800 miles on mule-back, and across the frightful passes of the Andes in mid-winter. The British soldiery thought that it would be but a march of triumph, and so it should have been but for Whitelocke. One hundred and ten British sail supported the land forces. Monte Video had fallen to Auchmuty after a brilliant skirmish under Colonel (afterwards Sir Denis) Pack, Beresford's alter ego, who had also escaped from Buenos Ayres.

---

[1] On January 28th, 1808, Lieutenant-General John Whitelocke, commander-in-chief of the expedition against Buenos Ayres, was brought before a general court-martial in the Great Hall of Chelsea College. Gen. Sir Wm. Meadows presided over a court of nineteen generals, including Sir John Moore, who on the 18th of March adjudged "the said Lt.-Gen. John Whitelocke to be cashiered and to be declared totally unfit and unworthy to serve His Majesty in any military capacity whatever." The king, in confirming the sentence, directed "that it be read at the head of every regiment in His Service, and inserted in all regimental orderly books with a view of its becoming a lasting memorial of the fatal consequences to which officers expose themselves who in the discharge of the important duties confided to them are deficient in that zeal, judgment, and personal exertion, which their Sovereign and their country have a right to expect from officers entrusted with high commands."

On the 28th of June, 1807, the British disembarked 36 miles from the capital. The weather was bad, and heavy rains made the march to Buenos Ayres very severe. The two advanced brigades, under Craufurd and Lumley respectively, were placed under Major-General Leveson-Gower. On the 2nd of July they came across the enemy. Leveson-Gower executed a clever flank movement, seized the bridge leading to the eastern quarter of the city, charged the defending battalions, and completely routed them. Then was the moment to push on. Buenos Ayres would have again been ours, without another blow. But Whitelocke's superior order was fatal. He had been slow in organizing the attack, he had badly chosen the place and time of disembarkation, and now he imposed further delay in the hour of victory. He was leading the main body by a circuitous route, and in the meantime an improvised resistance was organized by the City Council. Three days were allowed to elapse. At 6.30 on the morning of the 5th of July a Royal salute was fired. It was the signal for attack. Whitelocke had the choice of three alternatives for advancing on the citadel. He chose the worst. The force was divided into a central body and two wings. The left attack was to the north under Auchmuty and Lumley; the right, to the south, under Craufurd.

The British troops advanced at the double, without firing a shot, according to Whitelocke's orders. The flanks carried the Retiro on the north and the Residency on the south. It was a short-lived success. Further advance was stopped by a murderous fire from well-chosen and well-concealed positions. But again the British pushed on. At 10 o'clock the cheers of the fleet greeted the planting of the Union Jack on the east, the south, and the north. The day was apparently ours. But at 11.30 a large hostile column advanced against Craufurd, supported by the guns of the fortress. That turned the tide. At 2 o'clock Craufurd was compelled to replace the British standard by a flag of truce. He had received no support. The guns were decimating his force, and with 46 officers and 600 men he surrendered. Whitelocke, with the main body, was likewise repulsed with great loss. At sunset the defeat of the British was complete. They had lost 1000 killed and wounded, and 1000 prisoners. But 5000 or more still remained, independently of the naval force, and the Residency and other positions were still in British hands.

Liniers, again chivalrous, proposed the surrender of all prisoners, and the free embarkation of the British troops. The alcalde thought this course much too generous, and that the complete evacuation of the River Plate was essential. To this Whitelocke would not agree. On the 26th a quarter of an hour was given him to accept before the reopening of hostilities. The minutes sped. The Argentines attacked the Residency, and were repulsed with heavy loss. Still all might have been retrieved, but Whitelocke sent a flag of truce to accept Linier's conditions. In the evening the convention was signed, and in two months the British evacuated the River Plate.

What their ill-directed swords failed to accomplish their ships and their merchants have since won. Ten Republican flags float over South America, instead of the Union Jack. But British capital has developed, and is developing, the continent, and the energy of British merchants has effected the peaceful conquest of an El Dorado for British trade.

The following letter from Major-General Sir Edmund du Cane, K.C.B., from the letters of his father, of the 20th Light Dragoons, will be read with interest on this subject.

Queen's Gate Gardens, 24 April, 1894.

MY DEAR VINCENT,—I return with many thanks the Whitelocke Court-Martial and the companion novel "Ponce de Leon." I am very glad to learn all about those British transactions in South America, which are so little mentioned in histories that one knows nothing of them. My father's regiment, the 20th Light Dragoons, was detached from the Cape after its capture with some others, 38th and 54th I think, at Beresford's request when he found his force insufficient. But he surrendered the day this relief left the Cape, as they afterwards found. They landed and took Maldinaldo, a little way from Monte Video, and when Sir S. Auchmuty came with his relief expedition they assaulted and took Monte Video. This led the Spaniards to march the 71st Highlanders, and the other prisoners captured in Buenos Ayres, up the country, intending to take them 600 or 700 miles.

When they had got about 100 miles, Beresford and Pack, the Colonel of the 71st, escaped. My father said the Spaniards treated their prisoners very badly, cut off their ears and used them as cockades. Whitelocke could have taken Buenos Ayres as Monte Video was taken, but he was not a man of capacity, as I judge from the court-martial. The 71st hated surrendering, and said they would rather die with arms in their hands. My father's account was that they surrendered with all the honours of war, and then the Spaniards took them prisoners.[1]

Yours truly,

E. DU CANE.

---

[1] The "Highland Light Infantry Chronicle" for 1894, the quarterly magazine of this glorious regiment, reproduces the Journal kept at Buenos Ayres in 1806 by Captain Pocockc of the 71st. It gives much interesting information, as does "Ponce de Leon," of which the hero is Lieut. Gordon, one of the prisoners, concerning a little known but eventful incident in British history.

III.

THE PARIS OF THE WEST.

Buenos Ayres, October 30th, 1893.

South America is a land full of surprises. The telegrams published in Europe led one to expect that the condition of Buenos Ayres would be anything but agreeable to a tourist. They spoke of revolutions, arrests, and general disturbance. Even the day before we were released from an utterly unnecessary quarantine the state of siege was prolonged for another sixty days. We were fully prepared therefore, to find everybody armed *cap-à-pie*, and all ordinary occupations and amusements suspended. But nothing of the kind. No one would know, from the appearance of things, that anything out of the common had taken, or was taking, place. There were no passport formalities to go through. The Customs House authorities were extremely polite and anxious to avoid giving trouble —indeed, too much so in the case of some of the passengers. The streets of Buenos Ayres were crowded with people, bright, gay, and full of life. They reminded one much of Bucharest. Successfully that little capital of Eastern Europe imitates Paris, Parisian life, Parisian habits. With equal, indeed greater, success Buenos Ayres does so in the Western world. By comparison, our large provincial cities of like population (500,000) are funereal. The shops are full of the latest novelties. There are great cafés and restaurants. Within 500 yards of each other an Italian opera, three French dramatic companies, and two Spanish theatres are each drawing crowded houses. Arcs of gas lamps across the street opposite the theatre doors make the causeway as light as day. There are as many minor music-halls as in London. But in one respect Buenos Ayres surpasses either its French prototype or our metropolis of five million people. The detection of crime, and its adequate punishment, may leave, indeed, much room for improvement. Not so, however, street decorum. After nightfall, disorder is strictly confined to a special quarter, well patrolled by police. Elsewhere a constable stands at each corner where four blocks meet of a hundred houses each. From quarter of an hour to quarter of an hour one "fixed point" whistles to the next "fixed point" that all is well with him. If he receives no answer, a horse is waiting patiently by the kerbstone, ready saddled and bridled, and he rides off to render assistance.

The pride of Buenos Ayres is, however, the Park of Palmero. Thither on Sundays and Thursdays everybody who is anybody resorts. If he has no carriage of his own he hires one—not a cab or greasy fly, but a really smart turn-out. Equipage after equipage tears along the Florida and the wide avenues leading to Palmero. It looks as if life itself depended upon getting there first. In "the drive" three pair or five rows of carriages crawl along at a foot's pace, the ladies, in smart toilettes, doing credit to their natural beauty, and not a few men, too, taking the air in a close brougham. On special evenings the park is lighted by electricity, and the carriage carnival is prolonged.

Every Sunday there are races, and very well managed, too. The horses are, for the most part, descended from English blood, many of the best being bred by Mr. Kemmis, on his 18,000 acre "estancia" at Las Rosas. The betting is all by "Pari mutuel," under official management. There is said to be a good deal of foul play among the jockeys, all natives, and on this account the large British sporting population in the Argentine capital sticks to polo, cricket, tennis, and football. It mingles, indeed, but very little, if at all, with the Argentines, either in athletics or society. In some ways this is to be regretted; in others it is a good thing. It places a barrier which might be often lifted to mutual advantage, but maintains the individuality of race which has had so powerful an influence on the good name of Britain in foreign climes. Argentine society is attractive in many ways. The men are generous, hospitable, and prodigal in their expenditure, when they have any money, and possibly more so when they have none but what they have borrowed. They are, more than in Europe, the lords of creation. This affinity with the East is found in other directions. The ladies are handsome, well dressed, and well behaved, enjoying little freedom as girls, and not much more as wives. A feeling is springing up against this, but it is not making much headway. The depression is a useful excuse, for ladies' amusements are expensive. Of the depression one is reminded by unfinished palaces and unfinished public works. The walls were put up at the time of boom. Then came the crisis and the crash. The workmen were taken off, and the bricks alone remain as monuments of madness. One piece of enforced economy is to be regretted, namely, the stoppage of street paving. The granite roadway of the narrow streets is in the most lamentable condition, painfully cruel to the brave little horses drawing the crowded tramcars, agonizing for those who take any other conveyance. The pavements are fairly good, but they are so crowded that people have practically to walk in single file, and the noise from the vehicles is deafening. I have mentioned the exclusiveness of the English (over 5000 in number), with their Hurlingham Club, and other physical associations. Perhaps it is partly founded on the great distance between the suburbs of Flores, Quilmes, and Belgrano, all equally popular. But the insularism is not confined to sport and games. It finds valuable vent, also, in a pretty church and an admirably-managed British hospital. But there is one game in high favour in Argentine circles, a manly one, and pretty to see. It is the game of Pelota.

A long fives-court holds the four players, two on each side, severally armed with a long scoop-shaped basket or "cesta," fastened on the right hand at the wrist. It drives the ball at a tremendous pace, and the skill and activity involved are great. The betting is heavy, not only on the merit of the rival sides, but often on individual strokes, especially in the competition between six or more persons, playing two at a time, each missed stroke turning out the one in default. But for the size of the court required it would not improbably become a popular game in England. The Spanish professionals are in great favour, and receive large salaries. But it is said they are rarely able to play well after twenty-four years of age.

It will be seen that, despite revolutions, dictatorship, and martial law, Buenos Ayres is a pleasant place to live in. The evil tidings which make not a little sensation in

London are frequently learned by the residents from the European papers, when, three weeks old, they come to hand. A more difficult task it will be to make clear the causes underlying these commotions, which, however exaggerated, are ruinous to the country and fatal to the essential influx of capital and immigration.

IV.

ARGENTINE POLITICS.

Mendoza, November 7th, 1893.

It is a difficult task to understand Argentine politics. Men who have been years in the Republic give the most contradictory narratives. I will not, therefore, pretend to be able to weave an absolutely correct account of the present position of affairs from the tangled skein. But I have had the advantage of personal communication with the leading men of the several parties, and the most experienced of the foreign residents. I will try to give a general deduction from their views.

In the first place, it will be asked, What was the meaning of the "latest" revolution? The numerical definition is essential, for, unfortunately, the history of Argentina as an independent Republic is an almost continuous record of revolution and civil war. The same may, indeed, be said of its neighbours in South America. The Spanish dominion was no doubt oppressive, destructive of trade and progress. But, at all events, it gave the people subject to it a master, and prevented the endless striving of every man after power, which has been the cause of all these internal disturbances. Of parties now there are legion, surrounding each politician with tongue more fluent, or hand more adroit, than his fellows. The most prominent are known as Roquoistas, Juaristas, Mitristas, Trigogenistas, and Modernistas. I am sensible of having omitted many. No doubt Mulhall's "Dictionary of Statistics" enumerates them. But as the Representative House numbers only some seventy-two members, I think there must be some parties consisting of one man alone. What are the principles dividing these numerous groups of ambitious politicians? It would be difficult to explain otherwise than by a negative. It is not possible to gather what is the individual aim of any one party, which are the problems which separate them, beyond this:— power is the aim, tenure of office the governing principle. It is true that the Partido Nacional, now in office, embraces the Juaristas and Modernistas, of which the actual President of the Republic (or his son) is titular leader, as well as the followers of General Roca. They are termed the Conservatives, while the Union Civica is mainly manned by those known as Radicals.

The "latest" revolution was the work of the Radicals and their leader, one Dr. Alem—a greatly discredited personage. Programme they had none. General disorder was apparently their *mot d'ordre*, and herein they not a little resembled the Socialists and Radicals of England. They went about crying for vengeance against corrupt servants of the State, and herein they did well. But the means they adopted were more than suspicious. Happily, the energy of Dr. Quintana, the Minister of the Interior, was more than they bargained for, and although the cost was great—close on a million sterling—and the bill has yet to be paid, the storm never made serious headway. It is astonishing how lightly men talk in Argentina of revolutions, and how little attention they pay to them, lightly heeding that, although they rarely endanger life or property, being frequently little more than a street brawl, they are greatly magnified in passing through the cable to Europe, and greatly damage the credit and prosperity of the country. The reason for these frequent revolutions is not far to seek. One word expresses it—"Humanity." Far too few people are killed, far too few people are injured. This humanity causes a revolution to be regarded as a harmless amusement, a sort of theatrical parade or ballet. Still worse, those who have caused all the trouble for their own ends, even if they have at the moment been in military, naval, or civil employ, are rarely punished. The execution of persons guilty of a political offence is forbidden by the Argentine Constitution, and as wide an interpretation is given to the term "political offence" as by the apologists for the dastardly attempts of the Fenian dynamiters to murder innocent men, women, and children. The commanders of the two Argentine ships of war who recently sided with the revolutionists, and used their guns and men against the nation, were sentenced by court-martial to death. A few ladies sign the petition for clemency, invade the Chamber, carry it through the Lower House, and, of course, the President yields. He thinks that he may be in an analogous position some day, and one good turn will deserve another. Thus, so long as the revolutionist has nothing to lose and everything to gain, there will be revolutions.

This false "humanity" is not, however, the only cause. The other is an excessive army and navy. What in the world the Argentine Republic, with a native population of only about 2,090,000 of all ages and both sexes, wants with over 1400 naval and military officers, no man can conceive. Of course they have little to do besides enlivening the streets and restaurants with their exceedingly smart uniforms, and, as a necessary consequence, they give much attention to politics, or, rather, to the rivalry of parties. They have to be reckoned with by every Government, and hesitation about some pension or privilege might bring about an immediate revolution, and the chances of its temporary success are usually even. Argentina has no external enemies. Chili, Paraguay, Uruguay, and Brazil have far too much to think about at home, or are too weak. All Europe wishes peace and prosperity to the Republic, and too many Europeans and natives are interested in the country to permit aggressions by any single state. The best reform the Argentine Legislature could possibly institute would be a reduction by two-thirds of the army and navy. As it is, the 7000 men on a peace footing of the former, and the 34 ships of the latter, while of little use against the foreigner, are a perpetual menace to the internal welfare of the Republic.

The labour, too, of the men is lost to agriculture. They are of fair physique, docile—"better than their uniforms," said General Campos, the Minister of War, in response to a compliment on their appearance. The National Guard, having a paper strength of at least 500,000, would be ample for the defence of the country, if properly organized. That a reduction of the army and navy would be attended by a revolution goes without saying. But General Roca, formerly President, and the leading man in the country, could probably effect it. Unfortunately ill-health compels his retirement for the time from active political life. Not improbably the same cause may bring him ere long to England for rest and change. He should receive the warm welcome he deserves. His support of the present administration is essential to its existence. The President, Dr. Luis Saenz Peña, is an amiable man, with a rare reputation for honesty, but also for paying undue heed to the advice of a political son. He is not, moreover, a strong man, and has no knowledge of Europe. His election was accidental, and he has had, and has, a very difficult task in reconciling conflicting interests in his cabinet, guided by men of more ability and experience. His earliest effort was the exclusion of General Roca and his friends. The support, therefore, of General Roca at the present time is the more praiseworthy. That it is strong or enthusiastic is not to be pretended—indeed, it was described to me by the representative of a Continental Power as that of a "slanting pillar." It is given wholly in the interests of public order, for which the Minister of the Interior, Dr. Quintana, a statesman of great ability and much administrative power, is responsible. If a coalition Ministry could be formed, embracing General Roca, Dr. Pellegrini, with that other former President, the national historian, General Mitré, the proprietor also of the most influential newspaper, together with Dr. Quintana and Dr. Terry, the miscellaneous parties now undermining the interests of the State by their divergent views and individual ambitions might be absorbed. There is really nothing to divide them, and the necessity for political tranquility is so paramount that, if such a combination were possible, it would be the surest guarantee for the future of the country.

Unless this, or something analogous, is formed, no one can predict how long the present state of affairs will last. The existing Government is, doubtless, anxious to discharge its duty honourably. But whether it is strong enough to do so is an open question. There are not wanting causes of disturbance. Four provinces at the present time are being administered by the National Government through an Intervener, owing to the failure of the local administration. The need, too, of a steady course of administration is the greater, by reason of the composition of the people. The population for a land ten times the size of the United Kingdom is one fifth less than that of London.

Of the 4,000,000, no less than one-third are in the city and province of Buenos Ayres, covering only a twelfth of the area of the Republic. The foreigners and the children of foreigners equal, if they do not actually exceed, the native Argentines. They may be said to compose at least three-fourths of the commercial and industrial population, and the most valuable part of the landed interest is rapidly passing also into their hands. Hitherto foreigners have taken no part whatever in Argentine politics. They have left them entirely to the natives, the natives again leaving them almost entirely to a small section of the community, for the most part lawyers and others eager for spoil. There are many Argentine gentlemen of high character, wide culture, great intelligence, and large estate. They shun politics like the Plague. The vast majority of the native peasantry avoid them equally. They only want to be let alone, and do not care even to vote. Together these two classes, the Argentines of position and the Argentines of industry, with the foreign proprietors, merchants, tradesmen, and labourers, form a clear majority in the Republic. Provided the minority goes straight, the majority will be content to let it enjoy the sweets of office. But it is purely a question of time how long the majority will be content to be misgoverned by a minority, to have its business ruined, its debts unpaid, and general mistrust established.

The mistake of an over-zealous policeman—there have been a few lately at Santa Fé—a misdirected rifle, a few soldiers out of hand, or a party of marauding revolutionists, might bring about the change. No doubt a life or two would be lost; but the eventual gain would be great. England and Italy, Germany, France, and Spain have interests so great in Argentina in capital and men that, although content to allow the Republic to work out its own salvation, so long as Governments and revolutionists do not actively interfere with the foreign population and the peaceable pursuits of their callings, according to the Argentina Constitution, Europe could never allow any oppression to take place. In men, Italy is most concerned. There are in Argentina 700,000 Italians, and without them neither railway could be worked nor harvest gathered, nor cattle reared. There are 100,000 French—mostly shopkeepers, domestic servants, and shepherds. There are 100,000

Germans, mainly engaged in commerce. And there are 40,000 English, developing great tracts of land, furnishing brains and administrative power, and enabling the people to move from one end of the country to the other with the utmost facility. Behind these 40,000 British subjects are not less than 150,000,000*l.* of British money, which has made the country what it is. These are interests not to be neglected.

V.

ARGENTINE TRAVELLING IN 1827.

The following letter from the late Rt. Hon. Sir Harry Verney, Bart., written shortly before his death, aged ninety-two, gives an impression of Argentina in 1827.

Claydon House, Bucks,
December 28, 1893.

DEAR COLONEL HOWARD VINCENT,—I suppose that we were in the House of Commons together, and I therefore take the liberty of writing to you, my parliamentary life having been fifty-four years.

But before I was M.P. I made the journey which you describe in the *Globe* of Wednesday, the 27th, in circumstances different from yours. I had been ill from a sea voyage, without the riding and walking exercise to which I was accustomed in England, and my doctor advised a gallop on the pampa. I went from Rio to Buenos Ayres and Monte Video with that object. It was in 1827. After three or four pampas gallops, which restored my health, I was tempted to take a longer ride. I was warned against it by all at Monte Video and Buenos Ayres to whom I mentioned it. It was not the right time of year, it was impossible to cross the Andes blocked by snow, and travellers had been killed by the Indians which was the far greater danger. I replied I would see how far I could go, and that I should probably return in two or three days. Sir Woodbine Parish, who was either our Minister or Consul-General, was most kind in dissuading me. I was so fortunate as to find at Buenos Ayres a very intelligent, experienced guide, who had served under the Duke of Wellington —a Spaniard. The posts were five or ten or more leagues apart, each post house in a coral, round which was a broad, deep ditch and a small gun at each angle of the mud wall.

I recollect seeing one wall built of animals' heads; the mud wall could not be made to stand upright. Wild horses were caught. Every postmaster had three or four tropas of horses, each tropa 100 or 150 horses. When I arrived at a station the postmaster started off a Gaucho in the direction in which was a tropa. In half an hour, more or less, I used to see first the Gaucho's head in the perfectly clear atmosphere, his arm with the lasso, then the horses' heads, all galloping towards me. The postmaster drove into the coral a certain number of horses depending on the number of leagues to the next post house, and the number of my Gaucho party. The horses were very easy to ride, they seldom kicked or plunged. I rode many which had never been backed before. I always threw my poncho over the horse's head to blind him, while I forced the bit into his mouth and strapped my saddle on his back. When I jumped on his back holding the reins with the right hand, I pulled away the poncho from his head with the left.

My ride to Mendoza was, I believe, 1000 miles, and I think that I was fourteen or fifteen days. The postmaster used to tell me in which direction the Indians were supposed to be, and I always rode in a contrary direction. You speak of the summit of the Andes thirteen or fourteen thousand feet above the sea. I thought that it was 18,000. On the way I asked my guide how deep the snow was. He said 600 feet! Pray pardon this long letter.

Your faithful
HARRY VERNEY.

VI.

OVER THE CORDILLERA.

Santiago, November 10th, 1893.

The passage of the Andes is still somewhat of an event in South America. In winter it is a journey dangerous in itself, and at other seasons the discomforts surrounding it are great. Hence it is that so few persons in the Argentine have actually gone over the Cordillera. The native population is not much given to migration, and more especially when it is of a costly character. The foreigners in Argentina are not there for pleasure, and when opportunity for taking a holiday comes, they naturally prefer to go to Europe. These reasons make it exceedingly difficult to obtain exact information in Buenos Ayres as to the crossing of the Uspallata Pass, the best stopping places, and the precautions to be taken. There is, moreover, another reason, and that is the constant improvement of the route—the extension of the Transandine Railway, and the betterment of the accommodation. The experience of a couple of years ago becomes ancient history, interesting as a reminiscence, but valueless as a guide. We found ourselves, therefore, at Mendoza, so surfeited by the most contradictory counsels, that we were unable to decide which to adopt, and doubtful whether to believe any.

The first day's journey is simple enough. The Transandine Railway now takes passengers 100 miles on their way towards Chili. It runs two trains a week, along a smooth narrow gauge road—a triumph of engineering in not a few places. The first night has to be passed at Punte de Las Vacas, near which thousands of Argentine cattle, passing every year into Chili, rest awhile on their toilsome mountain tramp. The Transandine now lands its passengers six miles short thereof. In a month or so, Mr. Grant Dalton hopes to take travellers to the Inn itself. That will be a great convenience. But if the railway companies are going to make the Transandine route popular, they must do something more than provide two or three trains a week. They must enable their customers to obtain reasonable food and lodging. As it is, the hotel at Mendoza is a wretched affair, and the traveller is unfortunate who has to stay there more than a night. But it is a paradise compared to the wretched "posadas" on the Andean road. At Punte de Las Vacas the food is eatable, and the male and female dormitories, formed by mud walls, a mud roof, and a mud floor, have at least iron camp bedsteads. But at 7000 feet above the sea such "luxuries" are but scant preparation for an arduous journey. The Canadian Pacific has shown the way to open up a new country—that is by constructing the line, and putting up profitable hotels wherein to house travellers. The Transandine is more fortunately situated on the high road between two nations, the one largely dependent on the other for food.

From Punte de Las Vacas we had to start before the sun rose. The cumbré or summit of the Pass over the mountains was over twenty-five miles away, and it is scarcely possible to cross it after noon. In the middle of the day a violent gale usually blows, and often with such force that neither man nor beast can retain a foothold. The mules knew their way, and it was both impossible and futile to attempt to guide them in the dark. The sunrise was glorious, lighting up the snow-clad mountain peaks, one after the other, with a halo of glory. The absence of all vegetation and of animal life made the long ride, however, somewhat monotonous. One little bird accompanied us for hours. What misadventure brought it there was a mystery, and it appeared delighted to find another living thing. By seven o'clock we reached Puente del Inca, a natural bridge formed by rock, and near it some hot baths. The want of enterprise on the part of the railway became the more apparent as we looked into the hut, unable to produce even a cup of coffee, and much less breakfast. There was no alternative but to push on another three hours and a half to Las Cuevas. The road, fortunately, was fairly good, not too steep, and a couple of mules were able in most places to travel abreast. After riding seven hours, we naturally hoped for rest and refreshment before attempting to cross the Cumbré. But neither were obtainable, and the rising wind made the muleteers impatient of delay. The Argentine side of the Cumbré is very steep. But it presents no great difficulties. A zig-zag path, some six or eight inches wide, brings you to the summit in about two hours. True, it is like mounting a sugar-loaf. A fall would send both mule and rider thousands of feet to the bottom. But the sight at the top is an ample reward for all the toil, labour, and anxiety. It is magnificent and unequalled, as from a small level space, between 13,000 and 14,000 feet above the sea, you look upon giant mountain after giant mountain, mighty ravines, and impenetrable valleys, the atmosphere so clear that a dozen miles appear as a hundred yards.

We thought our troubles past now that we had safely surmounted the summit. But the worst was to come. The descent on the Chilian side is very steep, longer, and more precipitous than into Argentina. It was made far worse, also, by being deep in snow, which was totally absent from the heights over La Plata. The glare and rising wind were almost blinding, despite masks and glasses, and made it difficult to make out the narrow track of a preceding caravan, walled in on either side by several feet of snow. "Trust to your mule" is advice easy to give; but practice is necessary to follow it, and more especially coming down the side of a steeple, slipping here and sliding there, often sinking into a hole well over the knees. A man is more fortunately placed in the saddle than a woman, who has to meet the difficulties sideways. As one threads the narrow path, one says again and again : "How is it possible that two nations should be content in the present day to allow the communications between them to remain in this primitive state?" A very small sum would make and keep in repair a decent road. It is said that the matter is in contemplation. But the only signs of execution were on the part of the Englishman. The English have made and paid for the railroad between Buenos Ayres and Mendoza. The English have built the railroad from Mendoza towards the Andes. The English have made a considerable progress with a meeting railway on the Chilian side; and on the slopes of the Cumbré are vast quantities of material ready to carry out the bold plans of Mr. Baggallay and Messrs. Clark for a uniting tunnel so soon as the necessary capital is forthcoming A long ride it seems to Juncal, and when the twelve hours on mule back are over and the fifty kilomètres of the day's stage are accomplished, one feels that this passage of the Cordillera under present conditions is too physically exhausting, too hazardous, for pleasure. Nor is this view altered if you think to improve matters by going in a cart from Juncal to the Soldier's Leap. Those twenty miles down hill, over a narrow road, rocks and large stones constantly falling from the hills above into the foaming river below, and frequently resting on the road ledge, convey few agreeable reflections to the traveller. In four or five years, however, all this may be changed, and the sooner the better. If the Chilian Government guarantees the capital required for the completion of the railway, it is a guarantee which will be redeemed.

VII.

THE ENGLISH OF THE PACIFIC.

Coquimbo, Chili, November 16th, 1893.

The difference between Chili and Argentina is considerable. In the former one admires man, in the latter nature. This is speaking entirely from a practical point of view. So far as the picturesque is concerned, there is no comparison between the interminable plains of La Plata and the mountain scenery of Chili. Go where you will in Chili, from the frontier of Peru to Cape Horn, the Cordillera of the Andes form a background unrivalled in the world. In Argentina men can almost live without working, or, at any rate, by working so little as not to deserve the name of industry. In Chili laborious exertion is necessary for the sustenance of life. The necessary consequence is that in the Eastern continent there is idleness, apathy, and indifference, a disposition to leave things to take care of themselves, or to be developed by the foreigner. But on the narrow stretch of territory between the Andes and the Pacific, where floats for 2000 miles the Chilian flag, you find a sturdy independence and vigorous manhood. This strikes one almost as soon as you set foot in the country. Possibly the indifference of communication between East and West has not been without good effect.

Chili prides itself upon being the Eng'and of South America, and there is much in the comparison. Between Chili and her Republican neighbours there is a great gulf of character, in many respects as wide a one as between ourselves and the Greeks. We may well feel proud that Englishmen had not a little to do in the establishment of this vigorous state. O'Higgins and Cochrane, Arthur Prat and MacKenna are names justly held in reverence in Chili, and commemorated in street and statue. Nor are Englishmen exercising little influence now in Chili. I speak not of the 30,000,000*l.* of British money embarked in Chili, nor even of the great merchant houses which have made Valparaiso almost an English town, but of the sons of Englishmen who are to-day trusted leaders of the Republic. Edwards, Walker, Maciver, Ross are but a few of the British names in everyone's mouth. The Presidency of the Senate, the Leadership of both political parties, and many a place in the Legislature and the Civil Service of the State have fallen to them, not as Englishmen—for many of them have forgotten their fathers' tongue,—but as worthy Chilians.

The size, the wealth, the luxury of Buenos Ayres took one by surprise. Santiago de Chile is even more surprising. It enjoys none of the advantages of the Argentine capital in maritime position, as a great centre of import and export. Its trade is comparatively small, its foreign population insignificant. But wide streets, flanked with trees, large squares, fine public buildings, heroic statuary, the most splendid boulevard in the world, doubling in length and breadth " Unter den Linden " at Berlin, are calculated to fill the Argentine with envy. Best of all, this result has been achieved by independent effort, and not from the misapplication of unpaid loans from a too-confiding foreigner. There are, no doubt, defects in the Chilian, as in the English, character. Perfection is probably still very distant from her national and municipal institutions. But in South America the Chilian Government and the Chilian character stand upon an oasis. Alone among the daughters of Spain, alone even among the Republics of the world, has Chili anything approaching an independent Constitutional Government, responsible to the voice of the people. Her senators and deputies, and even the municipal councillors of the capital, are unpaid. They give their services, as in England, to the service of the nation, and a Parliamentary majority alone determines the tenure of office. We see, then, a republic formed, not on the model of the United States, which has produced such evil effects on the southern Continent, but a republic formed upon the English example, the Sovereign being substituted by an elected President. This one difference has been the source of Chili's greatest trouble, which gave her progress a blow, the effects of which are but too apparent at home and abroad.

No dispassionate person could travel through South America and not come to the conclusion that almost the worst monarch must be better than a system under which one man after another plunges nations into ruin and scatters broadcast distress and desolation that either in his own person, or that of his son, or that of his nominee, he may continue to hold the power he has once tasted as head of the State. This is practically the history of the infinity of revolutions which have afflicted South America since the time of the nominal independence of her several states. This was the story of Balmaceda, which read Chili a lesson so severe. The Chilian resistance to the Dictator was not a revolution as in the neighbouring republics. It was simply the resistance of the Parliamentary party to a Presidential autocracy. But as in freedom from internal quarrels, Chili has occupied an unique position in South America, so did she stand alone when fighting commenced. Argentines and Brazilians, Peruvians and Uruguayans, play at revolutions as at chess, and the only harm done is to their credit at the hands of cable manipulators. When, however, Chilian fought with Chilian he fought with that tenacity of character and firmness of purpose which distinguishes him from his neighbours. There were real bombardments and real battles, involving great destruction of property and vast loss of life. This riveted European attention the more upon the Chilian Civil War, and the memory thus planted is not to be lightly uprooted. It is not, however, easy to find any nation more united within itself at the present time, and no one could possibly be better fitted than President Montt to preserve this position of affairs. He is not a politician, probably he is not a statesman. His only desire is to be a constitutional head of the State so long as he can usefully serve in that capacity to the satisfaction of the nation. Of Liberal tendencies, he is indifferent to party, and did not hesitate the other day to honour the memory of a deceased Conservative Minister. I can liken him to no one so well as to the late Lord Iddesleigh. Of most modest demeanour, of most modest form of living, you see the President walking quietly in the Alameda, and say Chili is fortunate.

Nor is the similarity to England confined to form of government, and the connection with England by blood. It extends even to political parties in name and dividing line. There is the Conservative party led by the eloquent tongue of Señor Carlos Walker, with its dead hero, Portales, like Lord Beaconsfield in opinions and in some degree in face. As we sat in a box at the Municipal Theatre at Santiago, crowded from floor to ceiling, and saw the bust of Portales crowned on his first centenary with laurel by grateful dames, it was a Primrose League demonstration at Covent Garden for country, religion, and liberty. The Chilian Conservatives divide with Chilian Liberals as nearly as possible the voting strength of the country. They have the unbroken support of the Established Church of Rome in the most Catholic and religious country I have ever visited, and directed by an Archbishop of not less tact than skill. Upon the other hand, the Liberals hold most of the provincial offices, and although the President is determined, so far as he can, to prevent official interference with elections, and has not hesitated, despite his kindly nature, summarily to dismiss more than one offender of high degree, it is probable that in many places during the elections next March custom will prove stronger than innovation. The result of the election is, therefore, a matter of considerable doubt, and is looked forward to with great interest. The main question at issue is that of the Established Church. Clerical influence has undoubtedly been too strong, and is, many think, too strong still. The Radicals would disestablish the Church altogether, and cut off the annual subsidy it now receives of some 600,000 paper dollars. The Liberals would reduce it. The Conservatives support the old order—but as regards many of them, half-heartedly and with misgiving. Under these circumstances it is not improbable that a negative conclusion may be the result, and this will lead to a continuation of a Coalition Ministry as at present. It is well constituted under Señor Montt, a cousin of the President, as Minister of the Interior. Among its ablest members is Señor Venturo Blanco Viel, the Minister for Foreign Affairs, and it may well be hoped that under any circumstances his return to the Moneda, or Government House, is assured.

Rumours have of late been current in England of hostility on the part of Chili to foreign enterprise. It is not possible to ascertain that they have any basis of truth. The Chilians are anxious to do all that they possibly can for themselves, and to give employment to their own countrymen whenever possible. They cannot be blamed for that. The State owns the railways, and although they might be managed with greater profit and greater comfort by private enterprise, they give fair facilities for travel at economical rates. The tram lines in Santiago and Valparaiso are Chilian owned, and worked far better than in many other places—women conductors having among other things sensibly augmented the receipts. There are Chilian steamship lines, mines, breweries, and factories yielding handsome profits. But it is recognized that without European, and particularly English, help, capital will be lacking, and there is not the slightest indication that any step will be taken to destroy that confidence which has up to a very recent period been felt, not only in Chilian development, but in Chilian integrity.

VIII.

THE NITRATE FIELDS OF CHILI.

Pisagua, November 21st, 1893.

Ten millions sterling of British private capital! This is the sight we have just witnessed upon the Chilian desert. When, however, one speaks of the Chilian desert, it is of a region infinitely more productive of wealth than the most fertile district. These hills and valleys of arid sand, giving life to neither bird nor tree nor plant, which stretch for hundreds of miles along the western shores of South America, are rich in gold, in silver, and in copper, in sulphur and other products of the earth, but most of all in nitrate of soda and the productions therefrom. Many mines and fields have been worked and exhausted; many are being worked; many more remain to be discovered and developed. These deserts form, moreover, but the glacis thrown up from the bed of the Pacific to pave the road for future generations to tread towards the hidden resources of Bolivia and the almost unexplored regions of the interior.

The city of Iquique is proud of its wooden cathedral, its wooden theatre, its wooden houses, and the level roadway along the beach, whereon 20,000 people declare in evening walk that there are worse places to live in than this capital city of the rainless coast and the nitrate world. The freedom from rain saves them, indeed, from the troubles of the tropics in the Eastern Hemisphere. That damp heat which elsewhere renders movement a torture and life unendurable within the region of Capricorn is absent from the desert shore. The days are hot, but the nights are fresh and cold, and European children thrive here when from Asia they have to be sent home. Iquique lives, it is true, upon imported produce. Everything has to be brought from the south—even earth for the treasured flower of the English lady. But the supply of goods is plentiful over a waveless ocean. Water itself was for long dependent upon steamer carriage, but now English ingenuity and enterprise have brought down a plentiful supply from the bosom of the desert itself. To that same universal agency is practically due the city of Iquique, or, at least, everything conducing to its present prosperity.

First and foremost comes, assuredly, the Nitrate Railway —a triumph of engineering in itself; a triumph of good management in the hands of Mr. Griffin. Without the Nitrate Railway the nitrate fields could never have been developed, and although one can well sympathize with the nitrate owners competing keenly with each other against the high charges upon their goods, account should in fairness be taken of the hazardous nature of the undertaking in which investors sank their savings, the heavy expenses attendant upon a line with such steep gradients upon a soft foundation, and the years past of unremunerative labour. Perhaps more conciliation might have been advantageously shown in the adjustment of rates, and more account have been taken of the difficulties under which many of the nitrate fields are now labouring. But it is to be regretted that the Chilian Government should have thrown all its weight against the railway, and, interpreting after its own reading the conditions under which the two millions or so of capital was furnished, be lavishly distributing competing concessions. Such action can hardly fail adversely to affect fresh applications for funds from the London market, and make British investors in South America far more cautious than they have been in the past. Industrial development must be always a hazardous quantity, and if an exclusive privilege granted at one time is to be withdrawn, not on a legally declared "lapsus," but at the whim of a subsequent Presidential authority, the supposed monopoly is worth nothing at all as a security. It is possible that one or two of the works in the nitrate district may be able to provide for themselves a cheaper means of reaching the ocean than they at present possess. But it will be rather by temporary and transferable means than by an elaborate or permanent line. The conveyance of nitrate is, and will always be, the only source of income, and how long that nitrate will be obtainable from existing sources is a matter of pure conjecture. The enthusiast will declare the reserves equal to his lifetime—and that, indeed, may be long, but will probably be short. Of course, there may be a certain amount of stores to convey to the works, but the wants of the workers are few; and they are little tempted to travel, even by the nominal charge of a few shillings for the length of the whole of the present system of over 126 miles.

The Nitrate Railway serves about 300,000 acres of saltpetre ground. Thirty years ago they were estimated to contain some 63,000,000 tons of saltpetre, which, at the then rate of consumption, should last the world over a thousand years. But since then the world has changed. Its demand for nitrate has been enormously increased, and the Chilian Government, eager for the large export duty it levies of about 2*l.* 12*s.* 6*d.* a ton, or 2*s.* 4*d.* per quintal of 100 lbs., according to the rate of exchange, is anxious to force it upon a somewhat unwilling public at any price, regardless of the permanency of supply. Long ago the Indians recognized the agricultural value of nitrate, and in the beginning of the century half-a-dozen "oficinas" or works were established on the desert mountains of Tarapacà. In 1852 Mr. George Smith came out from Norwich to develop the industry, and by 1870 there were eighteen mills working, of which four were owned by Englishmen. By 1875 there were between forty and fifty. Peru, then Mistress of the Province and Queen of the Desert, saw the production increase, and with it the demand. The annual sale exceeded 4,000,000 quintals, and was evidently capable of being greatly increased. The Republic determined to turn trader, and expropriated the "oficinas," many of which were owned by Chilians, granting certificates of compensation. Fatal resolution! It lost the province. Within four years a pretext for war was found, and within three months of its declaration the nitrate fields passed for ever into the hands of Chili. The Peruvian certificates of indemnity sold for little or nothing. A title for 1000 silver sols, or over 180*l.*, found with difficulty a purchaser at Lima for 30*l.* But upon that depreciated foundation arose one of the most remarkable monuments of personal success within the generation.

Timely knowledge of the intention of the Chilian Government to honour the certificates by a re-grant of the lands they represented, with fortuitous financial aid to courage and foresight, were the steps from a lowly level to the throne of the so-called "Nitrate King." Largely under his auspices some 10,000,000*l.* of British money have been laid out in the nitrate fields of Chili. There are now over fifty works for the production of nitrate of soda, and half of them are in British hands, and others again in the hands of foreigners. This is not regarded with favour in the centres of Chilian patriotism, where it is forgotten that, although the Chilian has many virtues, although he is brave and laborious, quick-witted and eager, the possession of capital is not among them. If the foreigner has laid out millions in Chili, some of which may be productive, but many of which he will never see again, it has been on the faith of the honour of Chilians, whom the turnover of those vast sums has so greatly benefited. But for these investments of British money the nitrate industry would never have risen to its present condition, and production and knowledge would be far behind the existing standard.

What is a nitrate mill or oficina? To the slopes of the desert hill the "caliche," or raw material, is brought by mule cart or tram line. It has been dug out laboriously by blast and pick and shovel. Time was when it lay near at hand, but now the older works are approaching the further confines of their properties, and soon will begin the struggle for new grounds, now held by the Government. By tilt or other apparatus the crushing-machine is fed, and the product then passes to the boiling vats. In due time the sluices are opened, and down the pipes the charged liquor runs to the precipitating tanks. Thence, after the lapse of days, is taken the nitrate of soda, which, packed in bags of 300 lbs. each, is ready for export to fertilize more fertile fields. From the liquor again iodine is obtainable by due process, and the admixture of sulphur.

The staff of a nitrate oficina is not large. The manager and the heads of departments are usually of the nationality of the owners, and they live a comfortable, patriarchal life in a large roomy house at a fair distance from the works, dispensing hospitality generously, and enjoying not a little social intercourse with friendly neighbours. The workmen are Chilians, Bolivians, and Indians. They receive extraordinarily high wages, often 15*l.* or 16*l.* a month on piece work, and, as a rule, spend their earnings recklessly. Houses are provided for them, usually formed by a few sheets of corrugated iron, but they are more than sufficient shelter in the perpetual summer, and the most elementary rules of European cleanliness are almost impossible of enforcement. The desert provides no shops, and if it were not for the "oficina" store, the workman and his family would be able to obtain nothing. It may be a source of profit to the mill, and by charging goods against wages the " truck system " may be adopted. But it ensures some comfort at least to the housewife, and such is the demand for labour in excess of the supply that fair treatment is assured by natural process, notwithstanding that combination among the manufacturers which so exercises the Chilian official mind. Its object is the regulation of the output, and the development of consumption. These objects appear not only excusable, but absolutely essential in the common interest, and especially in the face of an export duty exceeding the cost of production. The merits of nitrate of soda can only be brought home to agriculturists by organized effort, and a wholesale output upon an unappreciative market can only prematurely exhaust the sources of supply, at a heavy loss to all concerned, except the receivers of the export duty, which amounted to 2,000,000*l.* in 1892, and should, unless evil counsels prevail, form a permanent source of income to the Santiago Treasury for many years yet to come. Unfortunately that profit to the Chilian Government is not shared by all those interested in the score or more of British nitrate companies. The majority of the shareholders are very distant from the nitrate fields, and had no idea of the proportion between the price paid for a property and its real value. The shares stand at 50 per cent. discount, and that probably represents a far more correct valuation. Even as it is, the business would appear to be overdone, and mills succeed mills far too quickly in a small area for large profits to be drawn. Everything depends, moreover, upon the extent of the unworked ground available, and this is a matter of speculation. As it is, there appears to be little. comparatively speaking, within the present radius, for nitrate caliche is fickle, and will have nothing to do with valleys or mountain summits in its choice of a home, but lies alone on hill slopes, most of which have now the appearance of having been overturned by a human earthquake. What is wanted is the geological chemist who will discover new zones or the means of producing more from the ground still available.

IX.

PERU AND THE PERUVIANS.

Pyta, December 1st, 1893.

It is affirmed by some enthusiasts, in spite of Columbus, that the riches of Solomon were drawn from Peru. However that may be, neither Inca nor Spaniard, neither Chilian nor Peruvian has in any sense exhausted them. The real development of the country has indeed yet to begin. The guano deposits, which yielded such enormous returns, may be in large measure exhausted. The nitrate fields of Tarapacà have gone for ever to the victorious arms of Chili. But Peru of its continental neighbours, has made least use of silver, and of copper, inexhaustible oil wells, vast regions for the production of tobacco, sugar, cotton, indiarubber, coffee, all the products of the tropics. There is only one obstacle to their being successfully worked, and that obstacle is Peru herself. The South American home of Castilian beauty, the seat of the purest Castilian dialect, Peru, with greater advantages than almost any of its continental neighbours, has made least use of them, and been even more distracted by internal troubles, the rivalry of presidential factions and political revolutions. The present time is no exception to the general rule. " Liberty, equality, and fraternity" are preached upon the platform and placarded upon banners, but stoutly denied in the street. The military despotism of Russia is mild compared to that of Peru. The streets of Lima are alive with red trousers and gold lace. Some two thousand officers with over 300 colonels constitute the "unemployed," and they are a far greater political danger and social trouble to Peru than the listless audiences on Tower Hill to England. The army is neither large nor formidable to a foreign foe. It has shown courage, but has always been outflanked. Its pay is small, and not paid. Its physique is indifferent, its equipment worse. The barracks of the capital are in a woeful plight, without a pane of glass. But at the street corners stand drowsy sentries, before the doorways of quiet citizens march patrols, ready on the slightest provocation to use their weapons against Peruvians. A recent review was made the occasion of a political demonstration. Four battalions marched past the President of the Republic, and went through half a dozen movements. The officers were given champagne; the men brandy. Addresses followed from his present Excellency, and the President Anterior, who placed him on "the throne," and who intends to succeed him. The troops marched back, shouting wildly for General Cacéres, and threw up their caps under the feet of his horse. He led them bravely in the Chilian war, but not to victory. His skill is reputed greater in the exercise of the financial opportunities of the Presidency than in the field. But the army, employed and unemployed, paid and unpaid, adores him, and looks to him for better times, and he is the military candidate for the succession of the actual President, his former subordinate and nominee, Colonel Bermudez.[1]

A few people, who were outraged by the spectacle of the garrison converting a review into a political demonstration and by public servants usurping the functions of the electorate, ventured, in answer to the "vivas" of the troops, to call the name of "Pierola." Señor Nicholas de Pierola is the Democratic candidate, and one with an equal public record. He has headed two revolutions, and been for a time Dictator. In a moment the city was placed under martial occupation. Strong parties occupied all the approaches to the Central Square in front of the Government Buildings, and no Peruvian was allowed to enter it. Between these two candidates for the Presidency, vacant in the middle of 1894, the struggle will wage fast and furious. There will be many encounters in many places, many arrests, many whippings, much tampering with personal liberty, and much illegality. The third candidate put forward by the Union Civica, Señor Mariano Nicholas Valcaved, President of the Chamber of Deputies, will not be a serious competitor. The Congress will be anxious to elect him, but a timely pretext will be found to dissolve it. In the rivalry between Cacéres and Pierola

---

[1] Since deceased.

there will be not a few individual sufferers. But the greatest sufferer of all will be the nation—Peru and her outside reputation. It is probable that the military party, assisted by all the influence of the Government agents throughout the country, will prove triumphant, and succeed in bringing about the re-election of General Cacéres. It is a result which need not be regretted by those abroad, who are interested in the prosperity and tranquillity of the Republic. The probability is that the success of Señor Pierola, although more popular with the people, would lead to much greater disturbance, and the more, having in view the strength and sentiments of the military party. General Cacéres will also afford a greater guarantee for a strong Government, and what Peru wants more than anything else is a strong Government. The Peruvian is amiable and generous, fond of amusement, and indolent, submitting to anything at the hands of authority, if authority is stable.

General Cacéres is, moreover, a man of travel, who knows that without foreign capital and enterprise Peru can do little or nothing for Peruvians. He is able to gauge at its proper value the irresponsible grumbling against the domination of the foreigner, and himself largely concerned, when formerly President, in the acceptance by the Republic in 1890 of the arrangements proposed by Mr. Michael Grace, Lord Donoughmore, and Mr. Eyre on behalf of the Peruvian Corporation, is likely to further their being loyally carried out. No country ever got rid of its foreign debt upon such favourable terms. Peru owed, for capital and accrued interest, upwards of 50,000,000*l.*, mainly to England. The Peruvian Corporation assumed the responsibility of the whole on approved terms, and gave Peru at the same time the benefit of an admirable administration of the railways and other property conceded in return. The choice of an Administrator-General was fortunate. In Mr. Clinton Dawkins, formerly of Her Majesty's Treasury, the bondholders have a representative who has commended himself to Peruvians as much by his ability, perseverance, and zeal on behalf of the common interest as by his personal tact. It will be most unfortunate for all concerned if any interruption should come in the Administration. There have, of course, been many and serious difficulties with the Government. But they are in a fair way of being satisfactorily settled. If, on the one hand, the Corporation is obliged to recognize that passing depression and temporary circumstances prevent Peru from meeting in full the stipulated annual payment of 80,000*l.* a year from the customs receipts in Callao, the Government sees, on the other, that it cannot, in justice, call upon the Corporation to expend the further capital it undertook to spend under a more auspicious condition of things, mutual compromise will be of mutual benefit. The time may be long, but it must come eventually, when the country will be able quietly to develop its great resources, and when by a prompt recognition of existing obligations and political quietude, the immigration of men and money will be considerable. Then the Peruvian Corporation will justify the hopes of those who founded it. In the meantime, its property is in first-rate order. The railways, despite the extraordinary engineering difficulties under which they labour, in the passage of the Cordillera in the Centre and the South, are in excellent condition—the permanent way good, the rolling stock sound, and the stations, to many of which are wisely attached excellent hotels, far better than on many other British lines in South America. The Oroya road is probably the most marvellous railway in the world. In 106 miles it rises on an ordinary gauge by a gradient of $3\frac{1}{2}$ to 4 per cent. without rack, pinion, or other system, to a height of nearly 16,000 feet above the level of the sea at the starting-point of Callao. It turns in this adventurous flight backwards and forwards upon itself times without number, describes " C's,'" " S's," and " V's " repeatedly, runs through half a hundred tunnels hewn out of tremendous mountains of rock, skirts precipices upon precipices, and traverses many a torrent. 40,000*l.* a mile was the price to Peru of this extraordinary work. When the Peruvian Corporation succeeded to the heritage, the line stopped at Chicla, 12,000 feet high. The track was in bad order, and unless it was pushed over the Andean summit towards the valleys of the Amazon could never be made productive. A million has been spent, and well spent, in repairs, on the extension, and in adapting the engines for Pacific petroleum instead of sea-borne coal. Mr. J. L. Thorndike, a Canadian, was the engineer, Mr.

M. S. Grace the contractor. The summit is breasted at 15,665 feet, and the line runs already for 30 miles to Oroya in the direction of the Amazon. It takes time to kill the competition of pack horse, mule, llama, and donkeys, costing little to buy and little to keep. But by an easy hand for a time, at least in the matter of rates, eventual success is certain. A large agricultural export to the rainless coast of the Pacific may be confidently expected to augment a growing mineral traffic. The population along the line is small, it is true, but little by little the people of Callao and Lima, and more especially the many visitors thereto passing north and south, will reap all the health and enjoyment that an extraordinary railroad offers in a land of perpetual spring.

X.

VENEZUELA AND ENGLAND.

Caracas, Christmas Day, 1893.

Venezuela is from several points of view an exception among her Republican sisters on the Spanish Main. In the first place, the country, in at least the metropolitan and accessible districts of the nine States, is extremely beautiful. Mountain succeeds mountain, and valley follows upon valley. In the second place, Venezuela alone has a gold and silver coinage, well designed, cast from vast indigenous stores of precious ore, and of equivalent value to the sovereign in the major piece, and to a franc in the minor. But the greatest exception of all is that Venezuela is "not in friendship with Great Britain." Fortunately, at most, one in ten millions of the Queen's lieges is aware of the fact, or the national trepidation might be great. This state of affairs has prevailed, however, for nearly seven years. It was on the 20th of February, 1887, that the Venezuelan Government wrote to the British Minister accredited to the Republic:—"Great Britain has progressively increased her own advances from the Essequibo to the Pomaron, the Moroco, the Waini, the Barima, and the Amacuro. Great Britain has therefore violated the rights of sovereignty and the independence of Venezuela. Venezuela must not preserve relations of friendship with a nation which has thus offended her, and in consequence suspends them from this day."

The British Minister, therefore, took his leave, and since that time British interests have been under the charge of the German Envoy. Fortunately for us, the Emperor William is represented at Caracas by a diplomatist of rank, fortune, and ability—Count Kleist, whose consort, the life and soul of the capital, is now endeavouring to build a Protestant Church. There are still, strange to say, some unbelievers in the visual fact the world over that "Trade follows the flag." The saying speaks for the "flag of sovereignty" alone. But it appears to be true also of the flag on the roof-top of a British Legation. Certain it is that since it was hauled down in Venezuela, British subjects and British trade have left, and been replaced by German. Five hundred Germans control the main channels of business, and more are coming. German competition is often exaggerated. But here, as in Guatemala, it is very real in its monopoly. There are two exceptions, however. The harbour at La Guayra was formed by an English company, and is managed by it. The railway breasting the 4000 feet from the sea to the capital in a wonderful circuit of 23 miles cut out of the precipitous mountain side, is also due to England, and a triumph of engineering. The railway to Valencia, on the other hand, is German. The concessionaire was Herr Krupp, and Essen made the rails, wheels, and axles. The capital was found by the Deutsche Bank and another. It passes through 80 tunnels on a 3 per cent. grade in its 70 miles or so. A great work, indeed, but not one to be interested in financially, despite the 7 per cent. guarantee—punctually "paid" according to South American rule.

But to return to the iniquities of Great Britain in "violating the sovereignty and independence of Venezuela." Where are the Pomaron, the Moroco, the Waini, the Barima, and the Amacuro to which we have "progressively advanced"? The Treaty Department of the Foreign Office has them marked on the wall. They are known in the great and thriving colony of British Guiana—the size of the United Kingdom—now so well administered by Sir Charles Cameron Lees. But elsewhere few British subjects know them by name, or could describe the course of the rivers they represent. They are all, however, well within the frontier line of British Guiana, as surveyed in 1841 by the engineer Schomburg, and it is rather Venezuela who has "progressively advanced" in her claims to the British territory, acquired from the Dutch by the Treaty of 1814. This frontier line is actually in British possession, and, whatever they say at Caracas, neighbouring Venezuelans are perfectly contented and happy that it should be so. Above all, there can be no surrender of the right claimed a

T

century ago, and re-affirmed by Lord Rosebery in 1886, to free navigation for the British flag on the Orinoco. This river, which was entered by Sir Walter Raleigh in 1585, is the second great water artery in South America. It is surpassed by the Amazon alone, is 20 miles wide at the mouth, opposite Barima Point on British territory, and is navigable certainly for 800 miles of its course. The Orinoco is fed by 436 rivers, leading to forests of wealth, as yet untrodden save by the Indian, and which we may well develop in friendly partnership. But, short of this, assuredly England would be glad to adjust any minor points of difference with Venezuela, and to see official concord again added to actual good will. The first step, of course, must be the renewal of diplomatic relations. This can only be done by the Government of the new President—General Crespo—conveying a distinct wish to that end, and a willingness to receive a new British Minister with especial and befitting cordiality. This is very desirable, as much from the Venezuelan point of view as our own.

Venezuela adjoins British Guiana for many hundreds of miles. This must be, whatever the exact boundary. But the Republic is also only, so to say, a stone's throw from another prosperous and bounteous British colony. By way of Trinidad alone can her northern citizens reach the banks of the Orinoco in anything like comfort and safety. A great emporium for trade is therefore Port of Spain, on the Gulf of Paria, approached by the narrow passage of "The Dragon's Mouth."

The Venezuelan revenue is mainly fiscal. That shows good sense. But the tariff is not framed on sensible lines. Sugar and articles of native growth are prohibited. In default of proper means of manufacture, native consumers fare very badly. On other goods the duty is enormous. The result is that sensible Venezuelans are alleged to have kept back the dues as long as possible, by holding their consignments from Europe in the warehouses of Trinidad until they were actually wanted. Possibly now and again an unpaid Venezuelan Custom-house official mis-read or forgot the text of the tariff. To meet this loss, real or imaginary, to deal a nasty blow at Trinidad, and another at Curaçoa, belonging to Holland, and analogously situated on the Atlantic seaboard, Venezuela imposed an additional tax of 30 per cent. upon all imports from the colonies, in the Atlantic, of any European Power. On the surface, France, Spain, and Denmark were affected as well as England and Holland. But as the colonies of the three former nations did no trade with Venezuela, the effect fell solely on Trinidad and Curaçoa. Most of all it affected Trinidad. This was in 1881. A vigorous Chamber of Commerce lost no time in protesting, and in invoking the prompt action of the Imperial Government. Protest has followed protest. The duties were imposed on May 3rd, 1882, and to this hour remain in force. Although one would not think it, from the stiff and brief despatches of the Colonial Office to the colony, Downing Street was not inactive. More than twelve years ago the Venezuelan Ministry was told by Sir Charles Mansfield that " Her Majesty's Government object to the application of the law, and that it was in contravention of the commercial engagement of 1834, which adopted and confirmed the Treaty of April 18th, 1825."

This ought to have been enough to bring about the rescindment of the impost—although general nominally, of British application almost entirely. But words are not followed in these days of peace by that persuasion which is legitimate when " right speaks with might." The trade of Trinidad with Venezuela fell off 70 per cent. In 1889, " Her Majesty's Government will not fail to take advantage of any opportunity favourable for putting an end to the present unsatisfactory state of affairs." But still the matter drifts on, to the mutual disadvantage of both Venezuela and Trinidad. Happily, the Minister for Foreign Affairs at Caracas is now a courteous statesman, Señor Don Rojas. He sees how unfortunate is the present condition of affairs. He sees that without British representation in Venezuela there can be no real development of the riches of his country by British capital, that without the advent of common sense, fair play, and respect for treaty engagements in the matter of trade with the British Empire, and every portion of it, but especially with Trinidad, there cannot be even an approach to a settlement of the boundary question, so vital to Venezuela. May Señor Rojas be able to exert a just influence over the President-elect and his colleagues, and by necessary, but in no sense humiliating, overtures, re-establish "the relations of friendship" with Great Britain, broken so ill-advisedly, to his country's injury, by General Guzman Blanco.

That ex-presidential autocrat and spoliator is now an exile from Venezuela. The provinces, towns, and streets named after him have been re-christened. High above Caracas is a so-called Hill of Calvary. High on "Calvary" stood a colossal statue of Guzman Blanco. The people threw it down, and pounded the pieces to powder. So may it be with his Act of "the suspension of friendship with Great Britain." Then up the hundred circular steps facing that Hill of Calvary will come each afternoon, with even lighter tread than now, the unofficial and octogenarian representative in Caracas of Great Britain. For nearly forty years Mr. Middleton served his country at foreign Courts. When, a quarter of a century ago, a pension was the reward of fidelity, Mr. Middleton, who knew every climate in the world, declared that of Caracas to be the best—a perpetual May, and yet so little visited from steaming Port of Spain—and there he would remain. His resolve has been faithfully kept and full of advantage to the pretty little capital. By his instrumentality in large measure is due many a good work, and not least of all a Society for the Prevention of Cruelty to Animals—a terrible need in South America, as well as the presence of a magnificent band twice a week on the marble-paved "Plaza." In the centre thereof is the statue of "Bolivar the Liberator," mounted on the fiery iron steed which does like duty in many a South American capital for many a Republican hero.

XI.

THE WEST INDIES.

"A Triumph of British Administration."

The normal idea of the West Indies is that they form an archipelago of islands close to one another, and united by summer waters. The reality is very different. Many islands there are—thirteen distinct possessions, several groups conjoining different islands. But they lie within a parallelogram 1100 miles from north to south—1000 miles from east to west. Communication between them, if only 40 or 50 miles apart, is uncertain and fitful, largely dependent on the fortnightly service of the Royal Mail Steam Packet Company, and more often than not across a stormy sea. Hence it is that West Indians, whether white or "café con un poco leche," or darkie, are stay-in-island people, know but little of their neighbours producing the same crops, and therefore with little mutual trade. When the official, the overseer, or the planter is entitled to a long holiday, he goes "home." The short vacations he spends at a more or less make-shift hotel on the shore, where the "beautiful north-easter" can blow over him all day and all night, and he can bathe perchance in a roaring surf.

West Indians are kind and hospitable. But they are very sensitive. Who would not be with a thermometer ranging from 70 to 90 degrees? They know their own island and the roadstead of Barbados. But they object to visitors forming any opinion concerning these British possessions as a whole. No prudent company would insure Mr. Froude if he again ventured among them. One writes therefore in fear and trembling. But let it be said at once that the greatest and most indelible impression the British West Indies make upon the political student is the magnificent example they present of the success, the justice, and the popularity of British Administration. It is true that their united 12,000 square miles form but one 911th part of the British Empire. It is true that the 1,350,000 inhabitants of all the islands put together, form but one 260th part of the population of the Queen's dominions. But their scattered position, from three to five thousand miles from Great Britain, the impossibility of maintaining any Imperial force save at one or two points, the circumstances attending their conquest and enforced peopling renders the task far more difficult than might be the case on a continent. But the success has been so great, so transcendent, that save for one or two minor and social grievances of an entirely transitory character, there is perfect peace, order, and contentment from the Bahamas in the north to Trinidad or British Guiana in the south, from Barbados in the east to Jamaica in the west, from windward to leeward. The supreme power is with the Crown, and good counsel comes from the Colonial Office, spoken through seven quinquennial Governors and sundry administrators. But the ordinances are of local initiation, of local enactment through many elected representatives, in some cases to two Houses of Legislature and of strictly local application. Public expenditure is wholly provided out of local taxation. Public order is maintained, and absolute security for life and property vouchsafed, by local police forces, and this amid a population freed by England, still capering in their joy at liberty, and as easily ignited by a misdirected spark as loose gunpowder. The world is illuminated by imperishable monuments of the Colonial genius of Britain and the justice of her rule. But nowhere is it more conspicuous than in the British West Indies. In this sense it is regarded by Spain, sore troubled by Cuba, the last remnant of a Colonial Empire as glorious, and more capable than that even of Britain. In this sense it is regarded by France, ever covetous of Colonial sway, but never succeeding, notwithstanding our example, in developing her few Colonies for the good of themselves or the Mother Land. Of this Martinique and Guadeloupe are instances in the West Indies, heavily subsidized though they are, and Indo-China in Asia. It is a fine thing, and one Englishmen may be proud of, that English is the universal language among a million negroes in the West Indies, to hear them declare themselves to be Englishmen, and talk of "Our Queen," and going "Home to England." Needless to say, that under such a condition of affairs it is absolute nonsense to talk at Exeter Hall, or anywhere else, about the oppression of the negro. A freer people is not to be found, or one with a clearer idea of asserting their rights to the extreme verge of verbal exaction and legal process. Education has done wonders on an intelligent foundation. The Church of England too may be proud of her work. She numbers a very large majority of the blacks among her sons. They are great church-goers, and numerous Protestant churches and chapels are well filled. Nor does the West Indian Christian, as in Hindustan and China, think Christian alcohol a cardinal article in the Christian creed. For an individual not to have seen a drunken man is nothing. But all authorities agree that the people are wonderfully sober, and an example to many a "cocktail" loving and "swizzle" ruined young Britisher. Morality, however, is on a different level. It has been said that there is no "immorality" among them, for there is no "morality." Legitimacy figures in some islands at 40 per cent. among the births. But this is declared high, and an earnest Dominican priest in Trinidad, where alone Rome maintains the ascendant, put it as low as 12 per cent. Corroboration of this is found on the notice board of the English cathedral at Port of Spain. It announces that baptisms are held:—

"Legitimate, Wednesday;
Illegitimate, Friday."

In the English sense there is no overcrowding—that is, of too many tenements in dark and stuffy courts. But nothing will prevent as many negroes as possible from shutting themselves up in a shanty soon after nightfall, closing the shutters, barring every air crevice, and remaining there until daylight. Do they then come out to work? Their fathers or grandfathers did. But that was under the lash. Their motto rather is "Work a little, play a little, eat a little, sleep a little." It is all "a little," except perhaps "the sleep," but especially "the work," and it takes but little in such a climate to support life. This undoubted indolence and want of perseverance, as also the absolute refusal to migrate from overcrowded Barbados to other islands crying out for labour, make the immigration of Indian coolies not only welcome, but an absolute necessity for Jamaica, Trinidad, and British Guiana. The Indian immigrant does exceedingly well, is under strict official protection, and rarely fails to save money.

One sometimes hears of the ruined condition of the West Indies. If it exists, it is most carefully veiled. The public finances are wondrously prosperous. The total annual revenue exceeds 1,800,000*l.*, mainly raised by Customs duties, against which there is not a word of complaint. The aggregate public debt is only 2,500,000*l.*, and has been spent to the last farthing in reproductive works. Compare this—as you may compare the splendid West Indian roads, the calm, the quiet, the contentment, with the impassable highways, the incessant revolutions with the state of affairs in any republic of South America, and you can but take national pride in the administration to which the result is due.

But there are other evidences of the material prosperity in the British West Indies than those already indicated, than the fields laden with sugar cane, and other tropical products, than the three-quarters of a million sterling in the Savings Banks, and they lie in

THE EXTERNAL TRADE.

It amounts to 12,000,000*l.* a year, practically 12*l.* a head, and of this one-half is with the British Empire. It is carried by seven million tons of shipping, of which six-sevenths are British. The trade with the Mother Country alone exceeds 14,000,000*l.* a year, and of this two-thirds consist of purchases by the British West Indies of the productions of British artisans. Ay, truly " Trade follows the flag." This circumstance must needs soften our *prima facie* view of the British West Indies (except Grenada) and British Guiana scuttling off to Washington the moment the McKinley Tariff Act came into force in 1890, and with the consent of the British Government and the help of the British Ambassador, concluding a reciprocity convention with the United States. They were required by America as a condition precedent to pull their tariffs to pieces. American goods had to be admitted free of duty or at vast reductions. Jamaica cut off 30,000*l.* a year from her revenue, Trinidad, 18,000*l*., Barbados, 12,000*l*., and other Colonies in proportion, at the bidding of Secretary Blaine. But colonial legislators were loyal to England. They reduced their duties equally as against her and the United States. The result has been an increase in British trade—a fitting reward for the disinterested zeal of Lord Knutsford, and a falling off—"from some unexplained cause," says the Secretary to the Washington Treasury—of American trade. A movement is being promoted by the St. Lucia Legislature to take the necessary steps to denounce the useless convention, as " having resulted in a large falling off of the revenue without any corresponding benefit to the planting interest, nor to the consumers of food, the retail price of which remains unchanged, and there being no other means of raising a revenue."

So far so good. But there is a dark spot on the British West Indies, and it is one of vital concern to the Empire. These beautiful and luxuriant islands, rich in products dear to France and America, are at present defenceless and undefended, save Jamaica and St. Lucia. If war should ever unhappily break out they must fall, at least temporarily, to any Power able for a time to wrest from us any portion of the sea. They may eventually be recaptured. But in any case enormous indemnities would be exacted, and they would have to be defrayed entirely from Colonial resources. Far better, far cheaper, far more patriotic to be prepared in time. There is a regiment of British infantry, a few artillerymen, and an engineer company or two in the West Indies, besides a fine battalion of the West Indian Regiment. Of what avail would their bravery be over so wide an expanse, if the sea were lost? It can only be held by the Royal Navy, and the claims of the Empire on Her Majesty's ships in a great war would certainly leave but a comparatively small squadron for the West Indies. There are local forces it is true, and all honour to Colonels Ward and Wilson and those who in Jamaica and Trinidad have formed volunteer corps. But the local forces all told only muster on paper 2200 men and a few old guns, which, if fired, or fireable, would only expose the towns to bombardment. Corps of submarine miners might, however, be well organized. The leading houses would more readily furnish the officers than to volunteer infantry, for on them would chiefly fall the penalty of neglect if an enemy were successful, and Colonial funds could well afford the necessary apparatus and the scientific control. Ships of war can only be kept away by the most powerful guns, equal to theirs, or by mechanical contrivances rendering their approach impracticable. The first cannot be provided. The latter can, and also an organized plan for working them. The British West Indies owe it to themselves and to the Empire to see to it.

C. E. HOWARD VINCENT.

R.M.S. Orinoco, off Barbados,
   Jan. 1st, 1894.

BRITISH COMMERCIAL INTERESTS IN SOUTH AMERICA.

Reports to the Chamber of Commerce and Manufactures of the City of Sheffield[1] *upon British Trade in Brazil, The Argentine, Chili, Peru, and Panama.*

XII.

BRITISH INTERESTS IN BRAZIL.

PRESENT CONDITION OF BRAZIL.

1. The present condition of affairs in the United States of Brazil is most unfavourable to obtaining any accurate information concerning the real condition of trade with the United Kingdom and its future prospects. I have, however, collected the best evidence on the subject which is possible under the deplorable circumstances of the hour. The Republic has been established barely four years, and they present an almost unbroken record of martial law, civil discord, and faction revolutions in the capital and the component States—a striking contrast to the peace, prosperity, and progress obtaining under the prolonged reign of the late Emperor, who was deposed and exiled in a moment, without cause or notice, at the whim of a handful of mutinous soldiers. As I write, the unparalleled beauties of the harbour below me are stained by the extraordinary

---

[1] At a meeting of the Council of the Sheffield Chamber of Commerce and Manufacturers held on Wednesday, the 9th day of May, 1894, it was resolved "That the best thanks of this Chamber be, and they are hereby accorded to Colonel Howard Vincent, C.B., M.P., for the valuable reports on Trade in South America which he has been good enough to send for the use of the Chamber."—W. H. BRITTAIN, President.

spectacle of the entire fleet being drawn up in rebel array against the National Government and Metropolis. Bombardment is only restrained by the threatened employment of force by Her Majesty's ships *Sirius*, *Beagle*, and *Racer*, and the war cruisers of France, Italy, Portugal, and America. Every cargo arriving in the bay, not protected by a foreign flag, is seized by the insurgents. Nor does this civil warfare, which has for the last six weeks paralyzed commerce, show signs of early termination, and, even when ended, there is not the slightest guarantee that internal peace will be long preserved, especially as in March next comes a new struggle for the headship of the Executive Government.

History of 1892.

2. "The history of 1892," says the American-edited *Rio News*, the most independent and trustworthy journal in the country, " is one long record of violence, arbitrary acts, and selfish schemes. Public credit and public interest have suffered almost irreparable injuries, and yet there has not been enough of patriotism, courage, and self-sacrifice to check the downward course of the nation. There has been less personal liberty than under the Monarchy, less respect for law, and less consideration for the good name of the country."

Foreign Trade.

3. Under such circumstances, it is not surprising that the oversea trade should be mainly in the hands of foreign firms. On the northern seaboard, from the mouth of the Amazon to the capital, the English take a clear lead. In Rio many of the coffee exporters are Americans, and in the Southern provinces the Germans preponderate. In Santa Catharina and Rio Grande do Sul, the latter are beginning to exercise a marked influence upon local affairs. As yet, however, but the fringe of the enormous riches of the vast territory of the Republic—twenty-seven times the size of Great Britain and Ireland, larger than the United States or Australia—has been tapped. There are few good roads, and communication is mainly confined to the sea, and the 5000 miles of railway, laid down largely by British enterprise, and greatly harassed by officialdom.

British Interests in Brazil.

COMMERCIAL INDIFFERENCE.

4. How little interest, comparatively speaking, is taken in the development of commerce and industrial prosperity by the Republican authorities is well illustrated by two circumstances. The first greatly affects the British flag and its carrying trade. On the smallest pretext a vessel is denied the right to discharge its cargo, or land its passengers, until it has performed quarantine and gone through certain ridiculous, but costly, performances for nominal disinfection at Ilha Grande, 60 miles south-west of Rio. This necessitates, in the case of a cargo destined for Para, an extra haulage on the double journey, of 4000 miles, and in the case of Pernambuco and adjacent ports for about 2200 miles, leading to an enormous increase in freights and augmentation in the price of the necessaries of life, many of which must be imported. The second is, by comparison, of minor importance, though eloquent in itself, namely, the publication only the other day of the trade statistics of 1890.

STAPLE PRODUCTS.

5. There are five great staples of commerce in Brazil—coffee and cotton, sugar and indiarubber, and tobacco. Of these, coffee is pre-eminent, and yields large returns. Eight million bags (worth over 20,000,000*l.*), of 60 kilos each, were exported last year, 1892, through Rio Janeiro, Santos, and Victoria. One-fourth went to Europe, excluding Great Britain, which took about 150,000 bags, and three-eighths to the United States. From the Amazon 5,000,000*l.* worth of indiarubber was exported, 1,600,000*l.* worth going to England, and double that quantity to America. But, valuable as are the bearing and possible coffee lands, rich as are the tropical regions in rubber extract and other natural products, they sink, it is thought by competent judges, into insignificance beside the capacity for the production of sugar.

HINDRANCES TO INDUSTRY.

6. Of the hindrance to industrial development by the want of roads and the inadequacy of the railways mention has been already made. But there is another greatly

restraining cause, and it affects not only the production of the staples, but also the exploitation of the undoubted mineral wealth. It is the want of labour. Not infrequently in some places a large part of a valuable crop has to be left on the ground for want of hands to gather it in. The population of the country is about 12,000,000, barely one-seventh of what it could well carry. "The outcome in considerable part," says a well-known Brazilian, "of an admixture of Indian, Negro, and Portuguese blood, the national character is gifted, it may be, by kindness of heart and amiability, but sullied by apathy, idleness, frivolity, and indifference, to a point not easy of conception." The 1,500,000 slaves, so impetuously emancipated in 1887 by the Crown Princess Isabel, when Regent during her father's absence, under the generous but ill-timed heart guidance of the Church, can scarcely be induced by most liberal wages to work steadily for more than a few days at a time. Having few wants, with no cold weather to face, revelling in the luxuriance of nature, they apparently prefer the freedom of urban indolence and alcoholic indulgence to equatorial labour.

IMMIGRATION.

7. Considerable exertions have been made to procure immigration, and 250,000 Italians, Spaniards, and Portuguese have been brought in within the last two years. They are the only European races adapted to the climate, but for the most part the immigrants seek only to accumulate a modest sum and to return to their homes. Negotiations are in progress with China. But there is nothing so distasteful to the prudent and conservative instincts of the Chinese as unsettled Governments. Of all immigrants, the most unsuitable are the English. The Emigration Bureau, in Westminster Broadway, cannot do better than continue to warn the English working man not to think of bettering his fortunes in Brazil. A few foremen do well in the recently established cotton mills, which will present fresh rivalry to Lancashire. But they are men of superior class, in receipt of good salaries on a contract engagement, and quite different from the ordinary emigrant.

BRITISH TRADE.

8. The total volume of British trade with Brazil amounts

to over 13,000,000*l.* a year, of which two-thirds consist in purchases from Brazil and one-third of sales to Brazil. This preponderance of import over export on our part is a new feature in the commercial relations between the two countries in the past twelve years, and one unfortunately often duplicated at the present day. In 1860 British exports to Brazil were double the imports thence. In 1880 they still exceeded them by 20 per cent. But while the importation from Brazil has quadrupled in the last 30 years, British exports have declined. Nor do we find that the whole volume of British trade with the Republic represents so satisfactory an increase as could be desired. While it amounts to about one-fourth of the total external trade of Brazil, British commerce, according to the eminent statistical authority of Mr. Mulhall, has increased only 6 per cent. between 1880 and 1891, while that of Brazil with the rest of the world increased 20 per cent.

Reciprocity Treaty with America.

9. In that year—1891—moreover, the United States of America concluded with Brazil a reciprocity convention well calculated to make the British results for the next decade still more unsatisfactory. The convention—the first of a series of twelve similar treaties already signed at Washington, a number the augmentation of which is now in active negotiation—secured the admission into Brazil on April 1, 1891, of fifteen standard articles of American production (including the old British staples of agricultural tools and machinery, mining and mechanical tools and machinery, all machinery for industrial and manufacturing purposes, and all railway construction material and equipment), "free" of all duty, whether national, state, or municipal, and a reduction of 25 per cent. in 2000 other classes of goods "on the tariff then in force or which may hereafter be adopted."

The consideration for this enormous advantage to the United States over Great Britain and the rest of the world, was the free admission of Brazilian sugars, molasses, coffee, and hides—articles America could not do without. It is obvious that the advantage of this treaty was and is entirely on the side of the United States of America, and this fact,

Brazil, in her wild desire to translate the American Constitution into Portuguese, could not then see, but now recognizes too late.

The question for us, though, is not what good this or other reciprocity treaties is likely to do for America or the other contracting parties, but what harm it is likely and indeed certain to do British trade in the long run: slowly it may be, but not the less surely.

INCREASE OF DUTY UPON BRITISH GOODS.

10. Already in 1892 the Brazilian Budget Law increased by 60 per cent. the duties on cotton and woollen manufactures, mainly derived from England, and by 50 or 60 per cent. the duties upon other articles of import. It is satisfactory to find that Sheffield cutlery has not as yet been seriously affected. But it holds its own only by enforced cheapness, and that too often means an undue cheapening of wages. Axes, hatchets, picks, and other articles in the manufacture of which we excel, are, however, being obtained from the United States. Whatever the result up to the present time, the undermining of British markets is a matter which requires most careful watching, and it is satisfactory that Mr. Harford, Her Majesty's able Secretary of Legation, is giving close attention to the question in Brazil.

It appears that the American sales to Brazil of cotton goods and manufactures generally have doubled, while those of hardware have trebled, and under date June 27, 1892, the American Secretary of State reports to the President:—"The condition of the export trade from the United States to Brazil during the last twelve months is extremely favourable, compared to that of Great Britain, which shows an enormous falling off in every line of merchandise."

PREPONDERANCE OF BRITISH SHIPPING.

11. Such advantage as British trade enjoys in the Brazilian market is mainly due to the superior enterprise and skill of our merchant marine. At least one-half of the foreign trade of Brazil is conveyed in English vessels. There are rarely less than from 70 to 100 in the harbour of Rio de Janeiro, and among other things they brought last year to

this port, principally from Cardiff, 454,000 tons of coal. As I count now the vessels in the harbour it appears that there is little besides the Red Ensign, and we can but feel that three Queen's ships – one cruiser and two small gunboats—protecting them from spoliation at the hands of the insurgent fleet, are all too few.

NECESSITY FOR A STRONGER NAVY.

12. The maintenance of a British Navy sufficiently numerous and sufficiently strong to protect the commercial fleets of England on every sea against any eventuality is the first and cardinal principle to be borne in mind by every Englishman concerned in the maintenance of our trade and industrial employment. It is gratifying to find that the United States, despite the superior commercial activity of her rulers and diplomatists, comes but fourth into the ports of Brazil, being surpassed by Norway and Germany, who together muster barely half of the British sail. Indeed communication between New York and Rio has now been surrendered by the Northern Stars and Stripes to the British flag.

FINANCIAL DIFFICULTIES IN BRAZIL.

13. Unfortunately in the actual state of Brazil it is not possible, despite careful inquiry, to suggest any special direction in which British trade could be advantageously pushed at the present time. The necessity for caution is only too apparent. Exchange which in 1889, under the Monarchy, was at par, or 27 pence per milreis, and only once fell below 20 pence, has now fallen to a fraction over 10 pence. Nor has it probably by any means touched bottom. The cost of this revolution, the third in four years, will be enormous directly and indirectly. One can but look with apprehension at the large figures of the annual interest due to England on account of Capital advanced for State and other purposes. Recovery may and probably will come in time from the disastrous results of the follies of the newly-fledged Republic, and not least of all from the indiscriminate and reckless launching in 1891 of banks, mining companies and industrial syndicates, and

the indiscriminate sale of Government concessions, contracts, and lands. But this happy era will only be attained when Brazilian politicians and the people generally remember that the riches of the country can be developed and the national prosperity secured only by putting into practice the motto on their standard—"Ordem e Progresso."

C. E. HOWARD VINCENT.

Rio de Janeiro, October 12th, 1893.

XIII.

BRITISH COMMERCIAL INTERESTS IN ARGENTINA.

MAGNITUDE OF BRITISH INTERESTS.

1. British Commercial Interests in The Argentine Republic are colossal. The officially estimated amount of Foreign Capital invested in the country comes to a thousand millions of gold dollars, or 200,000,000*l.* sterling. The real sum is probably considerably more. Of this external concern in the welfare of Argentina, at least three-fourths appertain to Great Britain. The whole of the fourteen loans contracted by The National Government, amounting to 44,000,000*l.*, were with one small exception raised in London. From the British Public—mainly, Provincial Governments have also obtained over 28,000,000*l.*, and Municipal Corporations close upon 5,000,000*l.* Upwards of 70,000,000*l.* have likewise been advanced for the construction of railroads, and 10,000,000*l.* embarked in Industrial Enterprises. A fair proportion of the 101 millions of gold dollars (say 20,000,000*l.*) obtained on supposed mortgages of real estate below value, by so-called Cedulas came also from Great Britain, although the loss which will ensue has to be shared by continental investors, especially in Holland. On the other hand the purchasers of landed property in the Republic, and especially of the large holdings, have been, and indeed still are, British subjects. In their hands too are to a considerable extent concentrated the Import and Export Trade, and the reliable Banking and other Financial Business.

CONSEQUENT NECESSITY FOR EFFECTIVE REPRESENTATION.

2. The recognition of these facts not only by the people of the United Kingdom, but also by Her Majesty's

Government, in view of the past, present, and future condition of affairs, is all-important. The representation of the Queen and Her Majesty's subjects should be commensurate with the magnitude of British interests, the number of British lives, and the amount of British property at stake. It is true that hitherto the " revolutions," as the incessant Republican contests for Presidential Power are designated, and which have been so disastrous to the welfare of the country, have not endangered foreigners to any appreciable extent. But it is a serious matter that while Argentina is in a state of revolution and of siege, while the condition of affairs in Uruguay is but little better, the River Plate, filled with British merchant shipping, should be left destitute of any vessel of Her Majesty's Navy. Events transpire rapidly. The unexpected is more certain to occur in South America than anywhere else, and I am but giving expression to the general feeling prevalent among more than 30,000 British subjects in the Republics debouching upon this vast estuary, when I say that it should never be left without one of Her Majesty's ships of size not inferior to the local vessels of war.

THE FOREIGN DEBT.

3. An arrangement has been entered into for the temporary reduction of the interest due on the National Loans amounting to 2,198,765*l.* per annum, by 648,000*l.* a year until 1898. This reduced interest, if not indeed the whole amount, Argentina is well able to pay. The customs Revenue alone should amount to some 3,000,000*l.* a year (the duties averaging 25 per cent. *ad valorem*) if properly collected by competent persons effectually controlled, and honestly administered, independently of local influences. There is fair ground also for hoping that a satisfactory arrangement will be made by Dr. Terry, the present capable and well-intentioned Minister of Finance, with regard to the interest on the 16,000,000*l.* of Railway Capital guaranteed by the State. But with respect to the Provincial and Municipal loans little hope can be held out, and still less with regard to the Cedulas. The three together amount to over 50,000,000*l.*, and it will be fortunate if any considerable proportion thereof ever reverts to the investors.

British Interests in Argentina.

DEVELOPMENT OF BRITISH INTERESTS.

4 The development of British Interests in Argentina has been coeval with the century. In 1804, the genius of Mr. Pitt, that great statesman, whose maxim was "British Policy is British Trade," foresaw the commercial future before South America freed from the Spanish yoke. Had more skill and better fortune attended the British arms at Buenos Ayres in 1806 and 1807, the Southern continent under the Union Jack would long ere this have eclipsed the United States in prosperity, and a richer Australia have been planted. In 1810, directly after the declaration of independence, English houses established themselves in the Argentine. In 1817 there were twelve, in 1823 thirty-six, and in the latter year half the shipping of the River Plate was British. The first agricultural immigrants were Irishmen, and they amassed considerable fortunes, their descendants being to-day among the most prosperous " estancieros " in the country. In 1854, British trade amounted to 2,600,000*l*. In 1884, Argentina took 4,800,000*l*. worth of British goods, and England imported from the Republic 1,200,000*l*. worth. This total has now been nearly doubled. Last year, 1892, the Foreign Trade exceeded 204 million dollars—export being, for the second time only in eleven years, in excess of the import. According to the calculations of Mr. Mulhall, the eminent international statistician and one of the oldest British residents in the Argentine, English trade increased between 1882 and 1892 by 105 per cent., while the whole trade of the Republic increased only 67 per cent. In the importation of woven and spun fabrics, of iron and steel, of building materials, of engines, Great Britain is well ahead, and they constitute half the imports. This result cannot be regarded otherwise than with satisfaction.

COMPETITION OF FOREIGN NATIONS.

5. At the same time, it is undeniable that the competition of foreign nations for the custom of the Republic has become far keener. The trade of Germany increased between 1882 and 1892 by 177 per cent., of Italy by 176 per cent. The total trade, however, of both of these competitors combined, with the United States and Spain thrown

in, was less than that of Great Britain. France (the largest purchaser from Argentina) comes next to ourselves, with a total trade of about 8,000,000*l.*, or one-third behind. It has gained, moreover, 29 per cent. in the ten years. I mention these circumstances in order to show that while there is every necessity for commercial and political vigilance on our part, there is no solid ground for the alarm which is frequently expressed that the Germans are beating us in Argentina. Certain it is that these indefatigable traders have made gigantic progress in many markets wherein, prior to German unity and the establishment of the German Empire, the British held the monopoly. Certain it is that by their never-wearying attention to details, to the study of local requirements in shapes, patterns, and colours, and their obliging readiness to do business in any language, currency, system of measurement, or quantity, and for a profit, however insignificant, they are absorbing more and more of the small trade. But in the major commerce, in large transactions requiring capital, in banking and in shipping, they are hardly yet to be considered as serious rivals.

FALSE MARKING OF FOREIGN GOODS AS BRITISH.

6. An allowance from all calculations must, however, be made with respect to the total volume of British trade, and whether compiled from our own or foreign statistics. This is necessitated, first, by a certain quantity of goods being unduly attributed to British origin or destination because they are conveyed in British ships; and secondly, because quantities of foreign-made goods, especially from Germany, are falsely marked with British names and trade marks, placed thereon either in Germany or England itself, after being imported from the Continent plain and unmarked, as unwisely permitted by British legislation. On this important subject I have addressed a separate communication to the Master of the Cutlers' Company, and cannot too earnestly commend the taking of prompt action to the early consideration of the manufacturers of Sheffield and other British centres. It is of especially vital importance to the cutlery, the iron and steel, and the dry goods trade in Argentina.

BRITISH RAILWAYS IN ARGENTINA.

7. Nothing has been more advantageous to British export to the Argentine than the development of the railway system of the Republic. It has, indeed, been overdone, the accommodation per thousand inhabitants being seven times as great as in Europe. Ninety per cent. of the railways belong to English companies, and as more than half of the twenty-seven have not lately been recovering their expenses, the loss is considerable. But improvement is now on the upward grade. Competing lines have been sanctioned to a ridiculous extent, and parallel roads supported without the slightest need by guarantees. Yet in the making of railway materials—engines, rolling stock, rails, &c.—British industry has been a great gainer. In locomotives and rails we are still well holding our own; but in passenger carriages (as in reapers, winnowing machines, ploughs, rakes, and forks) English manufacture is being eclipsed by America, and by Belgium in the supply of girders, columns, and of the thousands of miles of wire needed for the fencing of the permanent way, some of the companies, and notably the Central Argentine, one of the best managed lines in the world, and, I believe, the main line to the Pacific, under the administration of Mr. Dodds, of Sheffield, are now manufacturing for themselves, and will soon be independent of import.

BRITISH SHIPPING.

8. British shipping carries the greater part of the trade to and from Argentine ports. The number of vessels employed exceeds that of the entire world outside South America, and amounts to between three and four thousand a year, and of a burden approaching 3,000,000 tons. It is, therefore, of serious moment to find that while the products of Argentina are accorded in the United Kingdom precisely equal rights to those of Great Britain or Ireland, the English flag is deferentially taxed in Argentine waters. A vessel of 1000 tons register pays under the British flag over 20*l.* for entrance, lights, health, and wharfage dues, against only 6*l.* 15*s.* under the Argentine colours. It is not to be tolerated that the Union Jack should be thus compulsorily withdrawn from British shipping, and it will be interesting

to ascertain if this injustice has been effectively represented in the proper quarter. Care also should be taken that the interests of British shipping are not prejudiced by the extraordinary quarantine regulations frequently and capriciously enforced. While the utmost sanitary slackness prevails on shore, as much in the capital as in the provinces, vessels thirty, forty, fifty, and even sixty days out from England, with an absolutely clean bill of health, are subjected to long and vexatious quarantine on arrival in the River Plate.

AGRICULTURE IN THE ARGENTINE.

9. The greatest industry in the Argentine Republic is agricultural production. Indeed, it is the only one, for the total absence of coal, and apparently also of reliable oil wells, will for long prohibit any considerable establishment of manufacture. There are 22 millions of cattle, 75 millions of sheep, 4 millions of horses upon the fertile grass plains extending for hundreds of miles from the South Atlantic coast to the mountains. They show an enormous increase in the past ten years, as much in number as in quality, thanks to the importation of the best British blood, and, owing to the improved facilities, ox, sheep, or horse can be readily transported to Europe without loss of flesh. Kindness and space on board ship are remunerative. There are over 250,000,000 acres of land still to be taken up, and the greatest part of the entire area of the Republic is capable of transfer from pastoral to arable purposes, and especially to wheat cultivation. Fifteen years ago wheat had to be imported. In 1882 only 30,000 tons could be spared. Last year the surplus yield for export amounted to 1,300,000 tons. The export of maize, linseed, and flour has also increased enormously, and that of alfalfa or lucerne, which, growing knee high with long roots almost dispensing with rain, is becoming very considerable. The harvest now almost ready to be reaped will be greater than ever, and conduce to railway, industrial, and general prosperity. There is no fear of a field, perhaps fifty miles square, being spoilt in a night, as in Canada, by a degree of frost. The only enemies of the Argentine farmer are drought and locusts. The latter constitute frequently an army absolutely resistless and invincible, carrying everything before them,

devouring every green thing, and bidding man and all his machinery stand aside until they have passed.

ACQUISITION OF LAND BY ENGLISHMEN.

10. Many of the most successful "estançieros" are Englishmen and Scotchmen, while the Irish lead the way. The British have bought, and buy, the largest properties. Some districts, notably Cañada de Gomez, in Santa Fé (with a rural polo club of seventy members) are almost English. It is not uncommon for property, or even a flock or herd, to be farmed in shares—in thirds, fourths, or fifths. A share of the proceeds goes to the proprietor, with a liberal percentage for his capital; a share to the manager, and a share to the shepherd, his cottage and horses being allowed him, and his food from the flock, with what he can till. It is a system which produces excellent results for all parties, and more especially when vast distances make supervision impossible. Great fortunes have been made on "estancias," though often lost in other speculations, and a return of from 20 to 30 per cent. on the capital laid out is not rare.

The Italians, on the other hand, are becoming possessed of small holdings. They have purchased over 16,000 properties in the past seven years—about a third more than they sold. But the average value of each purchase was a little more than a quarter that of the 900 British purchases in the same period.

FOREIGNERS IN THE ARGENTINE.

11. This induces inquiry as to the number of foreigners in the Republic. The Italian-born population is estimated by the Royal legation at about 700,000, and Italian children, counted as Argentines by reason of birth in Argentina, at from 300,000 to 400,000 more. It furnishes the manual labour. Every year a large number of Italians come over for the Argentine harvest in the European winter, and return home for the Italian spring and summer. The service between Genoa and Buenos Ayres is the fastest there is. A good proportion remain, and find ready employment on the land and the railways. A percentage also become "colonists," or small proprietors. The number would be

much larger but for the political disquietude and uncertainty. It is a striking commentary on the pernicious effect of political turmoils that in 1890 the exodus of immigrants was only one-fifth behind the immigration, and in 1891 it was actually larger. Argentina has been far less successful than she ought to have been in attaching the immigrant to the soil of the country of his adoption, and for this squabbling politicians are alone to blame. Until greater care is taken to protect the foreign purchaser from fraud no great change can be looked for in this respect. The Republic may, however, be congratulated on tardy evidence of its desire to exclude foreign criminality from the territory. The conclusion of an Extradition Treaty with her Majesty's Minister and Government, thanks largely to the personal popularity in Congressional circles of Mr. George Welby, the Secretary of Legation, cannot fail, if actively pursued, to be productive of great mutual benefit.

The Spanish Colony, if "Colony" it can be called, considering that South America was under the Spanish flag for centuries, comes next, and after that the French, who largely compose the urban tradesman class, and furnish, from the Basque provinces, the best shepherds.

In point of numbers, the British rank but fourth, if indeed they do not take place numerically after the Germans. In great measure they are of very superior class—wealthy and able, at the head of vast enterprises and employing large capital. British skilled artisans are also numerous and in good demand as engineers, locomotive drivers, and foremen. But again, these, brought out on time contracts and gold salaries, are carefully selected men and of higher grade than the usual emigrant from our overcrowded centres. For him there is absolutely no opening in the Argentine Republic. The climate, the laws, the customs, the food, the lodging and the association are entirely unsuitable, and there are but few instances of success. On the other hand, women domestic servants are in great demand. But emigration to Argentina, except under the auspices of friends in the country, is not to be thought of.

Depreciation of the Currency.

12. The great obstacle to successful emigration lies in the depreciation of the Argentine paper currency—horrible

greasy stuff, tattered, dirty and torn, often carrying, it is said, infection in the five or ten cent. note, passing from juxtaposition to the skin of the beggar, to a person taking change in shop or tramcar, which, having regard to the awful paving of the streets from one end of South America to the other, is the only rational form of town locomotion. This depreciation—or rather the premium on gold, is not to be wondered at, considering the admitted issue of nearly 307 million paper dollars against a gold reserve, the most sanguine estimate can only put at about half that sum. There are national issues, provincial issues, and private bank issues. How little confidence the latter at least inspire, is illustrated by the refusal of provincial notes at the railway stations and post offices of the province itself.

Contrary to the theories of foreign professors of political economy, the reduced value of the paper dollar has neither augmented wages, nor the cost of living. A paper dollar, depreciated between 200 and 300 per cent., secures now very nearly as much labour and as much food as it did when it was at, or nearly at, par. The unfortunate emigrant only realizes the terrible difference, when desirous of converting the paper savings—the Italian can generally scrape together while the Englishman spends—into a European equivalent to send or take home.

The premium on gold is, moreover, of the greatest advantage to agriculturists. They pay for their labour, their food, and indeed for their holdings in depreciated paper, and they receive gold for their exported herds and crops. Its reduction would be firmly resisted by every possible means, and if sudden or violent, would entail serious disaster.

To the merchant, however, the result is very different. He has to pay gold for the foreign produce he imports, and he can obtain only with difficulty its equivalent in paper when he sells. The people do not understand why he should ask so many more "nationals" or paper dollars than formerly for this or that article, and dispense with it rather than pay the apparently enhanced price. The unaccountable fluctuation in the premiums are also productive of much speculation and great risk. There will be a difference of ten or twenty points in a few days or hours, and the utmost caution is necessary to avoid less.

Great Problem of the Future.

13. It will be gathered that the great problem before the Argentine Republic is the fast-increasing numerical and other superiority of the foreigner. There has not been any census for several years. But there can be no doubt whatever that fully one-half, and probably more of the four millions of people in a land ten times the size of the United Kingdom, are either foreigners or the children of foreigners, or of mixed marriages. This is proved by various circumstances. Of the births in the capital, containing an eighth of the whole population, purely Argentine marriages were in 1891 only $14\frac{1}{2}$ per cent. of the whole, and the births arising from such marriages only $10\frac{3}{4}$ per cent. The transfers of property from Argentines to foreigners are increasing. But few of the native landholders can resist the temptation to break up their estates. The Argentine is withdrawing every day more and more from industry and commerce. The capable upper class and the steady business people will have nothing to do with politics or the government of the country. This is unfortunate and lamentable, for it places political power largely in the hands of uneducated men, striving by every means, legitimate or otherwise, after their own ends. The people at large take little or no interest in public affairs. But a minute percentage concern themselves in elections, recognizing that under a democratic Republic considerable risk attends the exercise of the privilege of citizenship. The official mandate practically runs: "If the Government candidate is not returned by votes, let him be by bullets." Many think that foreign interests are too divided for any action on their part. Foreigners of all nations have up to the present wisely held aloof from Argentine political disputes, and in return they have not been seriously prejudiced either in person or individual property. But already there are signs of a coming change. The Italians are getting very strong, and they are absolutely indispensable to the every-day life of the community. If anything should occur, an act of injustice on the part of a petty judge, or the violence of an over-zealous policeman, a light may be set to a flame which will burn far and fiercely. The Italians, the English, and the Germans have interests in common, and they are shared by the French. Everything points to a

union in the future, and especially between England, Germany, and Italy, in South America as in Europe, for the good of mankind in general, and themselves in particular.

CONCLUSION.—CONSULAR COMMERCIAL REPORTS.

14. In conclusion, I must refer to the reports on the Argentine Republic, drawn up by Mr. Harris Gastrell, Vice-Consul at Buenos Ayres. They are full of valuable information, and have been prepared and published when it is still fresh. The advancement of an officer so zealous in the discharge of the duty towards British trade of Her Majesty's representatives abroad may be hoped for.

C. E. HOWARD VINCENT.

Mendoza, November 6th, 1893.

XIV.

BRITISH TRADE IN CHILI.

Difference between Chili and other South American Republics.

1. There is a great difference between Chili and the other Republics of South America. The latter are for the most part content to leave the development of their natural resources to foreigners, especially to English capital, and then to scramble out of the financial engagements contracted in any way they possibly can. The Chilian, on the other hand, is distinguished by a laudable feeling of personal independence. He is anxious to do what he can for himself. The organization of the country may still leave much to be desired. But Chili resembles England in more ways than one. Two generations have seen only a single "revolution." President Balmaceda thought, after his five years of legal office were up in 1891, to become dictator after the manner of South American Presidents. He was overthrown by Congress and a free nation after a sharp struggle. Chilian senators—elected in the proportion of one for every three deputies and a third retiring every second year, and Chilian deputies, elected triennially in the proportion of one for every 30,000 inhabitants, are not paid, and do not pay themselves in accordance with the usage of other democratic Republics. A "Walker" and a "Maciver," worthy sons of British parents, are proud to be Chilians, and respectively to lead the Conservative and Liberal parties on constitutional lines, and alternately to form ministries responsible, as with us, to Parliament, instead of to a Presidential autocrat.

The National Debt.

2. The lack of capital in Chili has been largely supplied from England, with satisfactory results, for the credulity of

the British investor has not been unduly taken advantage of, by the State at least. The Government loans are but five in number, and for only fifty-five million dollars, constituting an annual charge of two million dollars. For every farthing there is good value to show in the shape of 1106 kilometres of State railways, costing fifty-nine million dollars and bringing in a gross revenue of ten million dollars, notwithstanding exceedingly cheap fares and moderate rates. England overcame the engineering difficulties and supplied most of the plant. It is only now that Chilian drivers are taking the place of Englishmen, and it is proving a rather false economy in burnt boilers and tubes.

INTERNAL DEBT.

3. The Internal Debt amounts to fifty-three million dollars, which about represents the issue of State paper.

EXCESSIVE DEPRECIATION OF THE CURRENCY.

4. Notwithstanding the additional issues by forty banks (some of which are about to be amalgamated) of an aggregate of 115 million dollars' worth of notes, these figures compare so favourably with the financial condition of other South American Republics, and especially with the Trans-Andean External National Debt of 205 million dollars, and the Internal Debt of 307 million dollars, that the greater depreciation of the Chilian unit (it stands at about 16d. or nearly 300 per cent. discount) is difficult to understand. There are, moreover, no Provincial State Loans, which in the Argentine amount to 143 million dollars, for the Republic of Chili does not consist of a Federation of semi-antagonistic States, but is like the United Kingdom, one and indivisible.

REDEMPTION OF PAPER.

A law has, moreover, been passed for the total redemption of the State paper on January 1st, 1897, and the necessary machinery for the Mint has already been ordered. Already the small pieces up to 20 cents. are metallic. It is necessary, however, to add that the carrying out of the Statute will not be accomplished without great opposition, and especially on the part of the powerful agricultural interest, which is profiting largely by the low

External Trade.

5. The external trade amounted in 1892 to 142 million dollars, divided into 78 millions (say 12,250,000*l.*) of imports, and 64 millions (say 10,000,000*l.*) of exports. These figures show an improvement over 1890, and a very considerable one over 1891, the year of the Anti-Dictator tussle costing the nation 72 million dollars.

Britishers to the Front.

6. The greater part of the foreign trade passes through Valparaiso, with the exception of the export of nitrate of soda. The Britishers are well represented at this splendid port, yielding precedence on the Pacific only to San Francisco, not only in ships, 465 of 588,000 tons, out of 1258 of 1,343,000 tons, but numerically and in the Consulate-General. The British chaplain even takes an active and intelligent interest in the trade of his congregation. Holding the most reliable census tally, namely the cemetery gate, he is able to gauge rightly the frequent assertion that the Germans are ousting the English, notwithstanding that the great business firms of the latter occupy house after house, and their language is heard almost exclusively. There are about 100 deaths a year among foreign Protestants—50 are German, 40 are English, and 10 of other nationalities. The excess is entirely due to the greater proportion of German clerks. They are diligent and painstaking, good linguists, and disdaining recreation. Their high-spirited English colleagues are said, on the other hand, to prefer polo, tennis and cricket to the desk. In these they excel, and certainly the clerk leads a princely life to that he would follow at home. It ensures the good health necessary for posts of administrative responsibility, and from the hands of all nations these go in lion's share to Englishmen who will keep steady, and master foreign languages.

British Imports and Exports.

7. The principal British imports are printed white and unbleached cotton goods, woollens, carpets, hardware,

cutlery, rails and railroad iron, coal, candles, tea, boots and shoes, beer and spirits. They compose half of the whole trade. The principal Chilian exports are nitrate of soda (5,000,000*l.*), wheat (1,000,000*l.*), iodine (800,000*l.*), bar gold (100,000*l.*) and silver and copper each (800,000*l.*) and manganese. Three-fourths go, in the first instance, at any rate, to Great Britain. These facts show the close connection between the United Kingdom and Chili. The mutual trade has formed the subject of an important monograph by Senator Agostin Ross, late Minister to the Republic in London. Any proposition having its further development in view would probably be well received at Santiago de Chile, the finest city for its population (200,000) in South America, by the most sympathetic, capable, and stable government on the continent.

Customs Duties.

8. Indirect taxation is, in accordance with the rule of the universe, outside the United Kingdom, naturally preferred. The import duties press, however, heavily on many British industries. For instance, upon a case of Sheffield cutlery, worth 170 dollars 10 cents, they work out as follows :—

35 per cent. (some kinds are 25 per cent.) on $170 10 cents	$59.54
75 per cent. of $59·54 in paper money ...	$44·65
35 „ additional duty	15·12
Total duty	$59·77
Add 25 per cent. on $59·54 $14 89.	
This is payable in gold at the rate of 38*d.* per dollar, and after Jan. 1st, 1894, it will be increased to 50 per cent.	35.08
And	
Permits and Stamps	2·50
Discharging and labourers ...	2·80
Cartage and Despatching Fees ...	3·00
Total Customs Dues ...	$104·15

or nearly 6*l.*

The increase of the payment in gold is especially serious for British trade. There is, however, the slight consolation that machinery for use in agriculture, mining, and other industries is admitted free, as well as electrical and railway plant, or about a fourth of the whole.

Customs Revenue.

9. The Revenue from Customs Duties amounted in 1892 to nearly 48 million dollars, or eight times the total from the same source in 1878, the year antecedent to the war with Peru and Bolivia. The calculations of Señor Graña show that Chili has proved anew that "trade follows the flag." The Peruvian war gave Chili the new ports of Iquique, Antofogasta, Pisagua, Tocopilla, and temporarily, if not permanently, Arica. The four first-named produced in the tenth year of possession a trade of 50 million dollars, and a fiscal revenue in 1892 of $28\frac{1}{2}$ million dollars, compared to only 19 million dollars from all the old ports.

Chilian Military Expenditure.

10. There is indeed ground to fear that this gigantic commercial success, by force of arms, may unduly excite the naturally bellicose disposition of the Chilian, and especially in view of the martial weakness and internal discord of his neighbours. The expenses of the army and navy are ever increasing, and already exceed 15 million dollars a year, or one-third of the total expenditure. The nation numbers 1,300,000 males, and from these are voluntarily recruited three regiments of artillery, six of infantry, four of cavalry, and a corps of engineers, a total of 6000 men for a population of three millions, of whom 700,000 only can read and write. There is also a National Guard, consisting of 51,000 men in 78 corps. The officers, who are elsewhere in South America such a disquieting element, are less numerous than in other Republics. The generals are limited to ten, the colonels to fifty-eight. The Chilian navy consists of six first-class and six second-class vessels, with ten torpedo boats, the whole manned by 2050 sailors, with 189 officers. A new 6000 ton armour-clad is under orders from France, and the 18 steamers of the

Chilian Steamship Company (Sud-Americana) are available in case of need, receiving to that end a yearly subsidy of 200,000 dollars. The coasts are being fortified under the direction of Colonel Betzbold, late of the Prussian Engineers.

Steam Communication on the Pacific.

11. It may be mentioned that the Compania Sud-Americana de Vapores, above-mentioned, monopolizes with the Pacific Steam Navigation Company the coast trade between Valparaiso and Panama. There are no other means of communication between the nineteen ports. The coast is for the large part of the distance a rainless desert, but rich in metals. Every article of food has to be brought by sea. The fares and rates are enormous, and the profits in proportion. Three weeks are taken by each vessel to get over 2800 miles, and there should be room for a quick competing service running in connection with the Mexican, American, British, French, and Spanish mails from both sides of the Isthmus of Panama.

The Nitrate Fields.

12. The Chilian shareholders in the Sud-Americana, who employ English officers and engineers almost exclusively, do not naturally object to yearly dividends, ranging between 25 and 50 per cent. But some of them seek to inspire the Chilian people with a feeling of jealousy towards the few profitable British ventures in the nitrate fields of Tarapacá. Since they were won from Peru in 1880, 367 million dollars' worth of nitrate of soda and iodine have been produced, at a profit to the Chilian Treasury of 161 million dollars. This result has been mainly brought about by the outlay of 10,000,000*l*. of British money. The investments, taken as a whole, have produced and produce but an infinitesimal return. Very few of the over-numerous nitrate mills are paying a dividend to their shareholders. They were greatly over-capitalized, and are weighed down by the enormous Government duty of 2*l*. 12*s*. 6*d*. a ton, or over 100 per cent. on the cost of production. It yielded in 1892, 2,000,000*l*., on an export of about 800,000 tons, valued at 5,000,000*l*. Instead of taking up an attitude of hostility to the nitrate

manufacturers, which cannot fail to close the door against future British individual investment, the Government might well show practical sympathy with the heavy losses which have occurred, and concern itself with the preservation of the supply of nitrate of soda, and all it brings to the State, for the unworked extent of the fields is already more than doubtful.

Chilian Mineral Resources.

13. Chili has, however, one great advantage over her agricultural ally on the Atlantic. It lies not only in the possession of a vast mineral zone, producing gold, silver, and copper, with an invaluable mining population, but also in coal, permitting the successful establishment of manufacture. Chilian coal is used on the railways and the ocean, although somewhat foul and barely able to compete in price with English and Australian, cheaply sea borne as ballast for nitrate-fetching vessels. Captain Wonham, commanding H.M. Store Ship *Liffey* at this port (Coquimbo), has for instance 5000 tons of Welsh steam coal available for Her Majesty's ships on the station at about 25*s.* a ton.

Conclusion.

14. It remains only to be added that the British Colony in Chili numbers between 5000 and 6000 persons, and, so far as Europe is concerned, is exceeded only by the Germans, and that slightly. British trade shows a steady improvement, and is vastly ahead of every other nation. The external relations of the Republic appear to give rise to no present apprehension. The boundary questions with Argentina have been satisfactorily settled, and in a few years the English railway over the Cordillera may perhaps be completed, and an Atlantic outlet given to the Republic, which can hardly fail to continue to prosper, and so justify the confidence which has always been reposed by England in Chilian honour and common sense.

C. E. Howard Vincent.

Coquimbo,
    West Coast of South America,
        November 17th, 1893.

XV.

BRITISH INTERESTS IN PERU.

Decadence of Peru.

1. Peru was the prosperous seat for centuries of the great Empire in South America of the Incas. Then for three hundred years it was the capital province of the Spanish Dominions. To Peru came the produce of Europe. By Peru went out the riches of the continent. It was the great distributing centre. But now Peru has fallen from her high estate. The transition from Chili is great. It is another country, another race. The vigorous independence of the one is succeeded by the supine indifference of the other. The fault lies in the Government; but most of all in the people who make, or rather tolerate, such a Government. The letter of the Constitution declares it to be " democratic, representative, and based on unity." It is so in name only. In practice the Government is autocratic, dictatorial, founded in revolution, and based only on presidential unity.

Despotism of the Army.

2. The power for such an interpretation of a Republican sovereignty is derived from the Army. For external warfare, for territorial defence, it has been proved valueless. The Chilian swept all before him. Many a brave Peruvian was driven into the sea, owing to chiefs taking no precautions to secure their flanks or rear. The Army now consists of a brigade of artillery, three regiments of cavalry, and six of infantry—recruited by conscription with a Reserve formed of all Peruvians. The standing force is not excessive in numbers. But it is ill equipped and disciplined. A scarcity of officers it cannot complain of. The Peruvian loves gold lace and red trousers. There are reputed to be three hundred unemployed colonels. Certainly the officers

swarm in the capital. They are a constant danger to tranquillity and civil order, zealous in their cause, not scrupulous in their methods. The Presidency becomes vacant next June. Their candidate is General Cacéres, formerly President and Commander-in-Chief. They will probably carry him against the Congressional candidate, the President of the Chamber of Deputies, and the popular candidate, Señor Don Nicolas de Pierola, formerly Dictator. At the present time the victory of the military or stronger party may possibly be advantageous to Peru and her European friends.

The Peruvian Congress.

3. There is no difficulty in manning the Senate and the House of Representatives. Every department returns one or more senators, according to the number of provinces of which it consists. Each province returns a deputy for every 30,000 inhabitants. Every senator and deputy receives his journey expenses, and 1350 silver sols from the State in three equal instalments, at the commencement, in the middle, and at the end of each session. That a recipient may never be lacking owing to death or other disability, a supplementary senator and deputy is selected for each seat, who instantly fills the gap. One-third of each House is renewed every two years, but less by the voice of the people than by the will of the prefects and sub-prefects presiding over departments and provinces, and Governors over districts, at the word of the President. Peruvians of position or engaged in commerce give politics in consequence a wide berth, and personally they are wise. Others are of small account in a "republican democracy."

The Peruvian Debt and Peruvian Corporation.

4. In two respects Peru is superior to other South American Republics. She has made an honourable arrangement as regards her external debt, largely owing to the efforts of General Cacéres when President. The Republic has but to keep to it honourably. By the exertions of Mr. Michael Grace—of the firm of Grace, Brothers and Co.—the leading house along the Pacific coast, and

Lord Donoughmore, the Peruvian Government transferred its entire liability in respect of the three loans contracted in England in 1869, 1870, and 1872, to the Peruvian Corporation. In capital amount and interest the total came to 50,000,000*l.* From their charge Peru obtained complete exemption, ceding in return to the Corporation ten State railways, wildly and extravagantly built under sinister American advice; the guano deposits remaining after untoward French manipulation; the monopoly of navigation on Lake Titicaca, the main approach to Bolivia, sundry coast rights and public lands, and 80,000*l.* a year, in monthly payments, from the Customs receipts at Callao. The Corporation, under the able direction of Mr. Clinton Dawkins, is discharging its duties admirably, and has fulfilled all its obligations under the contract. Several new branches of traffic are springing up, the lines have been thoroughly repaired and pushed forward into the rich coffee lands on the Amazonian slopes of the Cordillera. Thus, great benefits will accrue to Peru if there be cordial co-operation between the Government and the Corporation. It is unfortunate that the fall in silver should have so depreciated the fiscal receipts as to frustrate the intention to meet the monthly cash payment in full. But no doubt mutual concessions will be satisfactorily arranged.[1]

Peruvian Currency.

5. The second advantage secured by Peru over her neighbours lies in the possession of a silver currency compared to a paper issue against value too often fictitious. The silver crisis has, it is true, depreciated the value of the Peruvian sol, and ten now go to the English sovereign instead of about six. This is untoward for the importer, whose rural customers cannot understand his altered charges, and dispense with his goods. But as elsewhere it is favourable to the exporter and to Englishmen engaged on contracts in Peru, among whom are many railway men who find the purchasing power of Peruvian money as regards domestic necessaries as great as ever.

There is also an Internal Debt of about forty million sols, contracted by various Presidents, to meet the coupons of

---

[1] This has now been accomplished.

which, some of the Customs receipts from alcohol and other matters are nominally allotted.

AREA OF PERU AND THE PROVINCES IN ABEYANCE.

6. Peru is estimated to contain over 400,000 square miles, and a population of 2,650,000. But these figures will be affected by the almost certain loss of the two provinces of Tacna and Arica in the course of next year. By the peace with Chili that Republic was to hold them until March, 1894, when a popular vote should be taken to decide their fate—the victor at the poll paying ten million sols to the loser. But in the absence of any power on the part of Peru to find the money, Chili will probably not feel bound by the conditions involving a probable loss, as Peruvian patriotism is sure to gain the day over self-interest. There is a talk of securing the good will of Bolivia, by giving her this one outlet to the coast in exchange for some other territory. But whether Chili will admit an inland State to the Pacific shore is doubtful.

IMPORT TRADE.

7. The statistics compiled under circumstances of no little difficulty by Señor Don Quesada, proprietor and editor of the leading paper, "El Commercio," and by Señor Don Rodriquez in a noteworthy official publication, show that in 1891 the import trade of Peru exceeded 15,000,000 sols, or about 1 sol, 84 cents (say 3s. 9d.) per inhabitant. Foreign goods paid an average duty of 39½ per cent. *ad valorem*, and produced a customs revenue of about five million sols, say 500,000*l*. Over forty-one per cent. of the imports came from the United Kingdom, and they provided two-fifths of the fiscal income.

These figures are satisfactory as regards our rivals, for the imports from Germany came only to 18.8 per cent. of the whole; from France only to 10.3 per cent.; and from the United States to but just over 8 per cent. They are less so, however, as regards ourselves, for in 1870 British trade with Peru amounted to 6,700,000*l*., and in 1891 to less than one-third of that sum.

Export Trade.

8. In the export trade Great Britain is the best friend of Peru. The total came in 1891 to 12,370,000 sols, and of this England bought to the extent of 46·9 per cent. of the whole, while Germany took but 8 per cent., and France 2 per cent. The chief articles of Peruvian export are sugar, cotton, wool, hides, and minerals. The latter include gold, silver, and copper. In 1891 ten million kilogrammes were exported, valued at 2,000,000 sols and paying Customs tribute of $35,000. Soon, under the influence of the Peruvian Corporation, this source of revenue will be greatly increased. Mineral oil is also being found in abundance. Already it furnishes the motive power for the railways, notwithstanding average gradients of $3\frac{1}{2}$ to 4 per cent. at half the price of coal. Coffee and cocoa are being planted and should do as well as in Brazil and Ecuador.

Shipping.

9. In shipping Great Britain is of course pre-eminent. Half the vessels entering the excellent port of Callao are British. The Chilian flag comes next, but in many cases that is the principal Chilian article on board. The ship is British built, the officers British, the stores British, and not improbably the cargo, besides the capital behind the flag.

British Advancement of Local Interests.

10. It is only natural that occasionally a little feeling may be aroused by this predominance. It has, however, on the whole, been of immense local advantage. In many instances the British residents have as great interest in the development of the locality of their adoption as if they were native born. They show it by munificent charitable donations from their earnings. In Valparaiso the Chilian Government, and in Lima and Callao the Peruvian Government, have recognized it by nominating British subjects to seats on the municipality. The good they have already been able to accomplish is considerable. May Buenos Ayres and other towns follow so excellent an example! I nothing else is done they will be able to show their colleagues

the imperative need of sanitation, and that good roads are at the root of prosperity, and of humanity towards that animal life, whose sufferings in Spanish America cannot be described.

IRON AND STEEL IN CENTRAL AND SOUTH AMERICA.[1]

11. Whichever way you turn in South America, British iron and steel meets the view. In every direction wasted British treasure is apparent. It is most conspicuous in the Argentine Republic. Brazil follows suit, and one trembles for the 100,000,000*l*. of British capital in that once prosperous empire, but now fast-decaying republic. How so many millions of savings could have been embarked on the faith of Governments so rickety, of Provincial Administrations so unsound, of Municipal Corporations so imaginary, to carry out the most ridiculous schemes, is a perpetual source of wonder to the traveller. It is to be hoped in charity that issuing-houses and boards of directors were equally ignorant, and that the blind only led the blind. But one result has been achieved, and one solid result remains. Some portion of the scattered millions found their way into British factories, some portion, in the shape of wages, into the hands of British ironworkers and artisans. Fully 75 per cent. of the lines laid down in South America were railed and equipped in the first instance from England, and this was at least a real and substantial advantage. In many cases this outlay is the only sensible thing connected with the companies, and represents the greater part of the available assets. It is interesting, therefore, to inquire in what position the British iron and steel trade stands at the present time in the South American market.

In every case the Custom-house returns give an advantage still to England, sometimes great and preponderant, but showing in almost every republic the gradual advance of our most formidable competitors—the United States and Germany. Occasionally here and there is a railway, the concession for which was obtained in France, and occasionally in this or that town there is a French designed and French made bridge. But it is seldom. Great Britain, the United

---

[1] Abbreviated from an article written for *The Ironmonger*.

States and Germany are the only rivals in the iron race—barring that Belgian supply of columns and girders which is met with to so large and regrettable an extent at home.

The railways, almost without exception, have been conceived by Englishmen, designed by Englishmen, and engineered by Englishmen. In equal degree they are to-day being managed by Englishmen, even when the original conception chances, unfortunately for the country, to be American or of other nationality. This was highly advantageous to the British iron and steel trade. An Englishman at home frequently buys foreign-made goods without thought or regret. But expatriation sharpens his patriotism. He is more English than at home, and likes to be surrounded by materials reminding him of the old country, and on the substantiality of which he can rely.

On some lines American locomotives are used; but by far the greater number of railroad-engines seem to be, or to have originally been, British made, at Leeds and Glasgow.

It should be borne in mind that, although locomotives are free of Customs duty by nearly every tariff, privileged importation entails so much difficulty with authorities struggling for every cent. which can be fiscally raised, that all the important lines, and, indeed, most of the others, have commenced to manufacture largely for themselves, and to build and repair their own locomotives and rolling-stock. The Central Argentine shops are the best I have seen, and on a very large scale.

In every case the superintendents, foremen, and many of the artisans are English. The two former are usually brought out on time contracts for two or three years—the foremen receiving from 15*l.* to 22*l.* a month. As regards the ordinary mechanics, there are plenty to be had of English as well as other nationalities without time engagements. A good man will easily earn from 8*s.* to 11*s.* a day, while living is very cheap and better than at home. But the great temptation is as to drink. In many yards and on many farm stations the Englishman has established a woeful reputation for his countrymen as regards sobriety.

In agricultural machinery there can be little doubt that the Americans have got well ahead with their comparatively cheap, light, attractive implements. Indeed, it would appear that, although Howards, Hornsbys, and some other great English firms show no lack of advertising enterprise, they hold their own more with threshing machines than anything else. As regards reapers, winnowing and sowing machines, ploughs, rakes, and forks, the Americans gain ground every day, and have almost established a monopoly. This is the opinion of Drysdales, Shaw Brothers, and other important firms at Buenos Ayres, while it is evident that Grace Brothers, with their chain of houses on the Pacific, and Messrs. Agar, in the Argentine, who mainly import from the United States, are doing an enormous business. It appears that the majority of English makers adhere, and, perhaps, wisely, to their system of turning out a really first-rate, strong, durable article, but far heavier than the American. But it should be borne in mind that in South America, of all places in the world, capital is scanty, and the great aim of one and all is to make money quickly and " clear out." This applies to the colonies too, where I have noticed the growing popularity of cheap and showy American implements.

In cutlery Sheffield wares and Sheffield trade-marks are predominant in every town and village. But not infrequently it is evident that the knife on which they are stamped never passed through the hands of a Hallamshire grinder. Germany is the great sinner in this respect, and Solingen the *locus delicti*. I am urging the Cutlers' Company to appoint, if only for a time, a travelling inspecting agency, with authority to set in motion the local laws in this respect, which even in Peru are more up to date than in most of the great countries who send diplomatic delegates to an International Industrial Convention, and do nothing further to promote honest trading. It must be admitted, too, that the Germans are very ingenious in "getting up" their cutlery, in the shape and finish, in the carding or casing, and produce a very plausible-looking article at an extraordinarily low price. That the edge turns and the steel breaks in a few days is a secondary consideration. The low purse is tempted by cheapness, and in the wholesale show-room I have seen the real and the false side by side.

I am bound, however, to add that while this increasing German competition is the bogie of every British merchant in South America, my own observation induces the belief that it is much exaggerated. Careful examination of the customs and shipping returns shows this. It is corroborated by the use of one's eyes in the shop-windows and upon the table of every hotel or restaurant. Verification, too, of the alleged German population in a place has more than once reduced it by one-half. It is certain, however, that the advance made by Germany in her foreign trade since she became a first-class empire with a strong foreign policy, and Ministers and Consuls protecting German trade, has been enormous. In the good old days, before the conclusion of the Franco-German war, and the commercial development in the United States after the civil war, we had these markets all to ourselves, and it is but natural that the old-established houses should lament the new era of competition on every hand in every line. It demands the exercise of the keenest vigilance, the greatest activity, the forcing of our goods through hostile duties by every possible means, and not least of all, the employment of energetic travellers of courteous manners, knowing at least three languages, and *most especially Spanish*, both colloquial and epistolary, and remunerated rather by a very liberal commission on results, than by daily allowance.

There is now no personal risk anywhere in South America, despite daily "revolutions" in one republic or another, to the foreigner, who takes ordinary precautions, is civil, and does not interfere with local affairs.

C. E. HOWARD VINCENT.

Panama, Dec. 8, 1893.

XVI.

THE PANAMA CANAL.

1. The attention of the Sheffield Chamber of Commerce having been drawn to the subjoined notice placed on the Order Book of the House of Commons,

> To ask the Under Secretary of State for Foreign Affairs, if, having regard to the development of British commercial interests in Central and South America likely to ensue from water communication being established through the Isthmus of Panama, Her Majesty's Government would be disposed to favourably entertain an invitation from the French Republic to the Great Maritime Powers to join with her in determining, by means of an international Technical Commission, the possibility of continuing the canal works through the opposing Cordillera, and thus completing the remaining portion of this vast undertaking abandoned by the original Panama Canal Company now in liquidation ;[1]

the following note was furnished of the facts concerning the magnificent efforts of the French people to connect the Atlantic Ocean with the Pacific through the Isthmus of Panama, for the good of International Commerce.

Trade Communication viâ Panama.

2. It is true that the plans made for a sufficient sojourn on the Isthmus in order fully to study local conditions were shattered by quarantine and other misfortunes. But thanks to Mr. Claude Mallet, Her Majesty's Consul at Panama, to Mr. Frederick Leay, Her Majesty's Consul at Colon, to the Hon. Secretary of the British Chamber of Commerce in Paris, to the courtesy of the Liquidators and Mandataire appointed by the French Courts, and the official documents placed at my disposal, I am able to give a general account of this wonderful enterprise, its past history, present condition, and future prospects.

It may be well recorded in passing, that the Spaniards, in

---

[1] The necessary answer of the Government was that until a communication was received from France on the subject it would be premature to express any opinion.

PANAMA CANAL WORKS

the early days of their American conquests, saw the vast influence to be exercised by the Isthmus Pass on international trade. More than one English filibustering expedition was directed to the narrow strip of land separating the two mightiest oceans of the globe. In 1836 the Government of His late Majesty King William IV. directed the attention of the British merchants in Peru and Chili to the importance of establishing communication with Europe *viâ* Panama. Its meetings assembled under the presidency of His Majesty's Consuls, the standard bearers of British trade on that distant sea-board expressed "respectful gratitude for such an unequivocal proof of the anxiety of His Majesty's Government to promote by every proper means the commercial interests of Great Britain, and unanimously concurred in the almost incalculable advantages and benefits likely to accrue from the establishment of the projected intercourse *viâ* Panama."

The Pacific Steam Navigation Company, running from the Bay of Panama to Valparaiso, and thence by Cape Horn to England, was an early result, and it still pursues a prosperous course. The next development was undertaken by American hands. In 1849 the State of New York authorized Mr. William Aspinwall and others to form a company for the construction of a railroad across the Isthmus. It was duly built, and still constitutes the only means of communication.

THE PANAMA CANAL COMPANY.

3. In 1876 the success of the Suez Canal directed the attention of those concerned in it to Panama. M. Bonaparte Wyse obtained a concession for making a canal from the United States of Colombia. In 1879 it was transferred to M. Ferdinand de Lesseps, who visited the Isthmus with a large staff. Under date November 15th, 1880, he addressed an open letter to France, and therein announced:—

(*a*) That a Technical Commission had declared a canal to be practicable.

(*b*) That the Suez Canal contractors had undertaken the work for 500 million francs.

(*c*) That a Share Capital of 300 million francs and a Debenture issue of 200 million francs would be sufficient.

(*d*) That a traffic of 6 million tons a year, yielding a revenue of 90 million francs, could be relied upon.

(*e*) That the annual maintenance of the canal would not exceed 35 million francs, and that 80 per cent. of the balance would suffice to give $11\frac{1}{2}$ per cent. on the investment, 5 per cent. being paid during construction.

Unfortunately this statement of affairs involved a spontaneous reduction on the cost estimated by the International Commission, of 1500 million francs. But the French public seeing the Suez Canal receipts increase eightfold between 1870 and 1880, and the Founders' Shares of 200*l.* quoted at 15,000*l.* (now worth 60,000*l.*) threw their savings into the venture. The 600,000 shares of 500 francs each were eagerly subscribed in March, 1881, and by further issues no less than 1,335,565,700 francs were altogether obtained, or in round numbers 53,000,000*l.* sterling. The work was to be completed in twelve years, and by 1884 the Colombian Government was advised that one-third had been finished, and two years later one-half. Possession was thereupon given of a portion of the land included in the Concession.

DIFFICULTIES OF THE COMPANY.

4. The difficulties which forced the Company to suspend payment in December, 1888, then commenced. The Chagres River, along the valley of which the course of the canal was in great part traced, rose sometimes from ten to twelve meters in thirty-six hours, and at such times the current towards the Atlantic ran at the rate of 2000 cubic meters per second. To dam the river, turn the river, use the river, were the remedies suggested. But one and all proved futile. Inundation succeeded inundation, and since the work has been given up the torrent has in some measure abandoned its natural bed for the artificial one of the canal.

THE CULEBRA.

5. But the Chagres is not the only obstacle to be surmounted. The Highlands of the Cordillera are encountered at the 23rd kilometer from Colon, and only give place to the Pacific lowlands at the 62nd. The mountain summit of the Culebra is 100 meters above the sea level.

It was intended to cut through it, but the soil proved soft and shifting, and the steep slopes much affected by not infrequent earthquakes. A fresh, highly competent, and impartial Commission sent out in 1890 by the Liquidators, reported that although a level canal was impossible, through communication might be perfectly well established by means of two locks. A further expenditure of about 40,000,000*l*. would, however, be necessary, including incidental expenses and interests until it was open for traffic.

POSITION OF THE LIQUIDATION.

6. In what position does the Liquidator—M. Pierre Gautron—find himself? Two months ago he lost by death the assistance of his able colleague M. Monchicourt, and his task is thereby rendered the more onerous. This day five months, namely, on October 31st, 1894, the Concession expires, unless before then a new company is formed to complete the work. In that event the buildings, hospitals, workmen's houses, shops, and sheds, which cost 52 million francs, will become the property of the Colombian Government; and the land—some 250,000 hectares—already conceded, reverts to the State. The machinery, which cost 150 million francs, and some of which is in fair order, may be sold, but will scarcely pay for removal. The 489 million francs said to have been spent on the 21 kilometers, already to some extent finished, will be absolutely and irretrievably lost. No other course will be possible, but to divide the assets in the hands of the Liquidator among the 400,000 bondholders. These assets consist of about 300,000*l*. in cash, as much as may be recovered from the old directors, M. Eiffel and others, against whom claims have been made for 50 million francs, the amount realizable from the sale of the machinery, and the value of 68,534 shares (out of 70,000) of 20*l*. each in the Panama Railroad, purchased at 150 per cent. premium, *subject always* to the claims of the Colombian Government in respect of 10 million francs it avers is owing to the Treasury by the Canal Company, and to any arrears due to the 47 French employés now on the Isthmus, and the maintenance charges, estimated at 4000*l*. a month. To the prospect of a return so visionary the bondholders naturally

prefer the formation of a new company, and are probably ready to make over to it, if formed, all their plant and assets in consideration of a deferred interest in the new undertaking.

A New Company.

7. Is the formation of a fresh company possible under existing conditions? In 1892, M. Hiélard, Vice-President of the Chamber of Commerce of the Seine, unsuccessfully endeavoured to organize one. Nor has M. Bartissol, a former engineer of the Suez Canal, been more fortunate. He placed before the liquidators various tempting and ingenious schemes, proposing to complete the canal in four years, carrying away the débris by a subterranean channel. But the Commission to whom the matter was referred, made an adverse report, and on March 30th last, M. Gautron broke off negotiations with M. Bartissol, whose primary aim was apparently the amelioration of the Panama Railway, and a much needed improvement in the ports of Panama and Colon. It is quite clear, therefore, that fresh capital in sufficient amount will not come from the French public. But as the late M. Monchicourt wrote to the Prime Minister on April 29th, 1892, "The French Government cannot remain indifferent to a work which would add greatly to the over-sea prestige of France, and the abandonment of which means the loss of the 1500 million francs taken from the purest national thrift."

Possible Action of France.

8. What action can the French Government take? The law of July last suspended all legal proceedings, and vested the interests of the bondholders in a mandataire—M. Lemarquis. But that is of no avail in attracting fresh capital. It must be drawn from abroad as well as from France under Governmental encouragement and superintendence. A condition precedent is indispensable—the determination by the highest possible scientific authority in the universe if the completion of the canal is practicable. The Commission sent out by the liquidators in 1890 declared that it could be made with two locks. Some of the best engineers of France were on that Commission. But

VIEW OF THE PANAMA CANAL. Page 322.

a yet higher tribunal, from an international point of view, is essential. France has been the pioneer. The losses have been French. Let France still take the lead and invite the Great Maritime Powers—England and the United States, Germany, Scandinavia and the Netherlands, Italy and Spain—to join with her in deciding if the natural difficulties presented by the Chagres River and the Culebra Mountain can be subjugated or not. An affirmative verdict from such a court would not find capital backward, as a traffic of not less than 4,000,000 tons could, it is thought, be relied upon even from the first, at a toll of about 10*s*. per ton, or 2*d*. per ton per kilometer. If negative, it is useless to throw good money after bad. An expenditure of 20,000*l*. by each of the Great Powers, and 10,000*l*. by the Minor States, would be more than ample for the expenses.

RESPONSE OF EUROPEAN POWERS.

9. How the Powers would respond, it is of course impossible to say until France has given the invitation. So far as England is concerned the development of all sea communications is beneficial by whomsoever made. The Suez Canal proves this. The greater part of the shipping on either side of the Isthmus is already British. Our interests in Peru and Chili are enormous, and the Canal would increase them. It would bring us new markets on the Pacific from Alaska to the Straits of Magellan. It would reduce the 15,000 miles from Liverpool to San Francisco by two-thirds. It would save 4000 miles between Plymouth and Peru. It would enable us to protect the new trade and cable route between Canada and Australia. It would give us an alternative road to the South Seas, to India, and the far East. It would be of the greatest advantage to Jamaica, Trinidad, Barbados, British Guiana, and our West Indian brothers. Like considerations in minor degree would weigh with France, Germany, and Italy, with Denmark, the Netherlands, Spain and Scandinavia.

ATTITUDE OF THE UNITED STATES.

10. The attitude of the United States of America might

be more uncertain. The Americans have, however, the most to gain by the making of the Canal, unless it be the peoples of the adjacent Republics. As all machinery and masonry, all tools and all the woodwork must be brought to the Isthmus, the greater part would be purchased in America. The sea distance between New York and San Francisco would be reduced by one-half, between New York and Peru by two-thirds. The question of competition with the Nicaragua Canal arises. The latter is finally declared to be impracticable with its 292 kilometers, against seventy-three between Colon and Panama, with its twenty-one locks and seventeen bridges, with the San Juan River not less treacherous than the Chagres. There is no doubt that American influence has been hostile to France at Bogota. But the feeling against the Canal being in the hands of "one" European Power would not apply to its being made by an International Corporation, on which America would be largely represented, and least of all to the scientific investigation preparatory to a recommencement of work.

The Decision of Colombia.

11. Only one other Power remains to be considered, and that it is true is the most important of all—the United States of Colombia—in whose territory is the Isthmus. But apart from the vast pecuniary and industrial interest Colombia has in the completion of the Canal, an equitable spirit of sound common sense has always animated, not only his Excellency the President of the Republic, but also the Government and Congress. As Dr. Nunez wrote not long ago to the liquidator—"the enterprise numbers many sympathizers in Colombia, and these sympathizers will increase in proportion as it is understood that negotiations are taking place with honourable and responsible persons." On December 6th, 1892, the Colombian Congress authorized the Executive either to modify previous contracts, or to conclude a fresh one without bringing the matter again before Parliament. The conditions of the present arrangement, made in April, 1893, with M. Mange, are certainly advantageous to the Republic, but perhaps not unduly so. They include the payment of 80,000*l.* for damages, and of

400,000*l.* for arrears, in addition to 10,000 shares in the Canal, the caution money of 750,000 francs deposited in 1878 being maintained. A further extension of at least twelve months beyond the present term, ending on October 31st next, would be necessary. But as there is no possibility of the Canal being made by any other means, it would doubtless be accorded.

Conclusion.

12. I have thus set out briefly, so far as I can, the present position of affairs, and the steps which I venture to suggest are essential to the carrying out of this great international undertaking. It can hardly fail, if completed, to prove of inestimable advantage to international trade, and in any case to Great Britain and Ireland.[1]

C. E. HOWARD VINCENT.

HOUSE OF COMMONS,
   May 31st, 1894.

[1] Those who desire more deeply to study the possibility of cutting through the Isthmus of Panama will find ample material, not only in the numerous publications issued by the Liquidator, 63bis, Rue de la Victoire, Paris, but also in the works of M. Bunau-Varilla, formerly Engineer-in-Chief, published by Masson, 120, Boulevard St. Germain; in "The Nineteenth Century" for February, 1892; the "North American Review" and "Nautical Magazine" for February, 1893; "Leslie's Popular Monthly" for March, 1893; and the "Atlantic Monthly" for October, 1893.

INDEX.

Aconcagua, Mount, 137.
Aconcagua River, source of, 112, 116, 117.
Advertising, novel form of, in Santiago, 127.
Agriculture in the Argentine, 296, 297.
Alameda of Statues, Lima, 172.
Alem, Dr., 245.
Amazon River, 184, 185.
Andes, crossing the, 93-121, 252-255; the summit of the, 109-112.
——— the "Lion of the," 119.
Antofagasta, 143, 144, 163.
Aquidaban, warship, 14, 15, 17-19, 26, 224-231.
Argentine Republic, the, a great custom of, 33; pampa of the, 34, 55-86; national game in the, 46, 47; nationalities in, 53; climate of, 57; religious fervour in, 123; politics, 244-249; travelling in the, 250, 251; difference between, and Chili, 256-260; British interests in, 291-301; foreign debt of, 292; British railways in, 295; British shipping, 295, 296; agriculture in, 296, 297; depreciation of the currency, 298, 299; the problem of the future in, 300, 301; capital of, see *Buenos Ayres*.
Arica, 163, 164, 312.
Aspinwall, 204.
Atacama Desert, the, 144.
Auchmuty, Sir Samuel, 236-238.

Bagallay, Mr., C.E., 93, 254.

Bahia, 9.
Baird, General, 233.
Barbados, 214-216, 279.
Beagle, gunboat, 14, 225.
Belgrano, Polo Club at, 38-40.
Benyas, Señor, vineyard of, 90.
Beresford, General, 41-43, 233-239.
Bermudez, Colonel, 268.
Bird Island, 2, 3.
Bizacha or prairie dog, 66.
Blake, Sir Henry, 209.
Blanco, General Guzman, 276.
Blue Mountains, 205, 211, 213.
Bog Walk, Jamaica, 211, 212.
Botanical Gardens at Rio, 23, 24.
Botofogo, suburb of Rio, 23, 24.
Bouwer, Mr., 61.
Boynton, Mr., and the *Aquidaban*, 17, 18, 228, 229.
Brazil; quarantine in, 7-11, 28, 30, 31; revolution in, 16-19, 221-232; British interests in, 283-290; present condition of, 283, 284; History of 1892, 284; foreign trade, 284; commercial indifference, 285; staple products, 285; hindrances to industry, 285, 286; immigration, 286; British trade with, 286-289; reciprocity treaty with America, 287, 288; financial difficulties in, 289, 290; capital of, see *Rio de Janeiro*.
Brazils, the convict settlement of, 5.
Brazilian nuts, 26.
Brazilian Submarine Telegraph Station at St. Vincent, 3.
Bridge built by Eiffel, 178.
Bridge of Hell, the, 180.

Bridge over Mendoza River, 106.
Bridgetown, Barbados, 214-216.
British Guiana, 273, 274.
British trade with Brazil, 286-289.
Buenos Ayres, 33-60, 257; San Domingo Church at, 34, 41-44; Royal Hotel at, 35; trams in, 35; street paving in, 36; policemen in, 36; streets and houses of, 36-38, 47; milk supply in, 38; suburbs of, 38-40; cemetery of, 44, 45; Mendicants' Asylum at, 45; water tanks at, 46; Flores, a suburb of, 47; post office at, 48; Tattersall's at, 47, 48; society in, 49; visit to the Opera at, 49; racecourses at, 50-52; the Paris of the West, 52, 53, 240-243; theatres in, 53; England and, in 1807, 41-44, 233-239; population of, 248, 249.

Caceres, General, 190, 268, 269, 310.
Calavera, 115.
Callao, port of, 167; lotteries at, 170.
Campos, General, 246.
Cañada de Gomez, 79, 297.
Canary Islands, 2.
Cape Frio, 9.
Caracas, 272-276.
Caracoles, the, 115.
Casalpaca Station, 183.
Casares, Señor V. de, 55-61.
Castle, Captain, description of nitrate manufacture, 155-157.
Cavancha at Iquique, 147.
Cazanova, Mons., Archbishop of Chili, 130.
Cattle; on the pampa of South America, 62; shipping at Valparaiso, 139, 140; Peruvian mode of boarding, 165, 166.
Cattle trade between Argentina and Chili, 93.
Celman, Juarez, 40.
Celman's Folly, Buenos Ayres, 45, 46.
Cemetery at Buenos Ayres, 44, 45.

Central Argentine Railway, workshops of, 69, 70.
Chagres River, 203, 320, 323.
" Chañar steppe," the, 80.
Chicla, 182, 270.
Chili, religious fervour in, 123, 142; climate of, 124; tramway companies in, 126; archbishop of, 129, 130; Roman Church in, 130; railway system of, 135; cattle in, 139, 140; war between, and Peru, 146, 153, 154, 162, 163; difference between, and Argentina, 256-260; nitrate fields of, 144-161; 261-266, 307, 308; British trade in, 302-308; national debt of, 302, 303; depreciation of the currency, 303; external trade of, 304; British imports and exports, 304, 305; Customs duties and revenue, 305, 306; military expenditure, 306, 307; steam communication on the Pacific, 307; mineral resources of, 308.
Chilian flag, the, 164, 165.
Chilian saddle, 100.
Chimborazo, Mount, 194.
Chorillos, bathing at, 169, 170.
Chosica, estancion, 176.
Cintra, 1.
Clark, Mr. Matteo, 118, 163, 254.
Climate; of the Argentine Republic, 57; of Chili, 124; of Valparaiso, 138; of Lima, 173.
Coaling stations, England and, 219, 220.
Cobra River, 212.
Colombia and the Panama Canal, 324, 325.
Colon, 204.
Coquimbo, 141; cathedral at, 141, 142.
Coal reef off coast of Brazil, 6, 7.
Corcovado, the, at Rio, 12, 25, 27.
Cordillera, the, see *Andes*.
Cordoba, 80-84; cathedral in, 81, 82; university at, 82; observatory at, 82, 83.
Corporation of Peruvian Bondholders, 175, 176, 269, 270.
Cousiño, Madame, 132-134.

Index.

Cousiño Park, the, at Santiago, 128, 129.
Craik, Mr., 61, 67, 69.
Crauford, General, 234-238.
Crespo, General, 274.
Culebra Mountain, 202, 320-323.

Dairy at Estancia San Martin, 58.
Dalton, Mrs. Grant, 94, 252.
Darwin's "Journal of a Naturalist," 64.
Dawkins, Mr. Clinton, 173, 176, 188, 269, 311.
Desert, the rainless, in S. America, 140-144, 148-154, 166.
Dickenson, Mr., 77.
Domingo, a car attendant, 61, 67.
Donoughmore, Lord, 269.
Du Cane, Major-General Sir E., 238, 239.

Eagle, an enormous, 105.
Earthquake at Mendoza in 1861, 89.
Eiffel, bridge built by, 178.
England; and Buenos Ayres in 1807, 34, 41-44, 233-239; and coaling stations, 219, 220; and Venezuela, 272-276.
English in Argentina, 53, 248, 249.
Ensenada docks, La Plata, 31, 33.
Erichsen, Mr., 160.
Estancias on the Argentine pampa, 65-67; life on, 71-77; *see also* Las Rosas, San Martin.
Eyre, Mr., 269.

Fencing round Estancias in Argentina, 66.
Fernando Noronha, island of, 5.
Fever, a dangerous, near Lima, 177.
Fireflies, 78.
Fishertown, 68.
Flores Island, 28.
Fonseca, Marshal, 222-224.
France and the Panama Canal, 316-323.
Fray Bentos, 30.

French, the, in Argentina, 53, 54, 248.
Froude, Mr., and the West Indies, 277.
Funeral procession at Mendoza, 89.

Galera, tunnel of the, 183, 184, 186.
Gama, Admiral S. da, 14, 225-231.
Gastrell, Mr. Harris, 301.
Gauchos of the South American pampa, 64, 75, 76, 87; in Santiago, 127.
Germany and the revolution at Rio, 17, 225, 226.
Germans in Argentina, 53, 293, 294, 298.
Gold in the Atacama desert, 144.
Gordon Town, 209-211.
Grace, Mr. M., 175, 269, 271.
Graveyard on the pampa, 64.
Green, Mr., 35.
Griffin, Mr., 147, 262.
Guano deposits, Tarapaca desert, 150.
Guayaquil, port of, 140, 192-196.
——— river, 192.

Haler, M. and Mme., 119.
Hawes, Mr., 154.
Hay, Sir John, 215.
Hayti, 213.
Hicks, Captain, of the s.s. *Thames*, 4, 26, 229.
Highlanders, the 71st, at Buenos Ayres in 1807, 41-43, 233-239.
Hispa, M., 117, 118.
Horse-breeding in the Argentine Republic, 60, 73.
Hotels in South America, 88, 89.

Ilha das Cobras, 14, 15, 227.
Ilha Grande, 8, 10, 285.
Incas, the, in Peru, 168, 309; industry of the ancient, 179.
Inca Lake, 115.
Indian burial place, ancient, 154; *see also* Incas.
——— village, 180.

Index.

Iquique, 145-148, 261; naval battle at, 146, 147; sea-walk of Cavancha at, 147; water tanks at, 148.
Iron and steel in South America, 314-317.
Irrigation at Mendoza, 90-92.
Italians in the Argentina, 53, 248, 293, 297, 298.

Jacmel, port of, 213.
Jacobi, Mr. (of Lima), 170, 171.
Jamaica, island of, 205-213, 281.
Jazpampa, oficina of, 160.
Jockey Club, the, Buenos Ayres, 50-52.
Juncal, 112, 114-118, 255.

Kemmis, Captain, Las Rosas Estançia, 48, 70-79, 241.
Kennedy, Mr., 135.
Kingston, Jamaica, 205-213.
Kleist, Count, 272.

La Cumbre, the summit of the Andes, 109, 112, 253, 254.
Lage, fort of, 13, 18, 27, 230, 231.
La Guayra, harbour at, 273.
Lang, Captain, 14, 26, 225-229.
La Plata, 30-33.
La Plata, island of, 196.
Las Cuevras, 105, 106-109, 253.
Las Palmas, 2.
Las Rosas, Estançia of, 70-79, 241.
Leay, Mr. Frederick, 318.
Lees, Sir C. C., 273.
Leones Station, 71.
Lesseps, M. Ferdinand de, 204, 319.
Leveson Gower, Major-General, 237.
Liebig's essence of beef, 30.
Lima, 167-174, 189-191, 267; architecture in, 168; cathedral in, 168, 169; the ladies of, 169; lotteries in, 170; surroundings of, 171; Column of Victory at, 171, 172; climate of, 173.
Liniers, Captain, 42, 235-238.
Lisbon, 1.
Llamas, troops of, 183.
Lloyd, Mr., 3, 220.

Locusts, swarms of, 71.
Lopez, Councillor, 132.
Los Andes, 118-120.
Lottery tickets at Rio, 22.
Lotteries in Lima, 170.
Lucerne, crops of, in Argentina, 76, 77.
Lumley, General, 236-238.

Mackay, Mr., 188.
Mai Island, 10, 12, 27.
Maipo, s.s., 138-144, 162, 163, 191, 196.
Mallet, Mr. Claude, 198, 318.
Manning, Cardinal, 130.
Mansfield, Sir Charles, 174, 275.
Mapocho, s.s., 192.
Mara la Plata, 138.
Marilio Dias, the, 25.
Matucama, 176, 186.
Meiggs, Mr. Henry, 165, 174, 175.
—— Mount, 184.
Mello, Admiral de, 14, 15, 17, 26, 223-232.
Mendes, Mr., 15.
Mendicants' Asylum, Buenos Ayres, 45.
Mendoza, 86-92, 94, 252, 253; earthquake at, in 1861, 89; vineyards at, 90, 91.
Mendoza River, 95-100, 106, 108.
Middleton, Mr., 276.
Miranda, General, 233.
Mitré, General B., 48, 233-239, 247.
Mollendo, 165.
Monte Video, 28-30.
Montt, President, 130, 131, 258, 259.
Moraes, Dr. Prudente de, 222.
Mount Christabel, Lima, 172.
Mount Meiggs, 184.
Mountain sickness (sorocche), 92, 112, 182.
Mules in Peru, 177, 178.
Munro, Mr., 80.

Negro, the West Indian, 279.
Newcastle, Jamaica, 210, 211.
Nichteroy, arsenal at, 14, 16, 227, 230.

Index.

Nines, Mr., 154.
Nitrate fields of Tarapaca, 144, 148-161, 261-266.
Nitrate, description of manufacture of, 155-157, 264-266.
Nitrate Railway, the, 145, 148-163, 262-264.
North, Colonel, and the nitrate fields, 152-155, 264.

Observatory at Cordoba, 82, 83.
Oficinas (nitrate works), 151-161, 264-266, see *Jazpampa, Paccha, Primativa, Sevastopol.*
Opera in Buenos Ayres, 49.
Organ Mountains, 13.
Orinoco River, 274.
Ormonde, racehorse, 60, 73.
Oroya Railway, the, 174-189, 270, 271.
Osa, Señor, 134, 135.
Ostriches, a flock of, 34.
Ouvidor, the, principal street of Rio, 23.

Paccha, oficina of, 161.
Pack, Colonel, 236-239.
Pakenham, Hor, Mrs., 38.
Palermo, park at, 50-52, 241.
Palms, avenue of, at the Botanical Gardens, Rio, 24.
Pai Island, 10, 12, 27.
Pampa of Tamarugal, 148, 151.
Pampa, the, of South America, 61-86.
Pampero, a (whirlwind), 78.
Panama, Gulf of, 197, 198.
——— Canal, 198-205, 318-325.
——— Isthmus of, 198-203.
——— Town, 197, 199.
Para, Royal Mail s.s., 197, 204, 205, 206, 214-217.
Parana River, 67, 85.
Paris, Buenos Ayres compared to, 52, 53, 240-243.
Parish, Sir W., 250.
Paton, General, 215.
Paysandu ox tongues, 30.
Payta, port of, 191, 192.
Pedro II., Emperor, 14, 22, 222.

Peixoto, General F., 15, 223, 224, 226.
Pelicans in South Pacific, 145.
Pellegrini, Dr., 51, 247.
"Pelota," national game in the Argentine, 46, 47, 242.
Peones, or farm servants on Argentine pampa, 66, 74-76.
Pernambuco, 6-8.
Peru; war between, and Chili, 146, 147, 153, 154, 162, 163; the conquest of, 168; finances of, 172, 173, 175; and the Peruvians, 267-271; Capital of, see *Lima.*
——— British interests in, 309-315; decadence of, 309; despotism of the army, 309, 310; Congress at, 310; debt of, 310, 311; currency of, 311; area of, 312; import trade, 312; export trade, 313; shipping, 313; British advancement of local interests, 313, 314; British investments in, 314.
Perugas, 177.
Peruvian Bondholders, Corporation of, 175, 176, 269, 270, 310, 311.
Peruvian mode of boarding cattle, 165, 166.
Pierola, Signor N. de, 268.
Pisagua, 161.
Pizarro, Inca chief, 168, 192, 198, 199.
Plate River, 28; sandbanks at mouth of, 29; estuary of the, 67.
Politics in the Argentine Republic, 244-249.
Polo Club at Belgrano, Buenos Ayres, 38-40.
Popham, Captain Sir Home, 41, 233-236.
Portales, Chilian minister, 122, 259; anniversary of the death of, 131, 132.
Port Royal, 205, 213.
Pozo Almonte, battle-field of, 153.
Prairie-dog, the, 66.
Prat, Arturo, a naval hero, 136, 146, 147.
Primativa, oficina of, 154-159.
Puente del Inca, 106, 253.
Puma, a, 86.
Pumá, island of, 192.

Punte de las Vacas, 94, 100, 101, 252, 253.

Quarantine in Brazil, 7-11, 28, 30, 31.
Quesada, Señor, 174.
Quinta Consiño, the, at Santiago, 132-134.
Quintana, Dr., 245-247.

Race-course at Valparaiso, 138.
Racer, gunboat, 14, 225.
Railway, the highest in the world, see *Oroya*.
Rain, lack of, at Iquique, 145.
Rainless Coast of S. America, 140-144, 148-154, 166.
Revolution in Brazil, 16-19, 221-232.
Rimac River, valley of the, 167, 176, 177, 180, 184.
Rio Blanco Station, 99.
Rio de Janeiro; harbour of, 12-14, 18, 21, 22; Naval arsenal at, 14, 15; bombardment of, 16-19, 221-232; suburbs of, 20; locomotion in, 21; streets of, 22, 23; Botanical Gardens at, 23, 34; fever in, 24; national holiday in, 25; population of, 225.
Rio News, the, 224, 284.
Roca, General, 51, 245-247.
Rojas, Señor Don, 275.
Rosario, 67-70; the Boulevard of, 68, 69; Cathedral in, 69.
Rosas, General, 40, 92.

Salto de Soldato, 117.
St. Antonio, island of, 2.
St. Lucia, 281.
St. Vincent, island of, 2, 3, 219-221.
Sandbanks at mouth of river Plate, 29.
San Carlos, gallery of, at Santiago, 126.
San Domingo Church, Buenos Ayres, 34, 41-44, 233-239.

San Luis range of mountains, 85.
——— province of, Argentina, 86.
San Martin, the Estancia, 55-61.
Santa Cruz, fort of, 13, 18, 19, 27, 227, 230, 231.
Santa Lucia of Santiago, 125.
Santa Rosa, 119.
Santiago, 120-128, 257; Cathedral at, 122-124; Boulevard in, 124, 125; Santa Lucia of, 125; streets of, 127; the Consino Park at, 128, 129; demonstration at Opera House, 131, 132; the Quinta Normal and the Quinta Consino at, 132-134.
Sarsena, town of, 141.
Secundo River, 85.
Selmer, Captain, 138.
Sena, Comte de, 48.
Sevastopol, oficina of, 151.
Sheep-shearing in Argentine Republic, 58, 59, 73-75.
Sheffield reports to Chamber of Commerce, *re* British Commercial interests in South America, 283-325.
Sibron, Admiral, of the French Navy, 225-230.
Silver-smelting works at Antofagasta, 144.
Sirius, H.M.S., 14, 26, 225, 228.
Skeletons on the South American pampa, 63.
Skemnor, Michael, 235.
Skunk, the, 77.
Smith, Mr. George, 263.
Soldier's Leap, the, 118, 255.
Sorocche, or mountain sickness, 92, 112, 182.
South America, horse-breeding in, 60, 73; the pampa of, 61-86; hotels in, 88, 89; the rainless desert in, 140-144, 148-154, 166; Chili, the England of, 256, 257; iron and steel in, 314-317; British commercial interests in, 283-325.
South Pacific, sunsets of the, 143; pelicans in, 145; steam communication on the, 307.
Spain and South America, 9.
Steel, iron and, in South America, 314-325.

Index.

Storm, a heavy, 78, 79.
Sugar-Loaf Mountain, 12, 20, 27.

Tacna, province of, 163, 312.
Tagus River, 1.
Tamarugal, pampa of, 148, 151.
Tarapaca, nitrate fields of, 144, 148, 150-161.
"Tattersalls" at Buenos Ayres, 47, 48.
Teneriffe, Peak of, 2.
Terry, Dr., 247, 292.
Thames, Royal Mail s.s., 1, 4, 5, 26-32, 166, 219, 229, 230.
Thorndike, Mr. J. L., 270.
Thoroughbred horses at San Martin, 60.
Tijuca range of mountains, 12, 20, 24.
Tolorzia Valley, 94, 103, 104.
Tramway companies in Chili, 126.
Transandine Railway, Argentine section, 84, 93-100, 185, 252-254; Chilian section, 118-121.
"Trapiche," vineyard of, 90, 91.
Travelling in the Argentine Republic 1827, 250, 251.
Trees in South America; Caroline trees, 87; Eucalyptus, 56, 65; Paradise tree, 71; thorn tree at Payta, 191; weeping willows, 56.
Trinidad, 275.
"Tuchero," a favourite Spanish dish, 59.
Tupungato, 112.

Uruguay River, 67.
Uspallata, plains of, 95, 97.
—— Pass, 181, 252.

Uspallata Station, 98.

Valcaved, Señor M. N., 268.
Valparaiso, 135-138, 304; monumental, 146.
Vaughan, Cardinal, 129, 130.
Venezuela and England, 272-276.
Verney, Sir Harry, 250, 251.
Viel, Señor Venturo Blanco, 259.
Vigo, 1.
Villalonga, Mr., 89, 92.
Villa Maria, 79, 84.
Villa Mercedes, 84, 85.
Villa residences at Flores, near Buenos Ayres, 47.
Villegaignon, fortress and naval depôt, 13, 17-19, 27, 225-230.
Viña del Mar, 137, 138.
Vineyards at Mendoza, 90, 91.

Walker, Señor Carlos, 259.
Wandelkolk, Admiral, 223.
Ward, Colonel, 281.
Wardrop, Mr., 31.
Water tanks at Buenos Ayres, 46.
Watmough, Mr., 227.
Welby, Mr., 49.
West Indies, the, 277-282; revenue of, 280; external trade of, 280-282.
Wetherall, Rev. Mr., 136.
Whitelocke, General, 42, 236-238.
Wilson, Colonel, 281.
Wyndham, Sir Hugh, 14-17, 25, 225-230.

Yellow fever, 31; in Rio, 24; a Guayaquil, 193.

FOR PUBLIC LIBRARIES.

"Newfoundland to Cochin China,

By the Golden Wave, New Nippon, and The Forbidden City,"

BY

MRS. HOWARD VINCENT

(Authoress of "Forty Thousand Miles over Land and Water.")

PROFUSELY ILLUSTRATED.

Opinions of the Press.

"One of the most travelled of modern English women."—*The Queen*.

"One of the brightest and most entertaining books of travel that have obtained publicity."—*Daily Telegraph*.

"A bright account of a second journey round the world."—*Times*.

"Written in a chatty style, and has the merits that belong to the impressions of a vigilant observer."—*Saturday Review*.

"Abounds in vivid impressions of many places and races."—*Leeds Mercury*.

Seven Shillings and Sixpence.

London: SAMPSON LOW, MARSTON & CO., LIMITED,
St. Dunstan's House, Fetter Lane, Fleet Street, E.C.

WORKS
BY
COLONEL HOWARD VINCENT, C.B., M.P.

A POLICE CODE & MANUAL OF THE CRIMINAL LAW FOR THE BRITISH EMPIRE.

receded by an ADDRESS TO CONSTABLES by the Hon. Sir HENRY HAWKINS, and adopted as a Text-Book by nearly every English-speaking Police Force.

Eighth and Abridged Edition.   Twenty-third Thousand.

Price 2s.; or 2s. 2d. post free.

EDWARDS, 83, HIGH STREET, MARYLEBONE, LONDON;
Or of any Bookseller.

THE "HOWARD VINCENT" MAP OF THE BRITISH EMPIRE.

Showing the Possessions of the British People throughout the World,—their Extent, Population, Trade and Revenue, &c.

For Public Institutions and Schools.   Price £1 1s.   72 in. by 63 in.

Inscribed with the Name of the Donor.

T. B. JOHNSTON, GEOGRAPHER TO THE QUEEN, EDINBURGH.

PROCÉDURE D'EXTRADITION.
Five Shillings.

HACHETTE ET CIE.

THE LAW OF CRITICISM & LIBEL.
Two Shillings and Sixpence.

EFFINGHAM WILSON.

RUSSIA'S ADVANCE EASTWARD.
Five Shillings.

ELEMENTARY MILITARY GEOGRAPHY, RECONNOITRING, AND SKETCHING.
Two Shillings and Sixpence.

KEGAN PAUL, TRENCH, TRÜBNER AND CO.

40,000 MILES
OVER LAND
AND
WATER.

By Mrs. HOWARD VINCENT.

The Journal of a Tour through the British Empire and America.

Third and Cheaper Edition.   3s. 6d., post free.

Opinions of the Press.

" Very bright and interesting."—*Morning Post.*

"Deserves and will receive an extended popularity."—*Daily Telegraph.*

" Most charming."—*Vanity Fair.*

" Chattily and agreeably written in pleasant and gossiping style. Open the volumes at what chapter you may, there is something to amuse and interest."—*The Queen.*

" There are few English ladies who have travelled as far as Mrs. Howard Vincent, and fewer still who could render their experiences in such a natural and interesting manner."—*Figaro.*

" An extremely fascinating book."—*Sheffield Telegraph.*

London : SAMPSON LOW, MARSTON & CO., LIMITED,
St. Dunstan's House, Fetter Lane, Fleet Street, E.C.

www.ingramcontent.com/pod-product-compliance
Lightning Source LLC
Chambersburg PA
CBHW030403230426
43664CB00007BB/724